Researching Youth

Existing books by editors

Andy Bennett
POPULAR MUSIC AND YOUTH CULTURE: Music, Identity and Place (2000)
CULTURES OF POPULAR MUSIC (2001).

Mark Cieslik
Cieslik, M. and Pollock, G. YOUNG PEOPLE IN RISK SOCIETY (2001)

Steven Miles
CONSUMERISM AS A WAY OF LIFE (1998)
YOUTH LIFESTYLES IN A CHANGING WORLD (2000)
SOCIAL THEORY IN THE REAL WORLD (2001)
Miles, S., Anderson, A. and Meethan, K. THE CHANGING CONSUMER (2002)

Researching Youth

Edited by

Andy Bennett
Department of Sociology
University of Surrey, UK

Mark Cieslik
School of Social Sciences and Law
University of Teesside, UK

Steven Miles
Centre for Cultural Policy and Management
University of Northumbria, UK

palgrave
macmillan

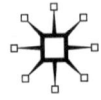

Editorial Matter & Selection © Andy Bennett, Mark Cieslik & Steven Miles 2003
Introduction © Mark Cieslik 2003
Chapter 10 © Steven Miles 2003
Chapter 11 © Andy Bennett 2003
Remaining chapters © Palgrave 2003

All rights reserved. No reproduction, copy or transmission of this publication may be made without written permission.

No paragraph of this publication may be reproduced, copied or transmitted save with written permission or in accordance with the provisions of the Copyright, Designs and Patents Act 1988, or under the terms of any licence permitting limited copying issued by the Copyright Licensing Agency, 90 Tottenham Court Road, London W1T 4LP.

Any person who does any unauthorised act in relation to this publication may be liable to criminal prosecution and civil claims for damages.

The authors have asserted their rights to be identified as the authors of this work in accordance with the Copyright, Designs and Patents Act 1988.

First published 2003 by
PALGRAVE MACMILLAN
Houndmills, Basingstoke, Hampshire RG21 6XS and
175 Fifth Avenue, New York, N.Y. 10010
Companies and representatives throughout the world

PALGRAVE MACMILLAN is the global academic imprint of the Palgrave Macmillan division of St. Martin's Press, LLC and of Palgrave Macmillan Ltd. Macmillan® is a registered trademark in the United States, United Kingdom and other countries. Palgrave is a registered trademark in the European Union and other countries.

ISBN 1–4039–0573–8 hardback

This book is printed on paper suitable for recycling and made from fully managed and sustained forest sources.

A catalogue record for this book is available from the British Library.

Library of Congress Cataloging-in-Publication Data
Researching youth / edited by Andy Bennett, Mark Cieslik, Steven Miles.
   p. cm.
Includes bibliographical references and index.
ISBN 1–4039–0573–8
1. Youth—Research. 2. Youth—Research—Europe. I. Bennett, Andy, 1963– II. Cieslik, Mark. III. Miles, Steven.

HQ796.R485 2003
305.235′07′2—dc21   2003046918

10 9 8 7 6 5 4 3 2 1
12 11 10 09 08 07 06 05 04 03

Printed and bound in Great Britain by
Antony Rowe Ltd, Chippenham and Eastbourne

Contents

List of Table and Figures vii

Acknowledgements ix

Notes on Contributors x

Introduction: Contemporary Youth Research: Issues, Controversies and Dilemmas 1
Mark Cieslik

Part 1 Youth Research in Context

1 Problems and Priorities for the Sociology of Youth 13
   Ken Roberts

2 Mods and Shockers: Youth Cultural Studies in Britain 29
   Phil Cohen

Part 2 Principles of Practice

3 Framing Youth: Reviewing Locally Commissioned Research on Young People, Drug Use and Drug Education 55
   Mathew Jones, Fenella Starkey and Judy Orme

4 Practice-based Research as Development: Innovation and Empowerment in Youth Intervention Initiatives using Collaborative Action Inquiry 66
   Barry Percy-Smith and Susan Weil

5 Onions and Apples: Problems with Comparative European Youth Research 85
   Fred Cartmel

Part 3 Reflections on Fieldwork

6 Ethnography in Practice: A Case Study Illustration 103
   Ruth Emond

7 Researching Young Women's Bodies: Values, Dilemmas and Contradictions 120
   Liz Frost

8   E-heads Versus Beer Monsters: Researching Young
People's Music and Drug Consumption in
Dance Club Settings   138
Karenza Moore

Part 4   Issues in Ethnography

9   Double Exposure: Exploring the Social and Political
Relations of Ethnographic Youth Research   157
Robert Hollands

10   Researching Young People as Consumers:
Can and Should We Ask Them Why?   170
Steven Miles

11   The Use of 'Insider' Knowledge in Ethnographic Research
on Contemporary Youth Music Scenes   186
Andy Bennett

Bibliography   201

Index   223

List of Table and Figures

Table

5.1   Methodological differences in EU research   89

Figures

4.1   Conceptualisation of linear approaches to youth
      policy interventions   74
4.2   A conceptualisation of co-inquiry-based approaches
      to youth professional encounters: bringing
      research into practice   78

Acknowledgements

This book is based on papers presented at the 'Researching Youth: Controversies, Issues and Dilemmas' conference held at the University of Surrey in July 2000. This was one of a number of events which have been organised by the British Sociological Association Youth Study Group (for details see: www.britsoc.org.uk). This study group was re-established by Mark Cieslik, Andy Bennett and Steve Miles in 1999 as a forum for youth researchers to discuss the latest work in the field of youth studies. Each year the study group organises one-day seminars as well as larger conferences, and further information on these events are available from the BSA website. The first volume of articles based on papers presented at study group events was published in 2002 (Cieslik, M. and Pollock, G. (eds), *Young People in Risk Society*, Aldershot) and further publications based on recent study group papers are forthcoming.

The editors wish to acknowledge the support of the BSA and also the many study group members who have contributed to the success of recent events. Most importantly, this book would not have been possible without the many young people who have participated in the various projects which make up this collection of papers.

Notes on Contributors

Andy Bennett is Lecturer in Sociology at the University of Surrey. Prior to studying for his PhD at Durham University, he spent two years in Germany working as a music teacher with the Frankfurt Rockmobil project. He has published articles on aspects of youth culture, popular music and local identity in a number of journals including *Sociology*, *Sociological Review*, *Media Culture and Society* and *Popular Music*. He is author of *Popular Music and Youth Culture: Music, Identity and Place* (2000) and *Cultures of Popular Music* (2001) and co-editor of *Guitar Cultures* (2001). Andy is Chair of the UK and Ireland branch of the International Association for the Study of Popular Music (IASPM) and co-convenor of the British Sociological Association Youth Study Group.

Fred Cartmel is a Senior Research Associate in the Youth, Education and Employment Research Unit based at Glasgow University and has written extensively on the labour market experiences of young people. He is presently involved in an investigation into long-term unemployment among 26–30 year olds, using a life biography approach.

Mark Cieslik is a Senior Lecturer in Sociology at the University of Teesside. Mark has been researching young people since the early 1990s when he undertook doctoral research into young people, schooling and social exclusion. More recently he has been involved in the evaluation of Education Action Zones as well as research funded by the Joseph Rowntree Foundation into youth transitions and social exclusion in the North-East of England. He is presently conducting a project into the relationship between youth transitions and basic skills. He is also co-convenor of the British Sociological Association Youth Study Group.

Phil Cohen is Professor of Cultural and Innovation Studies at the University of East London, where he directs the M^3 Research Laboratory. He is the author of *Rethinking the Youth Question* (2000) and numerous fieldwork studies on youth transitions, focusing on both real and imagined communities of gender, class and 'race'. This work is currently being edited into a new collection *Questioning Ethnographies* for Palgrave.

Ruth Emond currently works part-time in the Department of Applied Social Science, University of Stirling. The other half of her working week is spent as a social worker employed in a small project set up to provide a therapeutic service to children and parents who have experienced 'trauma'. In relation to research, Ruth has an interest in the group and friendship experiences of children and young people, particularly those in looked after care. Her PhD was an ethnographic study of two groups of young people in residential care and required her to live in the units for a year long period. Since completing her PhD, Ruth has undertaken research on young people leaving care and on young people in care and their experiences of education. She received a Marie Curie Post Doctoral Fellowship to undertake this latter piece of research at the Children's Research Centre, Trinity College, Dublin.

Liz Frost is a Senior Lecturer in Applied Social Sciences at the University of the West of England. Her main teaching areas are on mental health, and psychosocial approaches to identity. Much of her research in the last decades has been in relation to the issue of appearance and identity. From 1998 to 2000 this was particularly focused on the issue of young women and their uncomfortable relationship with their bodies. The idea that this might cause identity damage was explored in Frost (2001) *Young Women and The Body: A Feminist Sociology*. Currently Liz is researching the impact of consumer capitalism, particularly relating to the body and appearance, on the relatively new market of 'betweenagers' (children in the 8–12 years age range). Liz is also a member of the Home Office appointed Mental Health Act Commission.

Robert Hollands is currently a Senior Lecturer in the Department of Sociology and Social Policy at the University of Newcastle Upon Tyne, England and is the author of (with P. Chatterton) *Changing Our Toon: Youth, Nightlife and Urban Change in Newcastle* (2001); *Friday Night, Saturday Night: Youth Cultural Identification in the Post-Industrial City* (1995); *The Long Transition: Class, Culture and Youth Training* (1990) and (co-edited with Hart Cantelon) *Leisure, Sport and Working Class Cultures: Theory and History* (1988). His latest book (again with Paul Chatterton) is entitled *Making Urban Nightscapes: Youth Cultures, Pleasure Spaces and Corporate Power* was published in spring 2003.

John, Hood-Williams was a Lecturer at the University of Greenwich and published widely in the areas of the family, sexualities and gender.

His most recent publication was, 'Beyond Sex and Gender', with Wendy Cealey-Harrison (Sage Press, 2001). John Hood-Williams died in 1999.

Mathew Jones is a Senior Lecturer in Health and Social Policy in the Faculty of Health and Social Care at the University of the West of England, Bristol. He has carried out considerable research in the field of young people and drug prevention. His current research involves the evaluation of a school-based drug prevention initiative and the evaluation of a healthy living project and he has recently completed consultancy work for a local Drug Action Team. His research interests include young people, substance use, interprofessional education, participatory research and health inequalities.

Steven Miles is Head of Research at the Centre for Cultural Policy and Management at the University of Northumbria. He is author of *Youth Lifestyles in a Changing World* (2000), *Social Theory in the Real World* (2001) and *Consumerism as a Way of Life* (1998). He is also co-author with Malcolm Miles of a book on consuming cities shortly to be published by Palgrave. He retains a particular interest on the impact of consumption on young people's identities and their relationship to the city as a centre for consumption.

Karenza Moore is a Research Associate at the Centre for Research on Innovation and Competition (CRIC), University of Manchester, where she works with Dr Jason Rutter on the European Union funded mGain project, looking at mobile entertainment culture and concepts. Prior to this she was a PhD student at the Digital World Research Centre, University of Surrey. The title of her thesis is 'Versions of the Future in Relation to Mobile Telecommunication Technologies'.

Judy Orme is a Principal Lecturer in Public Health in the Faculty of Health and Social Care at the University of the West of England, Bristol. She is also the Director of the Research Centre in Public Health and Primary Care Development at UWE. She has carried out a significant amount of research focused on young people and drug prevention. She has co-edited two books in the field of health promotion and public health, the first *Health Promotion – Professional Perspectives* (2001) and secondly *Public Health for the 21st Century – New Perspectives on Policy, Participation and Practice* (2003). Her research interests include young people and risk – particularly drug prevention and alcohol use, the sociology of public health and public health in primary care.

Barry Percy-Smith is Senior Research Fellow at the SOLAR Action Research Centre at The University of West of England. Working across social and public policy arenas, his work centres on the use of 'whole system' action inquiry approaches to research and evaluation to support learning for change in social and organisational settings. His main interests concern childhood, youth, education, participation and citizenship. He has previously been UK Project Director for the UNESCO supported Growing Up In Cities programme, which involved young people and local officials in evaluating and improving local environments.

Ken Roberts is Professor of Sociology at the University of Liverpool. His books include *Youth and Leisure* (1983), *School-Leavers and their Prospects* (1984), *Youth and Employment in Modern Britain* (1995), *Poland's First Post-Communist Generation* (1995), *Surviving Post-Communism: Young People in the Former Soviet Union* (2000) and *Class in Modern Britain* (2001).

Fenella Starkey is a Research Associate in the Department of Social Medicine at the University of Bristol, where she co-ordinates a community-based randomised controlled trial of a peer-led anti-smoking intervention. Prior to her current appointment, Fenella worked at as a researcher at the University of the West of England for six years, undertaking evaluation work in the Faculty of Health and Social Care. Fenella has recently submitted her doctoral dissertation on participatory research with mental health service users as a strategy for empowerment. Her research interests include young people, substance use, peer education, mental health, and user participation in service development and in research.

Susan Weil is Professor of Social Pedagogy and Systemic Action Research and Co-Director of the SOLAR Action Research Centre at the University of West of England. Working predominantly in the health and education sectors her work focuses on the development of new forms of collaborative action inquiry in complex systems. She has recently worked with NHS Executives on whole system change and capability development projects. She is formerly Higher Education Research Director at the Office of Public Management.

Introduction: Contemporary Youth Research: Issues, Controversies and Dilemmas

Mark Cieslik

Introduction

This book sets out to explore some of the issues, problems and controversies facing youth researchers today. It is not a methods manual as such, but instead each contributor provides an account of some of the challenges they faced undertaking actual youth research and how these methodological issues were resolved. By grounding these methodological discussions in concrete examples of youth research, it is intended to provide the reader with an insight into what at times can seem a rather opaque process. By making transparent some of the dilemmas facing youth researchers it is hoped that this volume will go some way in aiding the research undertaken by the many students, policy-makers and practitioners now working in the field of youth studies.

Curiously, although young people have been at the centre of much research, policy-making and practice as well as being a popular area of undergraduate study, there have been very few texts exploring the methodological issues facing youth researchers (exceptions being Coles, 2000; McLeod and Malone, 2000). Though the burgeoning number of methods texts (May, 1997; Seale, 1998) and the smaller number of personal reflexive accounts of 'doing research' (Jupp *et al.*, 2000; King and Wincup, 2000) can prove useful for those embarking on a youth research project, such books do not always reveal the issues which are characteristic of the field of youth studies. For instance, the fact that the subjects of enquiry may be children or young teenagers has always meant that youth researchers have had to be sensitive to the issue of the unequal power relationships between the researched and the researcher. There is, therefore, a range of moral and ethical issues confronting individuals who investigate the lives of often vulnerable young people who lack the resources, social networks and knowledgebility of those conducting the research. The work of youth researchers has also been caught up in the fixation that the popular media have with the activities of young people. Researchers have had to tread carefully and bear in mind how their work may be represented by the media, and how this in turn may impact on the lives of young people themselves. Furthermore, youth research has also tended to be more of a field of study shaped by a multiplicity of theoretical and methodological traditions in the social sciences rather than a narrower disciplinary area of study (Sayer, 2000). Consequently this has posed challenges to researchers who have had to synthesise some of the competing theories and methods within sociology, psychology, cultural studies and criminology (Cohen and Ainley, 2000).

Recent social changes as well as theoretical and methodological developments in the social sciences have led to a reshaping of some of these older dilemmas together with the creation of some new problems and issues for youth research. For example, contemporary youth researchers are faced with the extension of the youth phase, in part as changing labour markets, welfare polices and attitudes towards personal relationships all impinge on the sorts of transitions young people make towards adulthood (Evans and Furlong, 1997; EGRIS, 2001). The growth of information and communication technologies together with the influence of processes of globalisation has also impinged on the lives of young people and, in turn, on youth research (Bynner, 1998; Green, 2002). These changes inevitably have implications for research into youth cultures and identities – more time spent on education and training, greater geographical mobility, the delaying of family formation, all point to the possibility of a reshaping of young people's patterns of association and cultural identities (White, 1999; Cieslik, 2001; Cieslik and Pollock, 2002). Wider developments in social theory and research methods, as we see with the influence of post-modern theorising, notions of risk, methodological reflexivity and biographical methods, have also come to inform the development of youth research projects (Rattansi and Phoenix, 1997; Evans *et al.*, 2000). Youth researchers therefore, have had to rethink earlier concepts of transition, youth culture and identity and hence the sorts of theories and methods that underpin contemporary youth research.

Furthermore, the 'youth industry' has grown remarkably in recent years and so the range and diversity of types of youth research and the problems associated with this work has expanded accordingly (Coles, 2000). There are youth studies students pursuing undergraduate dissertations, public and voluntary sector youth organisations evaluating their initiatives, a myriad of practitioners undertaking applied and action research as well as academic researchers drawing on a wide range of disciplinary influences in their projects. As this volume illustrates, all of these researchers are faced with difficult decisions about the design of their research – the sorts of research problem, theories and methods which will shape their work. Moreover, these technical issues over research design are joined by key issues of how to manage fieldwork relationships, how to organise the dissemination of research findings and the many political, moral and ethical concerns which emerge from undertaking research with young people.

Classic dilemmas in youth research: power relationships and the representation of young people

A long-standing issue with youth researchers has been how one negotiates between the various parties and their respective interests involved in the research process. At its simplest, one may have the classic situation of the lone researcher conducting empirical research into the changing situation of young people's lives, whilst the young people themselves are just getting on with living their lives. Even here, however, one has the ingredients for many of the classical ethical dilemmas one confronts when undertaking research. As Whyte (1955) observed in his studies on youth gangs, difficult decisions have to be made about the extent to which a researcher can participate in and document the lives of research subjects. As Winlow's (2002) recent research into criminality and the night-time economy has illustrated, there is an issue about how much of these activities can be documented in research reports before the project begins to jeopardise the position of respondents, the progress of the study and possibly the career of the researcher? Thus to what extent do researchers who are exploring, for example, criminality or other 'sensitive' topics have to negotiate with respondents about fieldwork roles, data collection and ultimately the censoring of some material during the research process?

These sorts of ethical issues around researching sensitive topics are highlighted by both Frost's chapter on body hatred and Moore's contribution which examines the issues of drug and alcohol use amongst clubbers. They both illustrate how researchers had to employ flexible, non-threatening fieldwork strategies that respected the concerns and interests of young people in the research settings. A sensitivity to issues of rapport and trust between the researcher and the researched was key to the generation of quality data and the successful completion of these projects.

Increasingly, however, as Jones *et al.* illustrate in their contribution to this volume, research can involve a multiplicity of parties and their respective interests such as government departments, local commissioning agencies and practitioners. Whatever the project, researchers have to rely on the goodwill of often vulnerable and impressionable respondents to provide data for their research, and hence researchers should respect the interests of the young people participating in the project. The various ethical guidelines of professional bodies such as the British Sociological Association have been developed for this very reason. Nevertheless, as Jones *et al.* suggest, the conflicting interests of different organisations may be very difficult to reconcile, and so the interests of young people (as well as the researcher) can be subsumed in the maze of political and ideological debate. In their example of research into drug use, the youth workers and the school authorities who were involved in the project had distinctive and irreconcilable philosophical and ideological traditions which led to problems organising the fieldwork as well as difficulties developing research instruments.

A further dilemma raised by contributors to this volume is how the research process involves the creation of a narrative by the researcher about the lives of young people which can then be used and adapted by others for their own ends. This distanciation of the products of research from the original research process and the lives of participants allows the users of research to creatively reinterpret the narratives which are presented in research reports. Hence, as Pearson (1983) and more recently Kelly (2000) have argued, the mass media and in turn the general public can construct stories which focus more on the 'spectacular lives' of a minority of young people rather than the mundane and humdrum experiences of the majority.

However, as Roberts argues in his chapter, youth researchers are also influenced by the mass media and by public opinion, and so youth studies predilection for studying 'spectacular' young people can pose a range of methodological problems. Roberts goes on to problematise the current fashion for research into consumption, arguing that such research problems abstract from the more fundamental transition processes which ultimately structure the lives of young people. He calls, therefore, for a more careful consideration of the sorts of research questions that currently shape many projects in youth studies, and a sensitivity to the relationship between research, mass media, government and other academic areas of study.

A number of chapters suggest that by focusing on youth who are young offenders, 'subculturalists' drug users, socially excluded, young mothers or truants, researchers can contribute to a subtle yet pervasive popular discourse about the lives of young people today – that somehow most are either 'in trouble' or 'causing trouble'. Lay observers, however, often overlook the empirical evidence that indicates that most young people do not fall into these categories, and so there is the problem of the popular misrepresentation of contemporary youth transitions and cultures. The concern about the role of research in this system of discourses–representations is that the power of these spectacular representations can have very real consequences for the young people themselves. Media frenzies over drug use, youth crime, the so-called emerging youth underclass can and do shape political agenda. These in turn inform policy initiatives which can lead to new punitive forms of regulation and surveillance of young people as we have witnessed for example in community curfews, new forms of school discipline and policing.

These problems and dilemmas cannot always be easily overcome. Research into 'ordinary' young people may be one solution (Jenkins, 1983; Brown, 1987; Roker *et al.*, 1999), though 'spectacular youth' are often at the heart of government policy agendas which shape the priorities of organisations such as the Economic and Social Research Council and the Joseph Rowntree Foundation from where youth research receives much of its funding. Some researchers have sought other ways of adapting to these dilemmas as we see in Ruth Emond's chapter in this volume, which discusses the concept of 'reflexivity' and its uses in youth research. Emond suggests that such an approach allows one to document and make transparent the complexities of the research process, particularly when negotiating the different interests of participants. In particular, she highlights the significance of the researcher's biography when undertaking qualitative research and how trust is central to the successful management of fieldwork relations. A reflexive approach allowed the various interests and perspectives of participants to be accommodated and documented in the processes avoiding some of the problems of misrepresentation usually associated with unequal power relationships in research.

More recent attempts to redress the balance of power between the various participants in the research-policy process has been developed by those using more participative methodologies (Butcher and Thomas, 2001). The chapter by Percy-Smith and Weil illustrates how efforts to involve young people in policy interventions led to much more positive outcomes for young people when compared to 'top-down' initiatives which were shaped by the target setting constraints of government agencies. The authors outline a model for successful policy implementation, evaluation and development which allows for negotiation between young people and practitioners over the goals and the processes involved in the policy initiative. This negotiation process or what the authors refer to as 'communicative action spaces' was central to ensuring that vulnerable young people were empowered to help themselves, and in the process avoided some of the more coercive elements of recent policy interventions in the lives of young people. These types of participative interventions surely have wider applications and raise questions about the conduct of youth research more generally.

The dilemmas of researching young people in late modernity

Though the traditional concerns of youth studies, such as inequality, transitions and cultures, are still central to much research, the impact of societal change on the lives of young people have impacted on the selection of research problems, theories and methods. The changing institutional fabric of western societies, processes of de-industrialisation, expansion of travel, tourism and migration, and the growing significance of youth to government policy have all contributed to a reshaping of youth research in recent years. As the key markers of adulthood now occur much later in life for most young people, the subsequent 'stretching' of the youth phase from the teens into the twenty something period has had a profound effect. The growth in Information and Communication Technologies (ICTs) has similarly transformed the experiences of young people, as has the growth in the ways in which young people can participate in forms of consumption and leisure-orientated activities.

Globalising processes have been particularly significant for contemporary youth studies with, for example, several projects examining the significance of the global reach of ICTs and the forms of travel and tourism for the patterning of youth cultures (Brah, 1996; Bennett, 2000; Carrington and Wilson, 2002; Hodkinson, 2002). The impact of global economic, political and cultural processes on the lives of young people around the world has also been the subject of much recent research (Roberts, 1995, 1998; Skelton and Valentine, 1998; Wallace and Kovatchev, 1998; Guerrero, 2001). Increasingly, therefore, commentators have called for the development of cross-national, comparative youth research which will enable social scientists to examine the changing lives of young people both at the societal as well as inter-societal levels (Heinz, 1999; Bynner, 2001). As Cartmel discusses in his contribution to this volume much of this comparative research has been conducted by quantitative researchers (Muller and Shavit, 1998; Gallie and Paugam, 2000). Moreover, the European Union which has needed data on the circumstances of young people in order to develop Europe-wide social policy initiatives has funded most of this research. Though offering a wealth of comparative data on issues such as social exclusion, unemployment, housing and crime, one problem with such policy-driven research he suggests is that it seldom leads to new theoretical insights. Drawing on his experience of undertaking Europe-wide surveys, Cartmel illustrates how there are also a host of practical methodological problems to overcome if one is to develop comparative survey research. What appear to be relatively simple issues such as questionnaire design and subsequent translation (so that they may be used in different societal contexts) can easily undermine the validity of the whole research process.

The extension of youth transitions has led some researchers to raise particular questions about the patterning of disadvantage and so theories around social exclusion have been central to much recent youth research on transition (Coles, 1995; MacDonald, 1998; MacDonald et al., 2001; Ridge, 2002). Furthermore, with government agendas and research funding agencies targeting 'youth problems' (such as crime, drugs, unemployment, educational under-achievement), much theorising has explored the relationship between the regulation, surveillance and enabling functions of state agencies and the lives of individual young people as we see elaborated through concepts such as citizenship (France, 1998, 2000; Helve and Wallace, 2001) and discourses (Griffin, 1993).

The concept of transition itself has undergone some revision in recent years, with some writers suggesting that it hinders research as much as enables it (Jeffs and Smith, 1998; Skelton, 2002). However, for many it still offers an invaluable conceptual tool for the analysis of young people's lives, albeit in a greatly revised form. Recent research has developed, for example, notions of cyclical, reversible and delayed transitions. (Craine, 1997; Du Bois-Reymond, 1998; Wyn and Dwyer, 1999). If research on transition has been remodelling some of the questions and theories which inform their work, it is only to be expected that these changes have impacted on the sorts of methods which many use in their work. Extended transitions pose a range of problems – snap-shot quantitative surveys over a short time-frame, which underpinned the ESRC 16–19 programme (see Banks *et al.*, 1992), abstract from the more long-term transition experiences which youth now currently undergo. Efforts to accommodate these methodological challenges for quantitative researchers are presently afoot with the establishment of new government-funded longitudinal surveys of young people. Qualitative research has also adapted to lengthier transitions with an increasing reliance on interviews with older subjects and the employment of techniques which can access the longitudinal experiences of respondents through life history, retrospective and biographical fieldwork methods (Chamberlayne *et al.*, 2000; Rees *et al.*, 2000; Roberts, 2001; Thompson *et al.*, 2002).

The emergence of extended transitions and wider theoretical developments in the social sciences has meant that youth researchers now seldom frame their research in the context of 'reproduction theories' as was often the case during the 1970s and 1980s (Willis, 1977; Hall and Jefferson, 1978). It is now more common for researchers to use theories influenced by post-structuralist critiques of earlier foundational thinkers as we observe with notions of post-subcultures (Muggleton, 1997, 2000), neo-tribes (Bennett, 1999) and lifestyles (Miles, 1995). Some have endeavoured to synthesise earlier Marxian, Weberian and Durkheimain traditions with more contemporary concerns and theorising as we see with concepts such as individualisation (Roberts, 1996), lifecourse theory (Irwin, 1995) and more recent efforts to develop a radical political economy approach in youth studies (Mizen, 2002).

For other writers, the extension of the youth phase suggests a greater range of possibilities for young people to explore their socio-cultural identities and forms of association (Miles, 2000). It is this question of the place of culture in the lives of young people today and how researchers may go about examining cultural practices which is the subject of Phil Cohen's contribution to this volume. In arguing for the centrality of culture to contemporary youth studies, Cohen develops an agenda for youth research which contrasts markedly with that of Robert's chapter. Nevertheless, both authors agree on the importance of actively involving and empowering young people in the research process, and Cohen in particular outlines the difficulties of presenting an authentic voice of youth to the users of research. The challenge for Cohen, as it is for Miles in this volume, is how research into contemporary youth cultures can provide an authentic voice for young people which can be empowering whilst at the same time providing an analysis which extends beyond the mere description of the meanings which respondents attach to their actions. As Miles illustrates in his chapter, this classic epistemological dilemma of research is particularly evident in research on consumption. For, consumption can at one level be a taken for granted, mundane everyday act, yet at another be imbued with complex meanings which illustrate the subtle ways in which young people participate in relationships with their families and friends, and also are connected to the economy. The danger, as both of these writers argue, is that the wider contextual concerns of the researcher may result in the 'overwriting' of the young people's experiences with those of the researcher's interpretations reducing the process to one where the research only allows for a crude ventriloquism to occur.

Chapters by Andy Bennett and Robert Hollands address many of these same questions but explore them through discussions of their work on music-based youth cultures and the night-time economy respectively. The significance of their contributions is that they illustrate how ethnographic research is still a popular methodological technique for addressing some of the epistemological dilemmas which face youth researchers. The production of high-quality data which accurately reflects the experiences of the respondents can be made possible by lengthy involvement with research subjects in fieldwork settings. Nevertheless, they caution, as many qualitative researchers before them have noted (Ball, 1998; Atkinson, 1990), that the development of roles which allow for 'insider accounts' are beset with their own challenges. In particular, as Bennett suggests, if researchers are long-term 'fan-researchers' does this closeness to the research topic undermine the analytical quality of the research? For Hollands, one way forward is the synthesis of ethnographic traditions developed by cultural studies and sociology which can allow for a more thorough understanding of the 'social relationships of fieldwork' and produce in turn a more adequate politics of method.

Structure of the book

The remainder of this book is divided into four sections. Contributions by Roberts in Chapter 1 and Cohen in Chapter 2 outline quite different agendas for the future of youth research, and these discussions frame the context for discussions developed by the other contributors. Roberts argues for the significance of transitions research today and details some of the difficulties facing those working from this perspective. In contrast, Cohen's contribution calls for the growing significance of the 'cultural' in youth research. In Section 2, the authors explore in various ways some of the difficulties of putting research principles into practice.

Section 3 provides a number of chapters which detail the experiences of undertaking ethnographic youth research. The final section of the book develops a discussion of some of the political and epistemological dilemmas that currently face researchers working in the field of youth studies. What all of these chapters aim to do is to illustrate some of the theoretical as well as everyday problems that confront youth researchers, and how some of these were overcome. Hopefully, this volume will go some way in aiding those about to embark on their own youth research project.

Part 1
Youth Research in Context

1
Problems and Priorities for the Sociology of Youth

Ken Roberts

Introduction

This chapter offers secure theoretical foundations on which the sociology of youth can build incrementally. It argues that:

1. Sociology must make its own youth questions, if necessary redefining the policy agenda, and that the discipline must stick to its own questions rather than absorbing or simply responding to the wider society's forever changing youth problems.

2. Sociology needs to prioritise its own youth questions. Two criteria are proposed: making a difference to individual young people's, and society's, future; and acting as a substructure vis-à-vis experiences in other domains. On these criteria it is argued that school-to-work and family/housing transitions have been, and remain, the core problems in the sociology of youth.

3. Established quantitative and qualitative research methods are no longer adequate and need to be adapted to engage with youth's current condition.

Youth as a social and sociological problem

Youth research goes round in circles. We never seem to progress. One reason will be the rate of circulation among youth researchers themselves. Newcomers are easily persuaded to seek fresh starts. Careers in youth research tend to be fragile. Some of the reasons apply in all the social (and other) sciences. For example, PhD students and research assistants may have to switch fields in order to obtain or maintain their employment. However, youth research has some special difficulties in holding its own. All youth researchers have alternative academic identities: as researchers into education, labour markets, gender, race, consumption or deviance, for example. And youth research lacks some of the ballast that holds practitioners in other specialisms. There are few degree courses dedicated to youth. The subject may be, but is not necessarily, even an option within degree courses in the basic social sciences. Moreover, there is no single youth work profession. The 'practitioners' addressed may be teachers, social workers, probation officers, careers officers, counsellors of various types, sports or arts specialists, or community workers. We could also include people from the music industry, fashion and the night-time economies. In some countries such as Britain there is no government department with 'youth' in its title. Youth researchers must therefore speak to a broader and more amorphous body of policy-makers. They cannot become sometime critics, and simultaneously protected clients, of a single, powerful government department.

Despite the above, youth research itself never flags. At present it is flourishing. In Britain it has been boosted by recent Economic and Social Research Council (ESRC) and Rowntree Foundation research programmes. The British Sociological Association's Youth Study Group has been revived. It is not difficult to see why. The vanishing youth labour market has not destroyed young people's transitions. There have been massive expansions in youth education and training. The youth lifestage has been prolonged (see Bynner et al., 1997a). The socio-cultural space thus created is being filled by new social practices. Intermediate conditions between leaving the parental home on the one side, and marriage and parenthood on the other, have been created: new types of households, and new types of couple relationships (see Heath and Kenyon, 1999). Furthermore the young singles scene is buoyant (see Hollands, 1995). Simultaneously, there are heightened risks of young people failing to progress, becoming socially excluded or an underclass. Sociologists are bound to be interested in establishing exactly what is going on. This chapter is a contribution to the ongoing debate on how this interest should be harnessed (see also Cohen and Ainley, 2000; MacDonald et al., 2001). It advises building on what we already know rather than searching for totally new paradigms which, in the long term, is likely to amount to no more than a temporary intellectual flurry.

Over the longer term, between the periodic peaks in sociological interest, youth research is sustained by young people posing constant problems for the authorities and adult society in general. It seems that if they are not unemployed or truanting then too many are getting pregnant too young, homeless, abusing drugs or up to some other mischief. Youth research is friendly territory for sociologists who like to work with their eyes down in search of social problems and their hands up seeking research funds. Research proposals which address or, better still, promise to find solutions to, youth problems are usually at least potentially fundable. This is despite our appalling track record in delivering solutions. Fortunately for all concerned, the symptoms of trouble, if not the underlying causes, change constantly. So there is a never-ending series of panics and calls for new diagnoses. The ensuing activity appears to satisfy everyone's need to be seen to be doing something. However, sociology cannot be content to allow the wider society to define its problems. For sociology, everything is a problem. Sociology needs to pose its own questions and develop its own knowledge-base from which, if necessary, to challenge policy-makers' definitions of 'the youth problem'. It may not be a problem for the wider society if young people accept and settle in modestly paid jobs where there are few intrinsic satisfactions or career prospects. For sociology, young people's compliance, if and when they are compliant, is a problem that cries out for explanation and closer scrutiny (as in Willis, 1977). Conversely, it may not be a problem for young people themselves (or society in general) if they drop out of education and training before government ministers think they should.

Youth is an especially rich research field for sociology because young people's lives impinge upon, or are impinged upon by, so many major social institutions. More than this, young people are either entering or leaving, or changing statuses within, the institutions. As such, young people's experiences can offer exceptional insights into the character and operations of the institutions, how these are changing, and the links and mismatches between them. There is no better age group for examining changing sexual codes, the development and stabilisation of sexual identities, social mobility processes, and the formation of new social strata. Youth researchers occupy a privileged position from which to intervene in broader debates such as the possible creation of an underclass or socially excluded groups (see MacDonald, 1997). While many of the relevant researchers prefer not to use the underclass label lest they be mistaken for Murray (1990, 1994) sympathisers, they rarely have difficulty in identifying a bottom group that is set apart by its frequent truancy, seriously disturbed family and housing histories, chronic unemployment, early parenthood and/or repeat offending (see, for example, Williamson and Middlemiss, 1999).

A hazard in having so rich a research field and in making everything into a problem is that sociology's youth agenda becomes enormous. So sociology needs to establish its own priorities. On what basis should we rank in (sociological) importance the various aspects of young people's lives? The following twin criteria may not be fully consensual, but they are likely to command a broad measure of agreement. Importance can be assessed, first, in terms of making a difference to the future lives of the young people concerned, and the future of their society, and second, in terms of which aspects of young people's lives operate as a substructure and govern their experiences elsewhere.

Key transitions

Most sociologists have abandoned trying to define youth in terms of chronological age. Nowadays we say that we study youth transitions which may occur at age 12, 16, 20, 30 or even when individuals are older than this. Youth is a life stage, neither the first nor the last, and as such is inherently transitional. It is impossible to conceive a genuine sociology of youth which does not study 'the transition', and from all the evidence that we now possess, or, at any rate, on my own reading of this evidence, two transitions stand out as clearly more important than others in terms of the criteria presented above. These are the transitions from education to work, and in family and housing situations.

Young people make many other transitions. Everything of sociological significance is different for adults than it is for children. Young people experience a thorough change. They become able to be politically active and influential. At specific but different ages they become legally able to have sex, purchase tobacco, and drink and consume alcohol in public places, and become subject to the adult justice system. They make the transition from having their alleged needs and wants provided for, usually by their families, to becoming independent consumers, able to buy things for themselves and to obtain credit. As they grow older, the state welfare system ceases to provide benefits via their families, or according to their alleged lesser needs as young persons, and recognises their full adult entitlements.

All these transitions are important, in their own ways, not least in the eyes of those directly affected, but the education-to-work and family/housing transitions have three elevating characteristics. First, it is the modern organisation of employment, and of family and domestic life, that creates the modern young person. Youth could not exist as we know it today unless the nuclear family was the normal residential unit with mates self-selected on the basis of mutual attraction, and unless formal education and (most) paid work had been extracted from family and community life. This is not to say that these arrangements never existed prior to modern times: only that the arrangements are normal in all modern societies, but were not so previously.

Second, the key transitions into employment and adult family relationships are not necessarily or always completed. Some people never establish themselves in jobs which will support an adult lifestyle. Some remain unmarried and childless, and continue to live in their parents' homes until the latter's death. Those concerned are still able to be recognised and accepted as, and to feel, adult. The crucial points are, first, that all young people are at risk, albeit to varying extents, of their school-to-work and family transitions not being completed in the sense of not leading to the 'normal' outcomes. Second, the lives of individuals who do not complete these transitions are certain to be different, arguably deviant, in many other respects. A degree of difference, including deviance, can be tolerated, and is arguably necessary in any society. Nevertheless, the third crucial point to be made here is that if the majority of young people failed to obtain jobs or to enter child-bearing relationships, the implications for the wider society would be momentous. Other transitions are rather different: most of them (like being able to vote) are accomplished simply by reaching a stipulated age, so the possibility of abnormal outcomes is eliminated.

Third, there is great variety in the types of employment and family/housing circumstances to which youth transitions lead. So how they accomplish these particular transitions has serious implications for the individuals' futures. The same cannot be said of some (though not all) of the other youth transitions. There are likely to be profound long-term implications depending on whether a young person experiences the justice system primarily as a source of protection or punishment. In contrast, it is not so evidently the case that whether or not a young person is politically active will make a significant difference to his or her future, let alone a country's. Moreover, all the other transitions are different in that, as argued fully below, exactly how they are accomplished depends largely on the manner in which young people make their education-to-work and family/housing transitions, whereas the reverse does not usually apply.

School-to-work and family transitions must therefore be the sociology of youth's priority topics. Unless these transitions are properly understood, nothing else is likely to be comprehensible. The priority topics are not neglected, but in neither case is there scope for slackening attention. The school-to-work transition was a major topic in youth research in most industrialised countries prior to Second World War. Unemployment and dead-end jobs were the big issues of that era (see Jewkes and Jewkes, 1938; Cameron *et al.*, 1943). Research interest eased in the post-war decades of full employment: the transition into employment had ceased to be a (social and political) problem. Interest revived in the 1970s and 1980s alongside the return of youth unemployment together with the training schemes and educational programmes that were introduced in this context (see, for example, Rees and Atkinson, 1982). Research interest has intensified, and has been partly refocused, by the now widespread view that human capital has become the crucial factor of production on which the competitiveness of national economies hinges. Hence the comparative studies of the proportions of young people achieving different levels of qualifications, receiving general education at upper secondary levels and beyond, vocational schooling, and employer-based and other types of training (see Shavit and Muller, 1998; Heinz, 1999). Comparative European research has taken some of its major recent strides in studies of the transition from education into employment. Important lessons of wider relevance have been learnt about the value, and also the difficulties and limitations, of these studies. The study of the school-to-work transition is currently in good shape, but there can be no let-up because evidence dates rapidly. For example, in Britain we need fresh research to chart how youth labour markets adjust to the recent rise in the proportion of young people progressing through higher education. Recent graduates cannot expect to equal the labour market achievements of earlier, much smaller, graduate cohorts. We also need to monitor the operation of the latest government schemes – Modern Apprenticeships and the New Deal, the introduction of Learning and Skills Councils, and the Connexions initiative, for example. We may have good grounds for suspecting that the new measures will work in much the same way as their predecessors, but such hunches always need corroboration.

Until recently young people's family and housing transitions were neglected by both youth and family sociologists. The standard research in this field used to be pre-occupied with the ages when young people first had sex, then, during the 1980s as HIV became an issue, whether their sex was safe. In many countries this situation changed in the 1990s. Housing and family transitions are no longer neglected. Research interest has been stimulated by the normalisation in northern Europe and North America of an intermediate stage between leaving the parental home and establishing a new child-rearing household, increased

Problems and Priorities for the Sociology of Youth 19

rates of separation, divorce and single parenthood, the contraction of the 'social' rented housing sectors in some countries, and the spread (and visibility) of homelessness among young people. We now have an impressive list of quality studies of young people's changing family relationships and housing (for example, Hutson and Liddiard, 1994; Jones, 1994, 1995; Pickvance and Pickvance, 1994; Irwin, 1995; Hobcraft and Kiernan, 1996; Kiernan, 1995; Heath and Kenyon, 1999). Even so, this research topic remains awfully immature. There is still a split between studies which focus on the material (housing) and those that deal with the socio-emotional, inter-personal relationships aspects of the transition, and we are nowhere near to having a robust typology of routes, leading to different adult destinations, and recruiting young people from different origins. Hence our limited understanding of the processes whereby some young adults become marginalised in housing markets, and how and why we are producing adult cohorts who are collectively failing to reproduce the population.

It is in the course of making school-to-work and family transitions that social class, gender and ethnic divisions among young people widen, deepen and are consolidated. These divisions are then reproduced in other areas of young people's lives – in leisure, politics, and experiences of the welfare and justice systems, for example (see below). This is just one respect in which it is impossible to explain what is occurring elsewhere until the substructure of young people's lives (their school-to-work and family/housing transitions) has been analysed properly.

Some writers (for example, Cohen and Ainley, 2000) argue that the entire transition discourse must be abandoned because, in these post-Fordist times, there are no longer secure and stable destinations towards which young people can head. They argue that cultural analysis is better able to cope with the current flux, but they are mistaken: their own analysis exaggerates the extent to which life has changed. Most people still marry and become parents. Death is still the most common terminator of marriage. In Britain there has been little change over the last 30 years in the likelihood of people feeling that their own jobs are insecure, or in the typical interval between jobs being entered and left (Burchell et al., 1999). Much that is alleged to be new, post-modern, is plain hype.

Citizenship

There are contenders for pole, or at least equal top position, in youth studies. One is the citizenship paradigm (see Jones and Wallace, 1992;

Bynner, 1997). This focuses on how young people may become increasingly active and influential politically, the welfare rights that they acquire or have withdrawn, and their treatment by the justice system. These are all important aspects of young people's lives. The argument here is not that they can be safely ignored. The position is rather that they are simply not pivotal in the same way as school-to-work and family transitions.

Youth is a period of transition in politics, welfare rights and justice. Young people's experiences in these domains are comparable to their experiences at school and work, and their family lives, in this respect. Another similarity, which needs to be highlighted, is that even though all young people may acquire the same legal rights at the same ages, in politics, welfare and justice they follow different routes which lead to different adult destinations. However, in the various realms of citizenship the particular routes that individuals follow are more governed by, than determinants of, their education-to-work and family situations. Everyone in present-day Britain becomes entitled to vote at age 18 unless they are certified insane or sit in the House of Lords, and for roughly a half of all adults this becomes virtually their sole political activity (Coxall and Robins, 1998). A quarter of adults are less active: they usually do not vote. The remaining quarter are more active, but in most of these cases their additional political activity is spasmodic, like signing a petition or writing to an MP or local councillor. Likewise, among young people the real political activists are a small minority even when participation in 'new social movements' is added to involvement in political parties (see Banks *et al.*, 1992). The activists were a minority even among students during the brief period in the late 1960s and early 1970s when many university campuses were in turmoil (see Blackstone *et al.*, 1970). Young political activists are an important group. Adult career politicians tend to be recruited from their ranks. So young people are divided into future leaders and followers, and nowadays the former are drawn almost wholly from the academically successful, university educated. Most young people who attend university do not become political activists, but virtually all career politicians are drawn from this subsection of the youth population. For the larger number whose main political activity is voting, their party choices depend more on their class locations than anything else. This remains the case even if the class-vote link is now weaker than in the past (see Sanders, 1997).

In terms of relationships to the welfare system, Europe and North America's adult populations also divide into two broad groups. On the one hand, there are those who use universal services and make additional provisions for their pensions, housing, and maybe their health care and children's education. On the other hand, there are those who use universal services plus means-tested benefits. Young people become divided into these two groups. Which they join has important implications for them, in both the short term and the longer run. The crucial point here is that which groups they join are inexplicable except in the context of their education-to-work and family trajectories.

Young people's positions vis-à-vis the justice system are basically similar. A minority enter careers in which they are variously treated and punished, while others come to regard the law, police and courts as their (effective or ineffective) protectors. Again, which group each individual joins depends primarily on his or her class and family background and trajectory.

Ultimately the citizenship paradigm flounders. Its issues are not unimportant, but they are not pivotal, and the sociology of youth needs to start from the right base. It is necessary to distinguish substructure from superstructure. Failure to do so, or selecting an inappropriate base, leads to the entire field of enquiry splintering into a bewildering array of issues, and a fragmentation of knowledge that obscures instead of exposing the forces and processes that are decisive in shaping young people's lives and futures.

Consumption and youth cultures

These are the further contenders for a pole position in youth studies. They have clearly become more important in the senses that young people collectively are spending more money than ever and have become a weightier consumer market segment. This is despite the decline in full-time youth employment. Somehow young people obtain the money from part-time jobs, parents, grants and loans to remain the most active age group in virtually every type of out-of-home leisure (see Roberts, 1999). As youth transitions have lengthened, teenagers' youth cultures have merged with larger young singles scenes where individuals who are in their late teens mingle with twenty- and thirty-somethings in pubs and clubs (see Hollands, 1995).

Young people's levels of income and spending depend primarily on their positions along the particular routes that they are following from education into employment (Roberts and Parsell, 1991). Their patterns of spending depend primarily on their family and housing circumstances

(Jones and Martin, 1999). In these senses it can be argued that their consumption is governed, structured, by other things. It may well be the case that these patterns break-up when we examine the fine texture of consumption – the particular places where young people congregate, the fashions that they wear, the music that they listen to and so on. In the 1970s the CCCS researchers (Hall and Jefferson, 1976; Mungham and Pearson, 1976) were able to show that youth styles were in fact class-based, but it can be argued that things are rather different today: particular types of music and nightspots nowadays create their own crowds, and the participants are often from diverse family and educational backgrounds (Thornton, 1995; Bennett, 1999). Thus, it can be argued, rather than expressing identities that are anchored elsewhere, consumption-based youth cultures are now the sites where identities are constructed (Hollands, 1995). Hence the case for granting these youth cultures a pole position in youth studies.

There is a sense in which it is necessarily true that young people's leisure activities are identity conferring. All social roles confer identities which enable the actors, and others, to recognise who they 'are'. However, some identities are more consequential than others. Consumption-based identities are often just Friday and Saturday night fun (Eygendaal, 1992). Some youth researchers may have taken youth cultures more seriously than their subjects. When consumption-based identities are not compartmentalised in this way, they are still most likely to be too transient to become a base for the actors' core views and feelings about their society and their own positions within it (Bynner and Ashford, 1992). This is not to urge youth researchers to ignore their subjects' leisure behaviour. Young people's leisure tastes and spending priorities always say something about their social condition, and their feelings about this. The point is simply that the rich material with which the researchers emerge remains incomprehensible unless set in context.

Identifying structures

It has been implicit throughout the above passages that the sociology of youth should identify social facts (to use Durkheim's terminology); patterns common among all, or particular categories of, young people. Since youth is an inherently transitional life stage, the search must be for common sequences of experiences which may be described as typical youth careers. We need typologies of (typical) youth careers in education and the labour market, housing and family relationships, politics, vis-à-vis the justice and state welfare systems, and in leisure and consumption. We also need typologies of childhood starting points and adult destinations. These are indispensable.

All this is most easily illustrated in the transition from school-to-work, but mainly because, up to now, this is the transition within which the search for career routes has been most intense. It is possible to identify typical sequences of experiences in post-compulsory education, training, employment and unemployment: routes which tend to recruit young people from particular family and educational backgrounds, and which lead to particular occupational destinations (see Roberts and Parsell, 1992). Describing these routes as trajectories recognises the operation of push and pull forces. For example, middle-class parents typically push their children towards higher education, while employers offering the best jobs seek and pull academic thoroughbreds towards them. Sociological common sense suggests that similar patterns and linkages will be found in young people's socio-emotional and sexualised relationships with peers, residential arrangements, consumption behaviour, and in their engagements with politics, the justice and welfare systems.

It is sometimes objected (see Evans and Furlong, 1997), first, that this kind of analysis mistakes the outcomes of individuals' choices and actions for structures which causally shape their lives, and second, that even if the structural agenda was appropriate in the past it has become less so today as a result of modern social structures loosening, and 'traditional' age, class and gender divisions blurring, in these flexible post-Fordist times. Nowadays, it is sometimes argued, their at best loosely structured situations require young people to be reflexive, to formulate goals, to take control of their own lives and futures, and navigate towards their chosen destinations. Researchers are sometimes invited to contribute to young people's empowerment by incorporating them as research partners and treating them as principal users of research findings. Rather than grouping young people according to their externally structured situations, it is suggested that the more realistic and productive course nowadays is to group them by the life strategies that they adopt (Wyn and Dwyer, 1999).

All this is largely a rerun of the 1960s and 1970s choice versus opportunity debates (see Roberts, 1975; Daws, 1977). The crucial fact of this matter is that, as always, young people continue to choose and navigate within constraints (structures) that are neither of their own making nor within their control. The kind of individualisation that has spread in these post-Fordist times is a structured variety (see Roberts *et al.*, 1994).

It is true that the choice and navigation metaphors accord with most young people's own thinking and discourses. Most attach great importance to being, and usually insist that they are, in control of their own biographies (see Evans and Heinz, 1993; Evans, 2002). This is not new. In the 1950s and 1960s young people accepted responsibility for their own occupational choices. Paul Willis' (1977) lads felt in control of their lives. Spanning the generations, a plain fact of this matter is that only a minority of young people have been able to decide what/who they wish to become well in advance, then implement their aims. This kind of active individualisation is class-based (Evans and Heinz, 1993). Most young people's biographies are individualised relatively passively as they make the best of the available opportunities. Many still remain very close to where they started out in life in both social class and residential terms. The extent to which the population has become mobile is easily exaggerated. It is still only a minority of young people who leave their parental homes for higher education, often for ever. In 1969, 56 per cent of Britain's 16–44-year-olds were still living in the same districts where they had been brought up. By 1999 this figure had fallen, but only to 46 per cent (Travis, 1999).

The proper job of sociology is not to compound, but to correct, the 'epistemological fallacy' to which young (and older) people, and even some youth researchers, often succumb (Furlong and Cartmel, 1997). This is not to take any particular side in a structure versus agency debate. Structure and agency are always implicated in one another. The crucial point is that sociology's principal concern must be with collective patterns. 'Rational choice theory' (Goldthorpe, 1998) may explain how structures are maintained and reproduced, but it cannot, in itself, explain the origins of the situations that make particular choices rational for the relevant actors.

Quantitative and qualitative methods

The real issue is not which is best but how to adapt both methods to contemporary conditions. Many youth researchers have a special affection for, and a desire to practise qualitatively. Doing otherwise would be a waste of opportunity by researchers who are close in age, and who are able to participate in their subjects' milieux, and draw on their own recent youth biographies. However, qualitative evidence from necessarily small-scale studies is most valuable when it can be set within the larger picture which can only be constructed from quantitative evidence from larger, and more representative, samples.

The ethnographic studies conducted at the CCCS in the 1960s and 1970s are among the crown jewels of British youth research (Hall and Jefferson, 1976; Mungham and Pearson, 1976). These enquiries demonstrated, or at least argued persuasively, that working-class youth cultures had a class base. This ended two decades of speculation about a generation war replacing the class struggle. There have been few outcomes from youth research which have equalled this impact. What is often overlooked is that the CCCS enquiries could be so revealing only because they were conducted at a point in history when the adult destinations of young people from different social backgrounds had become crystal clear. The investigations were conducted during the window of opportunity when it was known that the 1944 Education Act had failed, and that working-class children remained, in most cases, destined to fill working-class jobs. It was also the case that these young people were most likely to fall in love with, and marry, one another. The CCCS enquiries were conducted when all this was firmly established, but before the oil price spirals, economic restructuring and labour market turmoil led to a fresh generation of youth researchers contemplating broken bridges, a new limbo condition, and the creation of new career routes through new types of education and training (see, for example, Raffe, 1988; Ashton et al., 1989). During the brief window of opportunity all that remained was to explore the processes whereby working-class kids ended up in working-class jobs, and why they accepted their destinies (Willis, 1977). Before long, the number one youth research problem was once again to discover who was ending-up where.

Executing the necessarily large-scale enquiries that are needed to answer this latter question has become more difficult in these 'new times' because youth transitions have been prolonged. Many individuals are now in their late 20s or 30s before they marry and become parents, or have jobs which they are able and willing to occupy for the foreseeable future. How long the transition lasts varies from country to country. In Britain, despite the recent prolongation of their transitions, young people still appear to rush into adulthood compared with the more leisurely progress of their central European, not to mention their Mediterranean, counterparts (see Lagree, 1996). Modestly longitudinal studies, as in the ESRC 1987–89 16–19 Initiative which followed up its samples for just two years (see Banks et al., 1992), are no longer adequate. Increased longitudinality has been achieved with the 1958 and 1970 birth cohort samples, but a problem that arises is that by the time a cohort reaches age 30 or thereabouts, the situations and opportunities facing 16-year-olds have changed so substantially as to render the findings out-of-date. Cross-sectional surveys of young people of different ages, from 16 to 30, say, encounter the comparable problem that the current 16-year-olds' predicaments are unlike those faced by the 30-year-olds when they were 16. It would be hazardous for anyone to assume that today's university students will obtain similar labour market returns on their 'investments in human capital' as their predecessors in the late 1980s. Sequential cohort studies, like Britain's National Youth Cohort series but more longitudinal, would overcome these difficulties, but at enormous expense. Panels in which the subjects' ages vary, as in the British Household Panel Survey, could be the answer if the resources were available to continue or repeat such research indefinitely. A cheaper, and therefore probably more realistic, way of scanning prolonged youth transitions, will be a combination of forward-looking (what happens to 16-year-olds from different family and educational backgrounds?) and backward-looking enquiries (from where are those in specific positions at age 30 drawn?)

There is a comparable need to develop a contemporary equivalent to traditional ethnography. The CCCS researchers were criticised for their lack of attention to young women and ethnic minority youth. The latter omission has been rectified by subsequent researchers, but most girls' lives have never been amenable to participant observation. There are no sister enquiries to those in which researchers have contacted groups of young males who hang about and around their home neighbourhoods, where the fieldworkers have been able to share their subjects' conversations and activities. The young males' typical attitudes and preoccupations have thereby become known to the researchers, and it has been possible to generalise about the members of these peer groups because they have usually all been brought up in similar homes, attended the same schools, and faced similar future prospects. Girls' lives have never been as easily accessed, and the same applies nowadays to most young males. The places where young people hang about nowadays – pubs, music clubs and sports centres, for example – draw participants from many different backgrounds, who remain 'a crowd' maybe for just a few months, then disperse to various destinations (Thornton, 1995). Researchers get less pay-off from just hanging around. They can adopt the substitute methods normally used with girls (see Griffin, 1985) – detailed and repeat individual interviews – but this does not allow the subjects' lives to be observed, or their natural conversations overheard. Ethnographers can attach themselves to groups in schools and further education colleges, universities and training schemes, but these work based peer groups do not usually remain together throughout 'the transition', or even, in many cases, in their immediate outside-work lives (see Bates and Riseborough, 1993; Skeggs, 1997).

Comparative perspectives

Youth research needs to be longitudinal in perspective even when the methods are snapshot. Youth is an inherently transitional life stage, so all studies need to engage with how their subjects' lives are changing. It is also desirable, if not absolutely necessary, for the sociology of youth to compare youth transitions across time and place. The exercise itself always helps define sociological problems – distinctive features of youth transitions in particular places and at particular times – which then need to be explained. And comparisons themselves invariably suggest explanations.

Youth is rarely static in a historical, let alone biographical, sense. Life stage transitions create slack which can absorb tensions aroused by wider social and economic changes. Youth can be prolonged or shortened, hastened or delayed, and the same applies in later life. In recent decades in Britain, and in most other European countries, youth transitions have been extended. This trend could continue, but not indefinitely, and it will most likely be reversed at some point. What goes up must come down. It is not quite the same with youth transitions. These accelerated in many countries in the 1940s and 1950s when the typical ages of first marriages, and when young people began to earn adult wages, fell. Between the 1970s and 1990s transitions were extended (see Bynner *et al.*, 1997b). It is not inevitable, but it is possible, that before long youth will contract again. Even though the answers will change, the sociology of youth needs questions that will survive these cycles.

Developing the sociology of youth

The agenda for youth research sketched above may appear conservative. It is conservative, and rightly so, because the basic questions for the sociology of youth do not change. They need to be asked again in present-day conditions. Research methods need to be adapted but not jettisoned – we have a rather small basic armoury. We need progress, not more restarts:

> In psychology there are several comprehensive theories of youth, while sociology and pedagogy lack such theories. Sociologists use

ad hoc theories according to the specific needs of the actual research. Most often sociologists are happy with an ad hoc explanation of a certain youth phenomenon and do not seek a broader theoretical understanding of youth. Even the meaning of the concept 'youth' may vary in each sociological youth study (Puuronen, 2001, p. 11).

Constantly seeking new approaches, perspectives and paradigms is a recipe for stagnation – flurries of intellectual excitement which eventually evaporate, whereupon we discover that we are where we were before – no improved typologies, or more sophisticated theories about the links between different dimension of youth transitions, or between origins and destinations. We have foundations, an impressive track record of youth research, on which to build. Why kick past achievements away?

2
Mods and Shockers: Youth Cultural Studies in Britain[1]

For John Hood-Williams
Phil Cohen

Way back when

Youth research in Britain originated in two major public concerns of the immediate pre- and post-Second World War years: juvenile labour and juvenile delinquency. If the link between 'blind alley labour' and youth crime was always more assumed than demonstrated it was partly because the two areas of investigation followed quite distinct trajectories and their respective research agendas rarely converged. The study of delinquency remained the province of university settlement sociology and its politics of conscience (Richter, 1964); in this tradition, juvenile delinquency was seen very much in a community context either as forming part of a generationally transmitted criminal subculture, associated with what would later be called the 'under class' or as a peer sanctioned rite of passage involving defiance of adult officialdom. In either case it was an index of urban deprivation and the slum culture (Mays, 1954).

Studies of juvenile labour – mostly boy labour – were initially undertaken by economists with a specific interest in labour market theory and modernising the apprenticeship system (Gollan, 1937; Bray, 1980; Ainley and Rainbird, 1999). As customary rites of occupational succession in both skilled and unskilled trades began to weaken and finally collapse, to be gradually replaced by extended schooling and vocational training (Youth Training Schemes) in the 1970s, a new genre of 'transition studies' emerged led mainly by occupational or educational sociologists, and concerned with the deferred, broken, or otherwise problematic nature of school leavers' moves into the world of full-time work and adulthood. This has remained the mainstream tradition of youth studies ever since (Ashton, 1973; Bates *et al.*, 1984; Roberts, 1986; Finn, 1987; Raffe, 1988; Breen, 1991; Mizen, 1995).

This twin track development of youth research was largely dictated by the modernising agendas of successive Labour administrations, especially in the period of Wilson's 'white hot technological revolution'. Modernisation here meant eliminating the 'premodern' cultures of deprivation associated with the urban poor, and dismantling the casual labour market and hidden economy that was still based on pre-industrial forms of manual work (Marriott, 1991).

Whatever the gains in terms of consistency of empirical focus over an extended period, the result was a drastic narrowing of the theoretical perspective. The areas and methods of enquiry which elsewhere, in continental Europe and North America, came to dominate the field – psychoanalytically oriented studies of adolescence and historical investigations of youth, and especially student, movements – were effectively marginalised or ignored.

The early implantation of Freudianism and the equally precocious advent of the 'religion of youth' in the USA gave the world its first theoretically sophisticated model of adolescent psychology (Campbell, 2000). In Europe, the pivotal role played by revolutionary student movements in the formation of ethnic and civic nationalisms after 1848, gave the youth question a high intellectual profile from the outset and ever since it has remained the focus of novels (Moretti, 1987) and historical/sociological enquiry (Mitterauer, 1992).

There were no parallel developments in Britain over the corresponding period. As a result, the conditions simply did not exist for bringing together historical and psychoanalytic perspectives to create any wider angled focus on the youth question as occurred in the pioneering post-war work of Erik Erikson (1971) in the USA. Psychoanalysts like D.W. Winnicott offered interesting insights into the dynamics of juvenile delinquency and the role of therapeutic communities in their treatment (Winnicott, 1984), but steered well clear of meta-psychological pronouncements on the youth question itself. Some British historians focused on childhood and apprenticeship as part of a wider concern with the demographic revolution and the changing patterns of kinship and family formation in the transition to industrial capitalism, but again the youth question as such has been sidelined (Pinchbeck and Hewitt, 1969; Levine, 1979; Anderson, 1983).

In general, the mood amongst British academics was unsympathetic to any treatment of youth as part of a 'grand narrative' whether of the psyche or nation. The romantic excesses of 'sturm und drang' adolescence as themIf in European literature and sociology were widely believed to have led to fascism (Springhall, 1971). So instead of the exploration of the heightened emotional and sexual sensitivities of adolescence, or the heroics of youthful idealism as demonstrated in political movements, our post-war novelists and sociologists gave us close grained social(ist) realist accounts of the vicissitudes of growing-up working class in Salford, Liverpool, Glasgow, or London's East End. But then, as we know (or do we?), in the second half of the 1960s everything changed. As war babies grew up into angry young men, and then women, as the juvenile gave way to the teenager, something rather un-English (and not even quite British) happened (Roszak, 1969; Melly, 1989). A set of distinctive youth cultures emerged which were unmistakably home-grown but which also articulated changes occurring in what was coming to be known as the 'global village', changes which would see the onward march of Labour halted well this side of Blake's New Jerusalem, and put issues other than class on the political agenda (Mungham and Pearson, 1976; Seabrook, 1978). An everyday aesthetics built around youth fashions and popular music began to challenge the 'high culture' of the traditional English intelligentsia (Frith, 1983; Bennett, 2000); the spirit of the age was redefined in terms that would ultimately explode the parochial anglo-centric universe of discourse that had for so long dominated academic research. New epistemologies drawing on major currents in European Marxism, phenomenology and structuralism offered an alternative, subject-centred, mindset seemingly more attuned to the head mix of hedonistic body politics and radical utopianism, otherwise known as sex'n'drugs'n'rock'n'roll (Fornäs and Bolin, 1995; Pile and Thrift, 1995).

'English' community studies attempted to grapple with these 'exotic' new formations, but their accounts of youth phenomena increasingly lacked conviction (Wilmott, 1966; Parker, 1974). If sociologists of education were in a much better position to respond to the new conjuncture, it was partly because questions of knowledge, culture, ideology and power could hardly be kept out of the picture of what was happening to young people in the school system at a time when the issues of 'comprehensivisation' and 'meritocracy' were high on the political agenda (Jackson and Marsden, 1986; Young, 1994). The new research paradigms offered a way of linking the hidden curriculum of classroom knowledge with cultures of resistance to schooling in a way that offered an explanation as to why significant sections of the working class were losing out. Whether the focus was on codes of cultural transmission (Bernstein, 1974, 1996) or social reproduction (Bowles and Gintis, 1976) or their articulation (Bourdieu and Passeron, 1977), there was a concentrated attempt to produce more theoretically sophisticated but still empirically grounded accounts of schooling.

Yet, there was clearly more going on with Mods and Rockers, than could be explained by school counter cultures (Hargreaves, 1967, 1975), or how 'the lads learnt to labour' (Willis, 1977). What was lacking was an explanation of why and how these youth cultural forms had emerged just when they did. How were deep changes in the class structure affecting many aspects of social, cultural and political life in Britain in the 1960s and 1970s, re-positioning young people in the spheres of production and consumption (Gelder and Thornton, 1997)? And how did this in turn shape their relationships to the major institutions of state and civil society – the family, the school, the law, the communities of labour and leisure?

This chapter is concerned with how this conjuncture helped to shape the youth research agenda in Britain over the subsequent three decades. The next section traces the cultural turn in youth studies from the 1960s to the present and considers what has been gained – and lost – in the process. The following section examines what is at stake in returning the youth question to its origins in a new problematic grand narrative of modernity – how far does it help to interpret youth cultures as invented traditions of modernity, rather than as anticipations – or realisations – of the post-modern condition? Finally, the chapter looks at the current conjuncture and at some of the problems and possibilities associated with the emergence of a new kind of evidence-based youth policy centred on a more dialogic model of the research process than has hitherto prevailed. Could such a model help to renew theoretical debate around the youth question and at last overcome the marginalisation of youth studies – and young people themselves – in our public intellectual life?

The youth/cultural turn: from destiny to origins and back again

It has been argued that New Labour's 'cultural turn' in the 1990s was integral to its triumphalist vision of rebuilding the nation after the devastation of the Thatcher years. Less frequently noted is the fact that the project was from the outset heavily articulated to the youth question (Davies, 1999).

There was, of course, nothing new about equating the coming to power of a political party with the coming-of-age of a new generation pledged to rejuvenate civil society. In British politics, as we have already note, the generational card was first played by Disraeli over a century ago, and in continental Europe it has been a staple ingredient of both social movements and political discourse for much longer (Mitterauer, 1992). But Blairism gave this decidedly old-fashioned story a radically new twist by the simple device of appropriating the 'conquest of the cool' – that morphing of youth cultural values with 'soft' capitalism which marked the cutting edge of entrepreneurialism in the 1980s – and linking it to the advent of a new kind of cosmopolitan or multicultural middle class (Frank, 1997).

Unlike the 'Middle England' beloved of the Tory party, this stratum was largely the product of improved state education and training, and could therefore be rightfully claimed as the standard bearers of New Labour's self-proclaimed mission to deliver the masses to a fully fledged meritocracy (Blair, 1998). If this stratum could be promoted as the focus of a new narrative of national aspiration, it was because it was heavily concentrated in the so-called 'knowledge economy' (Landry and Bianchini, 1996; Leadbetter, 1997). Here flexible specialisation, impression management, horizontal networking – the Big Three 'need-to-do's' of the post-Fordist work regime – segued seamlessly into forms of life style innovation and reflexive 'self-invention' pioneered by post-war youth culture (Frank, 1997).

Youth-as-creative industry thus stood for everything that 'old Labour' was not: hip, sexy, individualistic, adventurous, enterprising, and above all open to the endless possibilities for niche marketing represented by multicultural capitalism. New Labour's logic was impeccable. After all, who would want to be identified with archaic institutions run by senile placemen, or, for that matter by middle-aged Marxists, in a world that capitalism has made safe for the permanent revolution of technologies and commodities? As for the unacceptable face of youth that is those who remained trapped in quasi-proletarian cultures of masculinity and manual labour, they – or rather their customary forms of solidarity and prides of place – quickly became the target of a whole series of special measures, from the big stick of youth curfews and zero tolerance policing to the carrots of 'Fame Academies' in the form of ICT and youth arts programmes designed to release the 'raw energy and hidden talent' of the underclass and put it to more socially purposeful, productive and profitable ends (Sefton-Green, 1998; DfEE, 1999).

Yet it would be wrong to explain the project of 'Cool Britannia', as simply a piece of inspired opportunism on the part of New Labour spin doctors. Its origins lie much deeper and further back. It was the emergence of the British New Left in the mid-1960s which laid the intellectual foundations for the cultural turn. Inspired by Gramsci's own version of the cultural turn, a group of Marxist historians, economists and sociologists around New Left Review developed an original critique of the roots of Britain's post-war malaise (Anderson, 1979). The failure to disseminate the conditions of prosperity beyond the traditional professional and managerial class, the lack of investment in private and public enterprise, and the refusal to modernise both economic infrastructure and political institutions, were all argued to be profoundly cultural in both cause and effect. Behind these conjunctural impasses lay a problem of much longer duration – the infatuation of the British middle classes with assimilating and preserving the aristocratic and imperial values of a traditional governing elite, values that were profoundly anti-industrial, anti-urban and anti-cosmopolitan in spirit and implementation (Wiener, 1985).

British cultural studies were born from this conjuncture, and almost its first move was to apply this style of thinking to the youth question. In the early work of the Birmingham school, the emergence of highly visible youth cultures – Teds, Mods, Rockers and Skinheads – in the 1960s and the erosion of customary transitions from school to work, provided key sites for both ethnographic and theoretical investigation inspired by a Gramscian analysis of popular culture (Hall and Jefferson, 1976; Hall, 1992). The detailed analysis of these new cultural forms was a way of looking afresh at dislocations in the post-war British social structure and challenging reductive economistic interpretations of class relations; at the same time it enabled cultural studies to distance itself both from the 'Eng Lit' tradition of condescension towards popular culture and the Fabian perspective of social reform associated with settlement sociology (Grossberg, 1997; Bennett, 2000).

The early CCCS work often proceeded from an identification with the marginal and 'outsider', influenced by notions of subculture and counterculture derived from West Coast deviancy theory; this was often grafted on to a more home grown concern with issues of popular literacy and working-class education raised by the New Left. The youth question brought these two sides of the story rather neatly together (Willis, 1977; Robins and Cohen, 1978; Brake, 1980).

Yet if cultural studies, in its own beginnings, used (white male working-class) youth culture as a sounding board from which to create its own distinctive 'voice', the field quickly expanded to include questions of gender and race. By the early 1980s, girls cultures and black youth cultures had become the site of important new work both theoretically and substantively (Griffin, 1985; Lees, 1986; Gilroy, 1987; McRobbie, 1991).

En route questions of class transformation/formation were rather left to one side. This was quite understandable given their association with the white malestream. Yet, this displacement of the class problematic was to have some unfortunate repercussions for the subsequent development of the field (Willis, 1990; Furlong, 1993; Munt, 2000).

More immediately, the linguistic and semiotic turn in the human sciences provided cultural studies with its main chance to put itself at the cutting edge of research. The study of cultural codes of every kind could now, it seemed, be put on a properly scientific basis. Teenage fashion, music, films, magazines and fiction would henceforth be treated as seriously as their more supposedly 'adult' counterparts (Lewis, 1992).

In retrospect, this move seems more like a false dawn than a fresh start for youth cultural analysis, but it did have the effect of encouraging more detailed studies of stylistic practices than had hitherto been possible (Hebdige, 1979, 1988). *Clash* lyrics and trainer ads, bedroom walls and shopping malls, scarf rituals on the soccer terraces and mating rituals on the dance floor, were all subjected to exhaustive scrutiny for what they might reveal about the process of 'revolt into style' (Melly, 1989). One, perhaps inevitable, result of these close-up 'storm and dress' youth studies was that the social contexts of family, school, work and community life that gave these practices their life historical depth and meaning, were pushed ever further into the background. But there was a socio-logic to this move.

With the demise of Punk, it was no longer enough to focus on 'spectacular deviance' – the visible and the audible – forms of youth culture (Frith, 1983, 1996). As the 1980s went on and signs of resistance became ever more subliminal, the quest for subtexts pushed researchers into ever more sophisticated ways of reading between the lines. Ethnography, with its realist epistemology and naive commitment to naturalistic observation of everyday social interaction was clearly not up to the task. The practice was virtually abandoned. At the same time, the limitations of semiology, and structuralism more generally, had become apparent once the play of substitutions within the code yielded evidence of processes of representation that could not be explained in purely linguistic terms. Just as the pleasure principles of much popular cultural practice remained incomprehensible (or a sign of False Consciousness) to 'ideology critique', so they proved irreducible to the analysis of binary oppositions. What was unsaid, unthought, unconscious, increasingly demanded the right to be spoken, thought and made articulate on its own terms.

Enter psychoanalysis as handmaiden to a 'new new' art, film and literary criticism. Cultural critics could now study the covert and disavowed strategies of authorisation at work in the image/text as symptomatic of everything that escaped the author's own conscious intentionality: from the genealogy of signatures to the epistemic zeitgeist, from the archaeology of knowledge to the most secret and perverse pleasures of the text, it was all grist to the deconstructive mill.

The advent of post-structuralism was singularly good news for armchair critics of popular culture. They no longer had to leave the security of the university bookstacks in order to perform Hegelian headstands on the high wire of Grand Theory. If there was no reality outside its representation and no referent beyond the internal play of signification, if meaning was continually deferred, every reading supplementary and inter-textuality ruled OK, then the work of cultural criticism became a never-ending quest to avoid the temptations of foreclosure by appealing to the social or the real (McRobbie, 1997).

Yet if all the world was a text and all the people in it merely quotations, some way still had to be found to tackle what was nominally outside the text but very much in the substance of what discourses of race, gender and sexuality insisted upon as their central reference point – namely the body. Courtesy of Foucault the formation of a corpus of texts into an institutionalised discourse of power might be related to a particular 'bio-political' strategy. With Lacan, it seemed that, conversely, bodies might be read as if they were texts, and hence subjected to a purely linguistic form of psychoanalysis operating behind as well as between the lines of desire.

Throughout the 1980s, cultural texts of every kind were thus laid out on the analysts couch; not in order to be dissected according to the old methods of moral anatomy (the good and important distinguished from the bad and trivial); nor to be cured of their prosodic ills, or 'reintegrated back into society' as the old style Modernists and Marxists preferred; but to be taken apart around the fault lines of unconscious identification which they provoked in the reader. By the bias of this new approach, students of cultural studies embarked on the toils of de-centred subjectivity and en route wrote themselves back into their PhDs as narrators of their own intellectual enterprise. But where would it lead them?

It might have indirectly provided a point of re-entry into the youth question. Post-structuralism drew attention to the effect of non-rationalised structures of feeling associated with the assumption of fully sexualised, and sometimes racialised bodies split down the line of their desires for the other. The discursive construction – and social performance – of adolescence as a nexus of imaginary identifications thus came more fully into focus as a discrete object of analysis. It was the rare achievement of John Hood-Williams to have pursued this line of enquiry, almost single handed, through the whole of his tragically short academic career (Hood-Williams, 2002). If this set of object relations went largely unexplored, it was because the lure of identity politics pulled in another direction.

Feminist and black cultural studies developed styles of autobiographical and memory work designed to explore more dramatic claims of historical injustice than the frustrations and impasses of growing up; in these highly politicised forms of self-narration, adolescence itself was often portrayed as little more than a rite of passage from primary (and hence unconscious) oppression to a state of greater political enlightenment (Hooks, 1992). From this vantage point, the insistence of the British School of Psychoanalysis on the subterfuges of the false self (not to mention the primacy of the mother/child dyad) were all too politically suspect. In particular, Kleinian theory was bad news for anyone who wanted to celebrate the socially transgressive nature of preoedipal object choices mandated by some versions of sexual politics, just as it had a lot of uncomfortable things to say about the conservative structures of oedipal revolt to those radical feminists whose attack on patriarchy took just this form (Alford, 1989).

By the mid-1990s, the textualisation of cultural studies was all but complete. The gains were manifest and multiple. It permitted cultural studies to install itself as a powerful intellectual force within university humanities departments and art schools, as well as to set up in business on its own academic account (Bennett, 2000). The technique of deconstruction spearheaded an internal critique of the human and social sciences for their complicity in the tyrannies of Western Reason, and hence, indirectly, helped cultural studies to establish its claims as a pioneer of post-colonial theory (Moore-Gilbert, 1997).

Yet the cult of textuality had its downside. For one thing, it failed to provide the intellectual tools or motivation to engage with the profound culturalisation of polity and economy that was taking place during this period. The growth of cultural industries and their deployment as part of a new strategy of urban regeneration was at the cutting edge of structural change in the 1980s. As capitalism went multicultural, en route helping to cement post-Fordist regimes into the remaining workplaces, the local state was left to pick up the pieces; the fragments of labour history or ethnography that were left behind on their doorsteps were converted into 'cultural flagship projects'; the post-colonial city dressed up in drag for the cosmopolitan tourist trade (Sassen, 1991; Cohen, 1999a).

The deeper implications of these changes for the class structure were for a long time ignored by cultural theorists. Despite the penetration of informatics into every aspect of social production, labour processes were still too unlike textual ones to be considered a suitable case for treatment. The fact that labouring bodies became increasingly sexualised and racialised in the iconography of popular culture went also largely un-remarked (Cohen, 1997a).

A further knock-on effect of textualisation was to further problematise any empirical research methodology. With feminist standpoint epistemologists denouncing the ethnographic interview as a version of date rape, and black anti-racists joining in with atrocity stories of participant observation as a simulacrum of colonial surveillance carried over from the days of plantation slavery, ethnographers went into hiding. Some hung up their tape recorders and retired hurt into the academic closet (or the library). Some purged themselves of 'other contempt' by engaging in prolonged bouts of critical textual deconstruction often spiced with strenuous acts of public self-flagellation. In the vacuum created by the disappearance of 'thick description', a new genre of quasi-sociological reportage emerged driven by the desire to authenticate or authorise the voices of oppressed (ethnic and sexual) minorities, whose experiences were recruited as support for ideologically driven agendas aiming at their liberation (Mac an Ghail, 1988; Mirza, 1992; Sewell, 1997).

At a time when the mainstream political culture in Britain was firmly dominated by the New Right, an alternative cultural politics emerged in which eco-feminism, gay politics and black perspective anti-racism celebrated their respective marginalities as a site of transcendence from the oppressive constraints of what was often seen as a more or less monolithic white, heterosexist power structure (O'Shea, 1998). En route 'race' and 'gender' were made equivalent to 'class' as identity constructs, despite their very different ontological status, not to mention their disparate provenance as analytic categories and sites of inequality (Skeggs, 1997). One payoff, of course, was that these instances could either be stacked up to constitute a hierarchy of oppression, or rendered down into a 'play of difference' without disturbing their essentialist construction (Fuss, 1989). Perhaps, a more productive result was that youth was definitively deconstructed as a unitary category – it was now definable as a specific site of multiply articulated identities, rather than as having some a priori meaning in and of itself (Hood-Williams, 2002).

Cultural studies thus promised to provide an intellectual space within which new social movements and identity politics as a whole might be critically assessed. Yet, in practice, the institutionalisation of the field as a distinct department of academic knowledge tended to militate against making this a remit part of any wider political agenda. Many of the leading lights concentrated on developing a unifying field theory in the shape of post-modernism, whilst ignoring the impact of Thatcherism on the political culture as a whole. But this apparent retreat from the wider agenda has to be understood in context.

Even though culture wars did not occur in British universities, on anything like the North American scale, there is no doubt that much cultural theory in this country has been devoted, directly or indirectly, to what student identity politics has put on the campus agenda (Nolan, 1996). This process of political involution intensified as the CS jargonaut began to roll; throughout the 1980s and the 1990s, the academic journals multiplied along with accretions of theoretical vocabulary and hierarchies of knowledge allied to their mastery; the development of an internal star system, fights over the canon and border disputes with cognate disciplines fuelled personal and professional rivalries within the field. Academic politicking increasingly took the place of more outward-looking pursuits. By the end of the century, the main preoccupations of the early phase of British Cultural Studies: changes in working-class life and labour, the methods of the critical ethnographic case study, the engagement with structural inequalities through initiatives in popular education, had all been definitively 'surpassed' or was it suppressed? Cultural studies had shed its roots in these 'parochial' (or was it politically grounded?) concerns and become a properly transnational and travelling theory, fit to explore and rule a post-colonial universe of discourse that was fully as hybrid as itself.

That however proved to be only one side of the story. In the 1990s, the narrative turn in the human sciences renewed interest in the everyday discourses and linguistic practices that regulate social interaction (Rampton, 1995; Widdicombe and Wooffitt, 1995); the rise of geography in place of a discredited historicism and the emphasis on social capital and network analysis gave an added impetus to the study of adolescent friendship patterns and peer group cultures as agencies of informal learning (Hey, 1997). Meanwhile, the advent of 'cultural flagship projects' and the building of whole new 'cultural quarters' in many downtown areas alerted many university administrators to the potential of cultural industries as a source of post-graduate employment. By extension cultural studies might now become a vocational subject, leading to jobs not only for those leaving university, but also help widen access to 'non-traditional' students who were in the vanguard of innovation in popular music, fashion and general youth style (Landry and Bianchini, 1996). For purely practical reasons to do with survival in an increasingly competitive academic market place, Cultural studies was forced to look beyond itself to the very questions that it had theoretically repressed as a condition of its academic success.

Meanwhile, on the 'New Times' or po-mo Left, it was time to rediscover youth as the site of newly fascinating 'multi-cultures' situated on the front lines of a transgressive and nomadic body politics, struggling to assert autonomy against the disciplinary structures of schooling, the homogenising powers of capital and the bureaucratic governance by the state (Melucci, 1989; McRobbie, 1994; Thornton, 1995; Giroux, 1996; Epstein, 1998). Youth cultures were 'cool places' where young people could come out of the various closets imposed by repressive normalisation, if only by hiding in the light (Skelton and Valentine, 1998; Macdonald, 2001). For some researchers, the seductive power of ethnography to add a little 'local colour' to the bare bones of sociological analysis proved a compelling motivation for its reintroduction, albeit often in a naturalistic rather than a critical mode (Bates and Riseberough, 1993; Blackman, 1995). For the more entrepreneurially minded, adolescent ethnicities provided a golden opportunity to lay claim to what was valuable in enterprise culture, and carve out a niche in the global marketing of 'youth culture' (Redhead et al., 1993; Polhemus, 1994). From both points of view, new lines of battle were drawn between those youth identities regarded as examples of healthy happy hybridity (and hence both marketable and political) and those which clung to pathological purities (bad for business and civic boosterism).

Along side this 'po-mo' tendency, and in some critical dialogue with it, another strand of work developed which attempted, with varying degrees of success, to relate this new agenda to an older tradition of youth cultural research (Brice Heath, 1983; Coffield, 1986; Hewitt, 1986; Cockburn, 1987; Hollands, 1990; Back, 1996; Cohen, 1997a). We are given detailed and often sensitive readings of how young people are making sense of changing class, gender and ethnic identities in the everyday contexts of their negotiation in peer groups, family relations, schooling, training and work. How to relate overarching explanatory paradigms to these thick descriptions remained a major problem. The two major ESRC youth research programmes that took place over the decade were especially disappointing in this regard. Despite the unifying themes of 'transition' and 'citizenship', the initiative generated a multiplicity of case studies, but yielded little theoretical advance in terms of integrating different intellectual traditions and disciplines (Banks et al., 1992; Jones and Wallace, 1992; Bynner, 1998). Within the sociology of education, however, several recent studies of 'youth in transition' have been more successful at putting together the theoretical and empirical sides of the research story (Ball and Maguire, 2000).

There was also some progress made in developing a more sophisticated and reflexive approach to ethnographic work, in particular to add some biographical depth through the use of audio and video diaries, photo-mapping, story making and guided phantasy (Cohen, 1997b, 1999; Walkerdine, 1997, 2001). At the same time, there have been important moves to use the Internet as an instrument of virtual ethnography to put the thesis of a multiple or post-modern identity to the empirical test (Buckingham, 1994; Sefton-Green, 1998). In future, the potential for using multimedia formats and online archives to disseminate youth research to wider non-academic audiences, including young people themselves, will obviously need to be fully explored.

Criminology, which throughout the Thatcher years had pursued the rigorous path of sociological realism, finally succumbed to its own version of the cultural turn, returning to the thematics of 'moral panic' through the narrative analysis of popular crime stories and the structures of feeling and phantasy which they articulate at the level of individual biographies, especially of crime victims (Hollway and Jefferson, 2000). Social historians have also begun to map out the changing discourses through which 'youth' has continually been reinvented as symbol or symptom of underlying tensions in British society over the last century (Pearson, 1983; Springhall, 1998).

Finally in the new century millions of young people are on the move from East to West, many of them in search of the material signs of a 'Good life' disseminated relentlessly through the mediascapes of the global cultural economy. Here youth culture is rendered synonymous with the affluent life style associated with cosmopolitan post-modernity (Appadurai, 1998). The idioms of youth culture have thus become a lingua franqua of shared aspiration across the world, but at the same time the notion of the nation as a crucible of identities is being given a new lease of life as a metaphor of diasporic belonging – and at precisely the moment at which its anchorage in the territorial state has been decisively destabilised. Here is a new nexus of contradiction defining the youth question in the era of globalisation (Amit-Talal and Wolf, 1995; Brah, 1996).

In at least some of this work the links between developments in cultural theory, social policy analysis and ethnographic research have, however tenuously, been maintained often in the face of pressures with academic life to the contrary. But how far does any of this work address the issue of what makes 'youth' a research question in the first place?

Back to the future: on modernity as invented tradition

From the very outset there was tension within the New Left between its culturalist and economistic tendencies (Black, 2003). There were those who read backwards from Gramsci and Lukacs to discover Hegel and the young Marx and whose main concern was to develop a critique of human alienation grounded in a cultural analysis of capitalist modernity. And there were those who wanted to hold onto the systemic concerns of classical Marxism with the political economy of exploitation and set out to enhance it with a more sophisticated analysis of modes of social production or social action. Today after a decade in which post-modern cultural theory and rational choice Marxism went off in different directions, there is once more a concerted attempt to bring the topics of alienation and exploitation back together and into a single conjunctural analysis of contemporary global capitalism (Hardt and Negri, 2001).

It could be argued that in its small way much recent youth research has attempted just such a reconciliation between cultural and structural analysis. The development of life course transition studies provided a compelling counterpoint to the quasi anthropological concern with exotic instances of deviance and difference. In this research literature, new biographical trajectories associated with class and gender positions are systematically linked to the changing regimes of schooling and work in the late capitalist society (Ball, 1998; Chamberlayne and Wengraf, 2000; Walkerdine, 2001). Although many transition studies continue to follow an abstracted empiricism, their findings, if not always their analyses, point up the complex patterns of overdetermination and discontinuity in young peoples' lives. Implicitly these studies address what makes the youth question so central to debates in the human sciences, namely that it is a question about forms of invented tradition and modernity – or rather of modernity itself as an invented tradition (Fornäs and Bolin, 1995).

It is this question which gave birth to the original problematics of social science at the end of the nineteenth century. At the time it was intimately bound up with constructing a binary opposition between age and youth. As Marx (1985, p. 234) put it:

History is nothing but the succession of the separate generations, each of which exploits the materials, the capital funds, the productive forces handed down to it by all the proceeding generations. And this, on the one hand, continues the traditional activity in completely changed circumstances, and on the other modifies the old circumstances with completely changed activity

Marx, typically, dialecticises the notions of tradition and modernity, without, for all that, abandoning their anchorage in the problematics of generation. Certainly the idea that youth is a unitary, and hence a unifying category has a history as long as that of modernity, and the two are closely linked. The invention of adolescence as a distinctive stage of the life cycle was part of the same discourse that challenged the 'dead hand of tradition' braking the 'engines of progress'. Over the last century, the 'condition of youth question' has assumed increasing importance as being symptomatic of the health of the nation or the future of the race, the welfare of the family, or the state of civilisation-as-we-know-it. For the last 50 years, young people have had to carry a peculiar burden of representation; everything they do, say, think, or feel, is scrutinised by an army of professional commentators for signs of the times. Generation X studies and teen coming-of-age movies continue this genre up to the present day (Lewis, 1992).

Nevertheless, the relation between youth as an invented tradition and what is sometimes called 'post-modernity' has overthrown many of the categorical assumptions of both classical Marxist and non-Marxist sociology, including the associations between 'youth' and 'the new' age and traditionalism (Phoenix and Rattansi, 1998). In the 'old' societies of the West, within which we must now include the United States, the Great Fear of ageing and the search for 'eternal youth' has produced an apparently unquenchable desire to 'keep up with new times' amongst all age groups, but especially amongst those over 40 who can afford it. As BIFF cartoons show us so wittily, post-modernism provided this 'new old' middle class with a ready-made template for an ironic plagiarism that enables them to pursue a masquerade of 'youthfulness' with a semblance of style. As a consequence, young people – especially those who are not able to enter into the middle-class world of studenthood – have to continually improvise fresh ways of asserting their difference from elders as well as from their more advantaged peers; increasingly, the most excluded young people re-appropriate 'youth' by adopting an implicit rhetori of progress and modernity, usually by assimilating new technologies of consumption and using them to restate localised prides of place. The trick is to be seen to be growing up faster, doing things sooner and going one bigger and better than those on the other side of the class and race tracks. For example, using a mobile phone provides a magical connection to a global information economy from which in reality the user may be cut off.

To own – or steal – a mobile may work wonders for the self-esteem of young people locked into structural unemployment, or petty crime, but their chronic prematurity in the realm of streetwise 'body politics' has increasingly gone along with the retardation of skills required to stake out claims to public amenity and resource in any wider and more civic terms. This predicament is today perhaps best exemplified by ageing 'home boys', young men in their twenties and thirties still at home, unable to make the transition to full-time work, a decent wage, or independent living as a result of the feminisation of many service sector jobs and the decline of manual labour. Pubs, parks and football terraces may still provide them with public platforms on which to perform more or less aggressively racialised styles of masculinity; but the painful fact of their redundancy – both as message and as material practice, is only amplified in the process. Home boys may be a special case but there are many more young people unable to make the transition to the kinds of mobile individualism demanded by the new cultural economy, who are no less stranded, and whose sense of frustration leads to less visible, if often more self-destructive patterns of response (Ainley, 1991).

This problem is found in an especially intense form within black youth cultures. The immense influence of African–American vernaculars in the evolution of popular music, in street fashions and in styles of body language is an everyday fact of contemporary youth culture (Gilroy, 1993). But it has fed off and reinforced processes of racial exclusion in schooling and employment to ensure that only a small minority of black youth succeed in making enough capital out of their own identity work to become part of the success story of the enterprise culture (MacDonald and Coffield, 1991). Significant numbers of Asian youth, now equipped with their own distinctive diasporic identities have found it somewhat easier to move onwards and upwards into the new multicultural middle class via higher education, even if these success stories only serve to underline the bitterness of the majority of their peers whom they leave behind on the front lines of racial confrontation in cities like Bradford, Huddersfield and Leeds (Brah, 1996; Centre for Social Markets, 2002).

Given the terms of this conjuncture, the 'classic' contradiction between the symbolic potency of the adolescent body associated with its sexuality, looks and style and the political/economic powerlessness of youth as a socio-legal category has to be revised (Irwin, 1995; Wyn and White, 1997). The binarisms that hitherto assigned family, community and peer groups to the side of 'tradition', and school, labour process, state and mass media to the province of 'modernity' no longer apply in any simple way and explanations that depend on them dissolve into incoherence.

This issue has been highlighted by recent attempts to construct a 'post-modern' sociology – or rather a sociology of the post-modern condition. Whether or not this project actually goes beyond the tradition/modernity distinction, or the essentialised categories of structure and agency which derive from it, remains open to doubt. However, for present purposes, it is enough to note the significant impact which this body of work has had in re-invigorating youth studies.

The work of Ulrich Beck, as elaborated by Anthony Giddens in Britain, has been one influential factor in this renaissance (Beck, 1992; Beck et al., 1994). Beck and Giddens argue that 'individualisation' and 'reflexivity' are all pervasive characteristics of 'late modernity', and that we are seeing the emergence of new forms of inequality based on the uneven distribution of risks, rather than resources. This analysis has provided youth researchers with a conceptual peg on which to hang a new generation of empirical transition studies (Furlong and Cartmel, 1997). The attempt to connect issues of citizenship, cultural entitlement and educational stakeholding in this new literature certainly represents an advance over previous work in the field. The danger of this approach, however, is that bio-political categories of populations 'at risk' are applied to those young people who conspicuously fail to adapt to the kinds of individualised reflexivity demanded by post-Fordist work discipline. This new 'youth underclass' bears a suspicious resemblance to the old one as far as its distinguishing features are concerned! In place of bad timekeeping and industrial sabotage, they are now accused to failing to master the arts of public impression management, or cope with multitasking and flexitime. The underlying principle of indiscipline remains the same.

Read another way, the youth-at-risk analysis tends to reinvent old-fashioned sturm und drang adolescence as symptomatic of a late twentieth century form of modernity from which any possibility of real political contestation has been eliminated at source. According to this view youth protest has not only been culturalised, it has been commodified to the point where it is entirely recuperated within the 'spectacle of dissent' (Frank, 1997). It's a familiar enough refrain, yet the emergence of the anti-globalisation movement, if nothing else, attests to continuing vitality of a political counter culture in which successive generations of students continue to play a major leadership role. Single issue campaigns, spanning environmentalism, cyber-activism, bio-politics and gay rights continue to be dynamised in the same way. This is a youth politics that is neither cool nor self-ironising, even if it is not entirely free from the narcissistic pull of feel good factors created around its own self-proclaimed idealisms. Here at any rate is a formidable counter narrative to the political cynicism that increasingly monopolises the media of public debate, albeit one within which young people who remain cut off from mainstream educational opportunity structures do not, once again, find their voice.

Finally the conflict between tradition and modernity is no longer intelligible as a conflict of generations. The generational division of labour based upon relatively stable patterns of apprenticeship to and/or inheritance of fixed assets and skills has collapsed (Cohen, 1999b). And so too have the normative frameworks of vocation and career that sustained a sense of lifelong investment in particular métiers or professions, and ensured the transmission of intellectual or cultural capital associated with their pursuit from one generation to the next (Sennett, 1998). Against this background the enlargement of adolescence, its encroachment on childhood and prolongation into what used to be adulthood is clearly both culturally driven and required by the collapse of secure strategies of social reproduction for all but the most privileged (Calcutt, 1998; Ball, 1998).

The current complication of structural inequalities and of the forms of self-narration through which they are actively negotiated clearly requires a radical rethinking of the youth question. Yet as we move into a period where joined up, evidence-based policy thinking is the order of the day, there is a crisis of confidence both within the academic community itself and amongst the public at large about the ability of social research to deliver really useful knowledge.

The dialogic imagination

It has been argued that if youth research in Britain has been largely a side-show, an adjunct to the more prestigious and mainstream sociologies of education, knowledge and culture, it is partly because youth policy itself has been marginalised in the development of governmental strategies. The youth service has always been a poor relation vis-à-vis the Department of Education and Science (DES) and the youth workers, where they have not been overtly hostile to theoretically grounded research, have tended to adopt a populist 'empowerment' model of youth advocacy that begs all the important research questions.

At the same time there will always be a demand for youth culture studies, if only because market research companies need to keep up with the latest consumer trends, whilst Generation X studies feed the curiosity of elders (who don't know any better) about what the young folks are getting up to when their backs are turned. Yet, perhaps for this reason there is a general sense of déjà vu about youth culture studies these days; and if it really is just telling the same old research story, this is hardly surprising given the continual recycling of commodified youth styles themselves (Miles, 2000).

If 'youth' is yesterday's news it is also partly because of demographic change. Given the current age profile of the British population, the government is understandably more concerned about how to tackle the pensions crisis than with funding yet another research initiative on youth transitions. In our audit society there will, of course, always be work for youth researchers carrying out evaluation studies of this or that programme aimed at the three Ds – druggies, delinquents and drop-outs – and we can rely on periodic moral panics whipped up by the mass media about 'yob culture' to create a demand for pop sociology (Acland, 1995). But in my view there are so many reasons why we should disentangle the youth question as far as possible from the behaviour and attitudes of this or that cohort of young people (Cohen, 1997a).

As an object of study, the youth question is about the place which ethno-biographical constructs of 'youth' occupy in the reproduction of the political, economic and cultural life of particular societies, now and in the past. Almost by definition, the youth question requires a framework of inter-generational and historical comparison. Empirically, this requires a three-point programme:

1. Comparing critical 'youth' experiences across generations, as well as across class and gender divisions.

2. Giving life historical depth to the analysis through longitudinal studies of a whole cohort, and biographical depth through intensive, psychoanalytically informed, case studies of individual adolescences.

3. Comparing constructs of youth and their meta-narratives in different historical periods and societies.

What kind of research methodology would be appropriate for such a programme? Clearly it would have to be interdisciplinary – it would need to bring together historians, sociologists, demographers, psychologists, ethnographers, narratologists and so on. And it would need to create a framework for negotiation between the bearers of local situated knowledge – the so-called youth informants – and the knowledge claims of the various academic disciplines. In other words, it would have to be *dialogic*.

Dialogics are currently at the cutting edge of moves to renew the sociological imagination. Starting from a critique of monologic research accounts centred on the fiction of an omniscient, authorial voice (Haraway, 1988), it has been argued that the discourse of the Other – other race, class, gender, generation and so on – is always and already present as both limit and condition of any sociological knowledge whatever (Cohen, 1997b; Hey, 1997, 2000b). In this view, empirical corroboration is an intrinsically dialogic process shaped by the play of difference; the attempt to suppress these dynamics by constructing some transcendent position of observation and judgement may be an ill-advised strategy for many kinds of qualitative research (Denzin and Lincoln, 1994).

Research dialogics have tended to rest on highly normative definitions. Those influenced by Paolo Freire (1970), following G.H. Mead and Alfred Schutz, see dialogue as a means whereby a *convergent* agenda of topics or unified world-view is arrived at as the basis of collective action. Biographical or ideological differences that cannot be articulated within this frame therefore tend to remain unvoiced. Action Research, it could be argued, still operates largely within this paradigm as does much feminist research which stresses the interview as an arena of *convergent* inter-subjectivity and feeling (Oakley, 1981).

Bakhtin's dialogism, in contrast, emphasises that *divergences* in voice, register, standpoint and power sustain topic elaboration, helping to resist narrative foreclosure associated with the pressure to achieve consensus (Bakhtin, 1994). Post-structuralists have claimed Bakhtin's notion of 'interanimation' between speech genres for their own paradigms of intertextuality, whilst feminist researchers have applied it empirically to understand how girls' discourses articulate positions of class dis-identification within friendship networks (Hey, 1997). The new sociology of knowledge has introduced experimental conversational forms into the presentation of research findings, the aim being to give space to the arguments going on inside the writer's head as well as in the wider research community (Ashmore, 1989). Michel Serres has developed a radically decentred version of dialogical pedagogy, focussing on the potential space of learning that exists in between the doxa of classroom knowledge and its object lessons, and the discourse of the Other that inhabits the interiority of the subject (Serres, 1997).

Some of these recent moves continue to see dialogics as a resource of playful, multivocal speech acts that subvert the formalised humourless monologues of power or 'political correctness'. However, this simple opposition has increasingly been challenged. Even within a single speech genre, such as the online chatroom for example, there are a range of positions and practices – from the discursive ingenuity of the 'wizard', to the compulsive repetitions of the 'blatherer' and 'spewer' or the pseudo participations of the 'lurker' and 'net geek'.

The evangelical tone in which some versions of dialogism have been pursued has rightly aroused scepticism amongst sections of the academic research community. Many remain unconvinced that putative methodological commitments to a more democratic research practice can *ever* escape the wider structures of knowledge/power that frame the relationship between universities and their informant communities (Clifford, 1986). As such, the attempt to create micro-worlds of discursive equality only prolongs the agony.

Despite these reservations, recent educational thinking would seem to indicate that *in principle* dialogic research, by offering informants a position of legitimate, if still peripheral, participation in the process of knowledge production may help enhance informant reflexivity and powers of articulation (Brice Heath, 1983; Lave and Wenger, 1991). This approach avoids the intellectual asset stripping that some have seen as characteristic of the traditional researcher/researched relationship without compromising the relative autonomy of the researcher's own account. But what are the conditions needed to obtain to ensure best outcomes?

There is evidence that dialogic interviews, where 'researcher' and 'informant' roles are periodically reversed, are easier to sustain where there are strong elements of shared cultural biography or parity of status between the partners (Portelli, 1997). This would mean that youth researchers should be in striking distance in terms of age and cultural background. Youth research is or should be mainly a young researcher's game. The development of the Internet may however be changing the rules (Jones, 1998; Hine, 2000). *Potentially* online discussion groups create virtual communities of informants linked to researchers via multiple channels in a way that undercuts many expert knowledge hierarchies. This communicative mode also challenges the simple normative model of dyadic exchanges and face-to-face communication upon which most theories of dialogism have hitherto been based. But so far, there has been no attempt to evaluate the direct uses of the Internet as a medium of interactive youth research nor has there been any systematic attempt to investigate what is gained or lost in terms of theoretical yield or empirical richness by the dialogic turn.

The focus on dialogics does finally point to a rich seam of empirical investigation. Feminist educationalists have recently produced evidence that girls' peer talk may be more dialogic than boys, but that mixed sex groups revert to mono- or duo-logic styles of address, talking past rather than to one another. Equally, black vernaculars have been argued to display strong codes of call and response, supporting 'in house' styles of multivocality (Hewitt, 1986; Rampton, 1995), although rap can also have a strong monotonal register linked to its afro-centric stance (Gilroy, 1993).

This brings us back to our starting point – New Labour's cultural turn and its implications for setting the agenda of youth research. The proponents of the 'Cool Britannia' project argued that kinds of subversive internal dialoguing associated with marginalised or minority cultures, with their elements of parody, transgressive ventriloquism and 'talking back' could *potentially* be converted into entrepreneurial forms of 'creative industry' (Landry and Ransom, 1999). This argument was part of an emergent consensus that the new breed of 'knowledge worker' had to think and talk dialogically, drawing creatively on others' ideas and experiences, especially when they are very different from one's own. In short, dialogic 'teamwork' was seen as the most generative context for producing innovative, problem-solving approaches and thus most likely to render timely ideas and products.

The transfer of dialogic models of 'smart knowledge' from economy to governance was central to New Labour's *'Third Way'* with its espousal of focus group politics and joined up policies designed to tackle entrenched forms of social exclusion amongst disadvantaged groups (Blair, 1998; Giddens, 1998; Pearce and Hillman, 1998). In the case of 'Cool Britannia', we therefore have a classic instance of government policy inventing a tradition of modernity in its own image in the attempt to create an all embracing rhetoric of societal rejuvenation (Rutherford, 1997). Perhaps, we need to consider just what New Labour and its cultural turn has delivered to those young people who have been left outside the once pearly, and now virtual gates of the 'knowledge society'. Are they being offered a narrative of aspiration with which they can realistically identify, or only an endorsement of what may already feel like the unwanted legacy of a historic defeat? On the answer to this question turns not just the fate of many young people, or even the success or failure of the 'New Labour' project, but the future shape and direction of British society as a whole.

Notes

1. Earlier versions of some parts of this chapter appeared in Ainley, P. and Cohen, P. *In the Country of the Blind: Journal of Youth Studies* (1999), in the Introduction to the North American edition of 'Rethinking the Youth Question' (Duke University Press, 2000) and in a paper given to a conference organised by the British Sociological Association Youth Research group in 2001. The sections have been considerably revised for the present text and I am very grateful to many students and colleagues for their help in this process. I would especially like to thank Valerie Hey, Pat Ainley, Valerie Walkerdine and UEL colleagues at the M^3 Research lab and the Centre for Narrative Research for their substantial contributions to this rethinking. I am also much indebted to earlier reviews of trends in youth research undertaken by Christine Griffin, Anne Phoenix and Ali Rattansi. None of the above should, of course, be held responsible for any of the views expressed here.

Part 2
Principles of Practice

3

Framing Youth: Reviewing Locally Commissioned Research on Young People, Drug Use and Drug Education

Mathew Jones, Fenella Starkey and Judy Orme

Introduction

Observing the considerable growth in the research of children and young people (Wyn and White, 1997; Christensen and James, 2000), a number of sociological commentators have drawn attention to the organisational and cultural conditions under which such research has been produced. Coles (2000) suggests that a review of 'youth research' can reveal as much about policy agendas, social concerns or the research process as it does about young people themselves. For example, research on young people has been employed to respond to moral panics, legitimate political agendas or contain public controversy (ibid.). Decisions with regard to research questions, the focus of inquiry and channels of dissemination are often shaped by dominant cultural representations of youth. These representations have tended to frame young people as, for instance, 'troubled', 'in trouble', 'at risk', 'less rational' or 'delinquent' (Jeffs and Smith, 1998; Miles, 2000). A common element to such representations is that young people are set apart from children and adults (Griffin, 1993), and characterised as being in a state of 'becoming' rather than 'being' (Wyn and White, 1997). In their review Jeffs and Smith (1998, p. 55) have contested these representations of young people:

> There can be no denying that some young people experience problems, but in these areas the question is whether the 'problem' is better approached as a 'youth question' or as an experience shared by people across a span of ages. When we come to look at 'teenage

pregnancy', 'youth homelessness', 'youth drug-taking' and so on, few of the pertinent dimensions of experience relate to any inherent qualities of 'youth'.

This critique suggests, therefore, that much youth research has tended to rehearse, or even amplify, constructs of youth that are present in other cultural spheres such as politics and the media. It is held that the active 'voice' of young people in research is, at best, heavily mediated through dominant cultural representations of youth.

This chapter draws upon this commentary as a reference for reviewing research on young people, drug use and drug education. The empirical basis of the chapter draws specifically on research and evaluation commissioned at the local level by statutory agencies. Four projects undertaken by the authors on behalf of four different statutory agencies in South-West England are used as case studies. These case studies are: a youth service-based peer education harm minimisation project; a school-based peer education drug prevention project; a youth service-based survey of young people's drug use; and a school-based survey of young people's drug use. An outline of each case study is provided in the boxed sections below.

A number of issues arising from the experience of conducting these projects are identified. These include: an adult-orientated research and policy context in relation to drugs, within which 'youth' become subjects of research; the framing of 'problems', for example drug use, in ways which may be at odds with young people's priorities; and tensions between the outcome-orientated focus of commissioning agencies and the process orientation of research participants. The themes underlying these issues may be common to much applied social research (Catan, 2002), evidence-based policy and practice (Farmer and Chesson, 2001) and programme evaluation (Pawson and Tilley, 1997). Nevertheless we suggest the focus of this chapter is timely given the importance ascribed to research evidence in the modernisation of public services – including young people's services – at the local level (for example, Department of Health, 2001; Health Advisory Service, 2001).

At the close of the chapter, we consider two methodological challenges for 'youth research' that arise from our analysis. The first challenge is concerned with promoting the active participation of young people in the research process. Secondly we consider the position of the researcher in relation to the research process. Whilst there is a growing literature on young people's participation (for example, Kirby, 1999; France, 2000) and role of the researcher in youth studies (for example,

Roche and Tucker, 1997; Catan, 2002), it is proposed that there exist specific obstacles and dilemmas when incorporating such practices into locally commissioned research.

Case studies

Case Study 1 Youth service-based peer education drug prevention project

> This project was a commissioned evaluation of year two of a three-year youth service peer education drug prevention programme (1996/97) in a county in the South-West of England. This programme was targeted at young people aged 16 plus and trained 15 groups of young people over the period of the year to develop and deliver their own drug education projects to other young people in youth centres and colleges, using a range of media to present their message. The project adopted an explicit harm minimisation approach.
>
> The young people attended a structured programme that included training, rehearsal and evaluation. The training phase of the project for the peer educators lasted for eleven months, with three months then allocated for the delivery of their project to a minimum of three other groups of young people outside the peer education project. The groups of peer educators were supported by dedicated part-time workers who were, in turn, supported by a central project team. The evaluation considered the planning process, the processes of recruitment, training and support, the organisational structure of the project, and the delivery of the individual projects.

Case Study 2 School-based peer education drug prevention project

> This study sought to evaluate a pilot peer education drug prevention project in a neighbouring county in the South-West of England. The project was organised by the Local Education Authority on behalf of the local Drug Reference Group and ran from July 1997 to April 1998. This project was based in two secondary schools, with ten young people from years 11 to 13 in each school taking part. The young people were supported and co-ordinated by the schools' health education co-ordinator, who in turn received central support from a schools' adviser in the local education authority.
>
> The young people received a programme of training, and then went on to work in school as peer educators delivering their lessons

Case Study 2 (Continued)

to years 7, 8 and 9. The model of peer education used in the two schools was slightly different. One school agreed lesson plans, which every peer educator then used. The other school gave the peer educators leeway to write their own lesson plans based upon drug education topics developed by the health education co-ordinator. The evaluation examined the organisation of the project, the training and support structures, and the impact of the peer education work on both the peer educators themselves and the classes they worked in. In addition, the research attempted to assess any changes in knowledge among the young people to whom they delivered.

Case Study 3 Youth service-based survey of young people's drug use

A survey of young people's drug use was commissioned in 1998 by a South West authority's Drug Reference Group and led by the local youth service in collaboration with the local social services department. This survey aimed to assess the prevalence and nature of young people's use of both legal and illegal drugs in the 11 to 25 age group, as well as young people's knowledge of and views upon sources of support and information relating to drugs issues.

The survey was conducted during January and February 1999 in informal educational or service settings, including youth centres, outreach youth projects, detached youth projects, voluntary agencies, mobile projects, Duke of Edinburgh schemes and social services settings. Agency workers carried out the survey following a briefing by the researchers, using a structured questionnaire in face-to-face interviews with young people. A total of 616 young people between the ages of 10 and 23 were interviewed over the six-week period of the survey.

Case Study 4 School-based survey of young people's drug use

This project was commissioned by a Drug Action Team and drew upon pooled local agency funds. The research sought to understand how young people's substance use in the authority corresponded to national trends, identify levels of awareness and knowledge regarding sources of support and information, and identify the views of young people with regard to local drug and alcohol-related issues.

> *Case Study 4* (continued)
>
> The study was conducted between November 2000 and February 2001. The fieldwork consisted of two components. Firstly half the secondary schools in the authority were purposively selected to take part in a self-completion questionnaire. One-thousand two hundred and twenty-five young people between the ages of 11 and 18 years completed the questionnaires in a school setting. Secondly in-depth interviews were conducted with 57 young people selected from a range of social backgrounds in the authority area. These interviews were conducted in informal settings outside schools. Two researchers undertook the survey and interview work with the assistance of school teachers, youth workers and social workers.

Key issues arising from the research and evaluation projects

The commissioning, design and implementation of these research and evaluation projects highlighted a range of issues relating to the way in which young people were conceptualised, consulted and involved in research.

Research and the commissioning context

Competing policy requirements

In a number of ways, the policy context oriented the commissioned research towards adult-defined agendas. Successive national government strategies on drugs – Tackling Drugs Together (Home Office, 1995) and Tackling Drugs Together to Build a Better Britain (Cabinet Office, 1998) – contain strong moral messages on the need to reduce the levels of drug use amongst young people. For example, the defining aim in the 1998 strategy in relation to young people stated the need 'to help young people resist drug misuse in order to achieve their full potential in society' (1998, p. 3). Emphasis is also given to the importance of research evidence in policy formulation; the 1998 strategy states 'our strategy must be based on accurate, independent research, approached in a level-headed analytical fashion' (1998, p. 11). The Health Advisory Service (1996) recommended that the commissioning of drug services for young people at the local level should be based upon locally determined assessments of need.

This policy environment created a tension for researchers between, on the one hand, a requirement to inform and underpin the moral and political imperatives of government strategies and, on the other hand, a need to maintain a credible and open value position in the research process. Both evaluations illustrated in Case Studies 1 and 2 operated in the context of a heavily politicised debate on the relative virtues of drug prevention and harm minimisation approaches to drug education.

Tensions with organisational accountability
A second set of issues arose from the local organisational contexts. At a local authority level the national strategies emphasised rationalisation, the efficient use of resources and accountability through the setting of 'clear, consistent and rigorous targets' (Cabinet Office, 1998). In this context the purpose of research and evaluation was heavily oriented towards the organisational responsibilities of agencies, for instance, in the production of baseline performance indicators. These tensions are also reflected in the research process. For example, the survey research in Case Studies 3 and 4 was driven by the monitoring cycles of local agencies and the need to resolve funding plans for specialist services. Young people's needs were primarily framed in terms of the orientation and capacity of local services.

Inter-agency tensions
National strategies placed considerable emphasis on partnerships and inter-agency co-ordination at the local level. In the case studies, commissioned research played a particular part in these agendas. Research acted as a vehicle through which agencies sought to negotiate their roles, responsibilities and access to funding. It also acted as an arena in which (mainly adult) interest groups sought to articulate ideological positions. For example, the evaluations in Case Studies 1 and 2 drew out debates on the boundaries between youth services and schools in providing drug-related education and support. Each service articulated somewhat different educational philosophies about how power relations between adults and young people should be conducted; schools tended to favour formal pedagogic methods while youth services were inclined to informal and voluntary association. All the case studies reflect Farmer and Chesson's (2001) argument that commissioners experience difficulties when attempting to integrate evidence into complex organisational environments.

Overall, therefore, the policy environment of the research could be identified as orientated towards an adult set of concerns, constructs and priorities. The national strategies were predicated on moral debates regarding the responsibilities of adults in political and organisational contexts. This context directly informed the funding briefs, research settings and destination of the research findings. Young people in these processes were located largely as subjects rather than agents.

The research briefs

An analysis of the research briefs can reveal as much about the predilections and the pressures upon commissioning agencies as they reveal about research subjects themselves. In the case studies, the following questions illustrate the research briefs that emerged from commissioning negotiations:

What are the patterns and nature of young people's drug use?
What reasons and motives do young people have for using or not using drugs?
What sources of information and advice in relation to drug use do young people value?
What kinds of interventions in relation to drug education are most effective?

These questions give some indications about the manner in which young people were both framed as *having* problems and *being* problems. Young people were identified as having potential problems in relation to the availability of drugs, their knowledge, attitudes and behaviour towards drugs, and access to support and education around drugs. Implicitly, however, young people were also constituted as being problems themselves through these research questions. All the case studies embedded a concern with eliciting the rationality of young peoples' (often covert) views and actions and with identifying interventions that will 'get through to and improve' this rationality. A subtext to this concern was an aim to fathom the rationality – or non-rationality – of groups of young people perceived to be at risk from drug-related problems.

Whether young people would necessarily identify the kinds of research problems illustrated in these case studies is open to question given that there were only indirect mechanisms for involving young people in the research process. In Case Study 4, it was clear that many interviewees perceived the answers to survey questions on drug prevalence and drug availability as self-evident. Interviewees often sought to raise alternative questions about policing, safety on streets or leisure facilities. Similarly participants in Case Studies 1 and 2 identified a number of personal rewards arising from involvement that lay outside the main focus of investigation such as increased confidence, and the development of practical skills. In all the case studies, constraints arising from the commissioning process tended to restrict the potential for incorporating participants' views into the research briefs. What *is* illustrated in the research briefs is how the commissioning process served to construct young people as possessing qualities, problems and needs that are, by implication, distinct from adults. Such representations tended to frame young people as possessing or presenting special problems. Jeffs and Smith (1998) suggest that considerable behavioural, social attitude and educational research (for example, Hendry *et al*., 1995; Goddard, 1997; Tennant, 1997) supports the argument that young peoples' problems, needs and modes of learning do not differ qualitatively from those of adults. In the field of substance use, research in the past decade recurrently yielded consistent data in response to questions similar to the ones illustrated in our research briefs; a wide variety of legal and illegal drugs were available and consumed by teenagers in patterns similar to those of young adults (for example, Parker *et al*., 1995); young people who have used drugs do not necessarily differ greatly from non-users in terms of their wider social attitudes (for example, Perri 6 *et al*., 1997); and young people remained consistently equivocal about the need for and the effectiveness of health education and support interventions – of whatever kind (for example, Roker and Coleman, 1997). Overall the research briefs illustrated in these case studies rehearse adult anxieties about youth, rather than build clearly upon the views of young people articulated in previous research.

Conducting the research

Tensions in the research focus between process and outcomes

Considering the research process, a particular tension relates to the emphasis within evaluation projects on outcomes as opposed to process. In Case Study 1, the funding body was keen for the evaluation to provide evidence of positive outcomes in terms of the project's impact on the young people to whom the peer education sessions were delivered. However, as the projects were primarily delivered in youth centres to whomsoever happened to be attending that evening, pre- and post-intervention testing to obtain such information was impossible in practice.

In contrast to the funding body, it was clear that the emphasis of both the youth workers organising the project and the young people participating in the project was on the project process itself. The year-long training and support and the benefits and pleasure they derived from that was what the young people themselves identified as important in the project. The relatively short space of time allocated for presentation of their projects to other young people outside the project tended not to be viewed as a priority by the peer educators. The peer educators felt that they had developed a range of skills from being involved in the project, including interpersonal and group-work skills, task completion, organisation, and decision-making, as well as increased knowledge about drugs and alcohol. All of these could be viewed as important outcomes in themselves. However, for a project funded specifically as a drug prevention activity, issues arise as to the extent to which the funding body would classify such outcomes as a 'success' in terms of influencing drug use. In the formal sense, young people participating in the project were characterised primarily as 'objects of change' rather than 'active agents'. Thus, the evaluation's commissioning environment tended to amplify the notion of youth as a state of 'becoming' – as opposed to a state of 'being' (Wyn and White, 1997).

'Top-down' and 'bottom-up' approaches to evaluation

A tension that affected the outcomes of research existed between 'top-down' activities with young people instigated by adults, and 'bottom-up' approaches instigated by young people themselves. The evaluations outlined in Case Studies 1 and 2 could be differentiated in this way: the school-based peer education drug prevention project was clearly a top-down initiative, with peer educators recruited and trained by a statutory agency in order to deliver adult-defined information to their classmates using pre-determined methods. The youth service-based project, on the other hand, although top-down in the sense that the overall project was initiated from outside the peer group concerned, was more 'bottom-up' in that the groups of young people were given considerable freedom over decisions about the information they conveyed and the way in which they conveyed it. This led to the use of a range of media, including plays, videos, music and games.

The top-down and tightly defined approach to working with young people proved easier to evaluate in terms of being able to identify consistent and therefore comparable outcome measures across the activities in which the range of young people were involved. This was an appealing prospect to funding bodies keen to demonstrate evidence-based practice in their strategic plans (Pawson and Tilley, 1997). However, this approach may conflict with the developmental needs of the young people themselves involved in the activities. A 'bottom-up' approach which involves young people in defining their own approach to projects and gives them freedom regarding the way in which they wish to implement these may be more empowering and result in a greater richness and diversity of work. Yet the approach may be far harder to 'measure' in terms of consistent outcomes. Nevertheless, Coles (2000) suggests that any move towards the 'holistic' involvement of young people in policy, research and programme evaluation cannot be conducted under fixed and imposed conditions.

Conclusions: commissioned research, active participation and the position of the researcher

There is a growing emphasis within the research and youth work communities both on encouraging young people to participate more fully as subjects of research and on exploring ways of actively involving young people in designing and conducting their own research (for example, Ward, 1997; Kirby, 1999; France, 2000b). The benefits of involvement in participatory research for young people themselves are widely documented, including personal benefits in terms of skills development and enjoyment, as well as increased democratic participation in decision-making processes and increased social justice with regard to expectation of action resulting from their findings (ibid.).

However, the evidence presented on locally commissioned research indicated that there were significant barriers to employing participatory methodologies. Commissioning agencies have favoured traditional adult-led projects that meet policy agendas, feed into strategic planning, and pursue predictable costs, objectives and timescales. As Kirby (1999) points out, agencies may be resistant to funding projects which change and evolve as they respond to young people's needs, and which have indeterminate outcomes. Recent government-sponsored guidance to local agencies (DrugScope/DPAS, 2001; Health Advisory Service, 2001) places renewed emphasis on the role of research and evaluation in the modernisation of young people's drugs services. Creating meaningful involvement for young people in such reforms requires a committed, skilled and flexible commissioning environment (Consumers in NHS Research Support Unit, 2000). Whilst local commissioning agencies may be receptive to the idea of participatory research, it is probable that they will struggle to integrate such initiatives into the modernisation agenda (Farmer and Chesson, 2001).

In these circumstances, researchers who seek to develop participatory methodologies are presented with some difficult dilemmas. Engagement with commissioned research risks complicity with pre-defined moral and political agendas, adult-orientated representations of youth, outcome-driven enquiry and top-down planning. Yet the role of the researcher is not simply confined to the production of evidence that can be accommodated by the commissioning bodies (Catan, 2002). The review presented in this chapter suggests that researchers have a role in challenging received agendas and supporting the involvement of young people through subjecting the conditions of research production to scrutiny.

4
Practice-based Research as Development: Innovation and Empowerment in Youth Intervention Initiatives using Collaborative Action Inquiry

Barry Percy-Smith and Susan Weil

The changing context of youth research, policy and practice

The current plethora of youth policy initiatives in the UK is challenging practitioners, policy-makers and researchers alike to think differently about how to develop and implement more effective intervention strategies. In turn, this stimulates reflection on the nature of roles and relationships between research, policy and practice. Catalysed by the Modernising Government agenda (Department of Health, 1998) and discourses of rights, participation, inclusion and citizenship, all of which accentuate the active role of young people in research and development processes, local service providers are now obliged to involve youth in the planning, monitoring and delivery of interventions (see, for example, Quality Protects, Children's Fund, Connexions). In the Planning Guidance notes for Connexions it states:

> Connexions Partnerships will involve young people, collect and act upon their views and be proactive in doing so. Involving young people is a necessity in order to provide a service based upon identified rather than perceived need, to enhance the self learning of young people about themselves, others and how organisations work... They (young people) will have a key role to play to ensure the service emphasises innovation and delivery that meets their needs (October 2001, p. 58).

This extract suggests the importance of an approach to practice which is based on achieving effectiveness and accountability through individual and systemic learning. As a result emphasis has also been placed on the importance of evidence-based practice to inform the development, implementation and monitoring of Connexions. Whilst noble in intent, the development of evidence-based practice has been constricted by particular interpretations of what constitutes evidence and a corresponding lack of resultant learning and development of systems and practice. Instead, it appears that evidence-based practice has, for the most part, become either a masquerade for involving young people or an iron rod of monitoring and accountability.

The central dilemma here is how to bring research and learning for change into the context of practice in ways that have meaning and impact within the lifetime of projects. So, often the expectations foisted onto practitioners are incongruous with the understanding and capability for learning and change they possess as practitioners, either as a result of the burden of existing workloads or assumptions underlying their own professional role and approaches to practice. As Stacey (2001) notes, 'the inability of participation and partnership concepts to consistently deliver meaningful outcomes that lead to positive personal experience and structural change...results from "ideological confusion" particularly around participation rhetoric within which accountability may be lost, confused or disguised.' Political rhetoric abounds about giving young people a voice, about social inclusion for young people, about New Deals for young people, about social responsibility and so on. But in spite of whatever value may exist in such rhetorical commitments, programmes, initiatives and professional practices concerned with enhancing the social and economic participation of young people, their desired objectives are not always achieved. It is our contention that part of the problem is that traditional systems and processes of research, policy-making and practice have been slow in changing to facilitate young people's involvement in ways that are generative and empowering for both individuals and systems. In spite of the changing context in which youth interventions are taking place, beyond direct youth work, there has been a lack of rigorous critical reflection on the changing nature of professional practice with young people and, in particular, the way in which research and learning for change can be facilitated in organisations, partnerships and systems involved with implementing youth social policy interventions.

This chapter makes a contribution to filling this gap by offering a rationale for, and insight into, 'new forms' of practice-based research with young people. Drawing on experiences from a cross-European collaborative action inquiry project[1] exploring strengths and limitations of education, training and guidance interventions for young unemployed adults, the chapter outlines how meaning and impact on youth policy interventions can be enhanced by adopting a 'new paradigm' of research in the form of 'co-inquiry-based practice' or socially contextualised knowledge generation (Gibbons, 1994; Weil, 1999). It is argued that, by bringing research into practice in this way, possibilities for more effective youth interventions can be realised.

Challenges for youth research and practice

Much youth (and in turn sociological and social policy) research has been couched within, or at least with respect to, discourses of social change (see, for example, Fornäs and Bolin, 1995; Bynner et al., 1997a; Furlong and Cartmel, 1997; Evans et al., 2000; Cieslik and Pollock, 2002). It is commonly acknowledged that risk, uncertainty and the dissolving of traditional social structures and modes of social affiliation are giving rise to increasing individualisation in the way young people navigate their lifecourse and, in turn, change the way the relationship between the individual and society is understood. The ascendancy of Third Way politics has recast this relationship in terms of a hybrid melange of conventional left/right doctrine melding individual freedom with social justice (Giddens, 2000). Yet at the same time the balance of social responsibility with rights sought within meta-policy narratives about active citizenship (Dwyer, 1998) have yet to make a real mark in the way they are translated into professional practice. Shifts in policy rhetoric in response to social change have been slow in giving rise to corresponding learning and change in organisations, partnerships and systems. So, often responses to youth issues focus attention on young people themselves and how they need to behave, change or act, with insufficient consideration of how society and in turn systems and organisations might be failing young people, and therefore how systems need to learn and change.

In his critical review of youth research, Cieslik (2001) argues for empirically grounded research which confronts the theoretical and methodological challenges facing researchers in the twenty-first century. In spite of the prevalence of individualising discourses within late modernity theses (Giddens, 1991; Beck, 1992; Furlong and Cartmel, 1997), social structures continue to exert significant influence on individual biographies (Wyn and White, 1997; Rudd and Evans, 1998). As Cieslik

(2001, p. 42), citing Archer (1982), goes on to argue: 'What new theories and concepts in youth research need to be able to do is allow us to explore how social structures and the agency of individual young people operate separately (at an analytical and empirical level) and how at the same time they are interwoven.' This is imperative if youth policy is to be effective in transforming relationships between youth and society and generating social outcomes which matter with respect to achieving goals of participation, citizenship and inclusion. Policy alone cannot bring about social change. Rather, the participation and empowerment of individuals as agents of change within the lived realities of their own everyday lives is critical to the successful achievement of meaningful social outcomes. Individual lives are not played out in a social vacuum, rather they are negotiated with respect to changing social, organisational and policy contexts. Yet conventional approaches to research, practice and policy development are based on hierarchical, top-down models of relationships between society and individuals, in which the latter are conveyed rights of citizenship only if they acquiesce in their responsibilities as articulated and laid down by the state (Dwyer, 1998; Percy-Smith and Weil, 2002). This is particularly evident with the New Deal for Young People, wherein under the guise of individual choice and opportunity, benefits are conditional upon the coercion (through the threat of sanctions for non-compliance) of young people into employment and training options as prescribed by the state. Instead of giving meaning to policy intentions in terms of new research policy and practice contracts with young people, much youth policy has been implemented against a backdrop of old standards of practice and thinking which have often failed to realise the potential espoused in policy.

Traditionally research has been conducted separately from practice and policy development in the hope that learning is fed back into the system. Cohen and Ainley (2000) acknowledge this in terms of the need to 'transcend the narrow empiricism of most traditional youth studies to create a third space within which "situated learning" can occur' (Lave and Wenger, 1991). The success or failure of youth social policy initiatives is dependent on how well they are implemented in practice. Competing ideologies and intentions are played out in practice as the implementation of standardised policy formulations driven by targets and performance indicators clash with young people's diverse cultural standpoints and lived realities. In critically reflecting on assumptions about youth transitions, Skelton (2002) highlights the limitations of linear concepts of transitions which frame youth policy responses, highlighting instead the need for research to hold on to the 'complexities and differences' that characterise diverse trajectories. Given the hybrid and customised nature of individualised identities, biographies and lifestyles in the risk society, Cieslik and Pollock (2002) draw attention to the need for individuals to become more reflexive about daily practices and the way individual subjectivities are negotiated. Whilst greater emphasis and recognition is now placed on individual agency, social and organisational structures still continue to exert considerable influence on individual lifechances (Wyn and White, 1997; Rudd and Evans, 1998).

A key question for youth research, policy and practice is to what extent the imperatives of individual agency enshrined in discourses of youth participation are facilitated within social and organisational systems and practices and how is individual agency reconciled with the reality of social and systemic constraints? With many professionals working with young people – such as teachers, careers guidance, employment, benefit and housing advisors – interventions and encounters have been framed on the basis of unequal power relations characterised by the professional (whom it is assumed knows what's best for the young person) and the young person (who gets socially engineered into politically safe outcomes). Ferguson (2001, p. 122), for example, reveals how: 'Adult reticence to take the risk of allowing young people responsibility for their own lives contrasts sharply with the attitudes expressed by young people themselves.' In a similar vein Barber (2001), in a study exploring young people's experience of participation, notes that 'feeling empowered' is perceived as a major priority by young people, rather than tangible policy outputs per se.

Sufficient evidence exists to demonstrate that professional relationships such as this are not conducive to the satisfactory engagement of young people in generating appropriate solutions (Kinder *et al.*, 1996; Janssens *et al.*, 2000; Wood and Forrest, 2000; MacKenzie, 2001; Percy-Smith, 2002; Percy-Smith and Weil, 2002). With the advent of the Connexions Service, the central role of the Personal Advisor (PA) and the imperatives of user involvement in service planning and delivery, greater attention has been directed to the critical role of the professional relationship with young people. Oliver (2002, p. 33), reflecting on the participatory methodology used in the role of the Connexions PA, highlights how 'the PAs have the potential to play a crucial part in the design and development of their own professional role and of the service within which they will operate.' However, she also suggests the need for encouraging cultures of participatory reflective inquiry beyond the role of the PAs. There are of course numerous examples of good practice working with young people in empowering ways, especially in local projects supported by voluntary sector organisations. Yet little seems to change in terms of moving towards more participative structures and processes for involving youth in learning and development in mainstream social systems. For example, in education, guidance for work, neighbourhood regeneration processes, local governance, the design and delivery of services for young people and environmental planning, the systems that exist tend to undermine the potential benefit of young people's participation and perpetuate the marginalisation rather than integration of young people.

There seem to be three issues which are key to whether young people are able to effectively work alongside professionals in research and development. First, that there is a prevailing culture which sees professionals as experts who, guided by prescribed policy objectives, see it as their role to act in young people's 'best interests'. As such, emphasis is placed on enacting policy in response *to taken-for-granted assumptions* about the nature of 'youth problems'. Second, prevailing conceptions of young people as in some way lacking the necessary capacity to participate means that they become subjects of, rather than participants in, research and development processes, leaving professionals as 'expert' guardians acting in 'young people's best interests'. Third, research, learning and action for change are often separated from the development and implementation of policy and practice. As a result the grounded, multi-faceted realities of young people's lived experiences can become circumvented in order to ensure the 'satisfactory' achievement of policy objectives. In so doing the focus of the intervention – young people's social realities – becomes disconnected from what takes place in practice. Research is so often seen as something someone else does separate from the work of practitioners with the result that cultures of practice, research and learning are so often absent.

What we are exploring here are ways in which we can differentially construct research and development processes involving young people, in ways that accommodate and respond to the tensions, dilemmas, disjunctions, diversity and power relations which exist in encounters with young people. The basic premise of this chapter is therefore that simple solutions based on singular agenda, partial perspectives and mechanistic (positivist) understandings of change, are ineffective in responding to the complexity of young people's lived realities. Instead there is a need for new models of practice-based research wherein young people and professionals are able to jointly and reflexively construct interventions based on inquiry into the complexities and disjunctions at play between policy imperatives and young people's lived realities within the real time of practice. In essence, we attempt to elaborate the notion of 'structured individualisation' (Rudd and Evans, 1998) through new forms of inquiry-based practice. To illustrate this, the chapter will draw on two scenarios illustrating different types of youth interventions in education, training and guidance for young people drawn from a two-year European research project.[2] We offer these stories to highlight some of the complexity at play in youth interventions but also to generate insights into some of the critical factors which can make a difference to the outcomes of such interventions and which therefore constitute facets of an 'alternative' practice-based approach to research with young people.

Scenario 1   Paradoxes of linear approaches to mainstream youth policy interventions: an encounter with New Deal

The rhetoric of New Deal is of a client-centred initiative tailored to each individual, designed to make a real difference to youth unemployment. The advisors I talked to expressed a high level of commitment to helping young people in a way that is meaningful for them. Yet in reality they are constrained by what is possible within New Deal. To learn more, I had been invited to observe meetings between New Deal Personal Advisors and young people in the New Deal office, if the latter were agreeable to this.

One of many encounters I witnessed was with Sean, a 21-year-old with no qualifications. His father was in prison, and he didn't get on with his family so he lived alone. He had come into the office because his money hadn't arrived. He looks stressed out. Apparently his money had been stopped because he didn't turn up to start on his Environmental Task Force (ETF) Option. The advisor had previously assigned him to other such 'Options', only for him not to turn up. The advisor is getting suspicious that he is fiddling the system. To try and find out more the advisor asks how he is paying his rent. Sean says he gets housing benefit but is living on nothing. His financial situation is causing a great deal of anxiety. He appears perplexed and angry and doesn't appear to know what to do. The advisor too appears to be frustrated by the situation as he seeks to mediate between policy prescriptions and the realities that Sean presents him. Sean is adamant he doesn't want to do the ETF option. Instead he wants to find work. The advisor tells him he doesn't have any choice now and has to do the Option saying: 'That's the way it is unfortunately'. This simple statement confronted me, as witness to this encounter, with the lack of scope within New Deal to be truly client-centred and to respond to the issues and dilemmas that individuals like Sean are grappling with. Instead the advisor felt obliged to use the power vested in him to enforce New Deal procedure in order to bypass the complexity of the issues at stake and to reach an outcome which fits in with the agenda and objectives of New Deal. Eventually, as a result of a lack of alternative options and because of his desperate financial situation Sean agrees under duress that he will go on the option. But he makes it clear he doesn't want to. He is still concerned about whether he will get his money or not so the advisor goes off to talk to seek advice from a colleague. The advisor returns, reports that his claim is going to an adjudication officer and then starts going through the necessary paperwork to refer him back onto ETF. Sean becomes increasingly more agitated and after nearly an hour the encounter ends and Sean leaves.

If we look at this more closely we see that neither advisor nor young person is empowered here. The advisor is precariously situated between meeting policy targets and responding to the complexity of the young person's lived realities, but with limited flexibility in how he can deal with such dilemmas. Dilemmas, tensions, ambiguities and disjunctions between the agendas of the advisor and the young person, policy intentions and what they are both experiencing in the real time of their encounter, proliferate in encounters such as this. There is *no communicative action space* (Kemmis, n.d.) in which to acknowledge the complexity of the problems and issues that have arisen and in light of this, to consider what might be possible in making the service more responsive to young people's needs and circumstances. Instead the impasse leads to the advisor using his power to leapfrog the messiness and impose a solution so as to produce a quick and simple solution which is satisfactory for the advisor and the system he serves rather than for the young person. The marginalisation of the client's position and the domination of the discursive space by the professional has similarly been noted elsewhere (see, for example, Stacey and Mignot, 2001). Such action however, gives rise to unintended effects for the young person in terms of failing to respond to the issues and dilemmas which are alive for him and as a result fail to bring about an outcome which is also meaningful for the young person. This is occurring in an initiative that has been designed to help young adults, who have been failed by social systems, to succeed. As Stacey and Mignot (2001, p. 38) argue there is a need to 'provide a discursive space within which to redress the balance of support offered to young people at the point of intervention'.

One of the paradoxes here is that the failure to take full account of the young person's context and the complexities at play means that Sean has not been empowered in his choices, actions and motivation. He is thus unlikely to sustain a commitment to the option he has been

74 *Principles of Practice*

given and as a result rebounds back into the system or out of it. Who gains here? This is of no benefit to either advisor or young person and undermines the original policy intentions of New Deal. This type of linear, instrumental and means/end interaction can be illustrated diagrammatically (see Figure 4.1). As Skelton (2002) argues, the limitations of linear approaches to youth transitions fail to acknowledge the level of complexity of young people's lives characterised by multiple transitions and diverse biographies and lifestyles.

The dilemmas of practice encountered here centre around the way in which the active participation of young people is approached. Third Way politics emphasises individual responsibility and active citizenship. Yet as Hall *et al.* (2000) argue, this tends to involve the pre-eminence of the professional (and in turn the state) agenda. However, in spite of policy rhetoric underpinning initiatives such as New Deal, critical discourses of citizenship highlight the lack of clarity in interpretations of active citizenship, in particular what active citizenship means for professional practice in relationships with young people. Hall *et al.* (2000) argue that reconceptualising citizenship within the context of

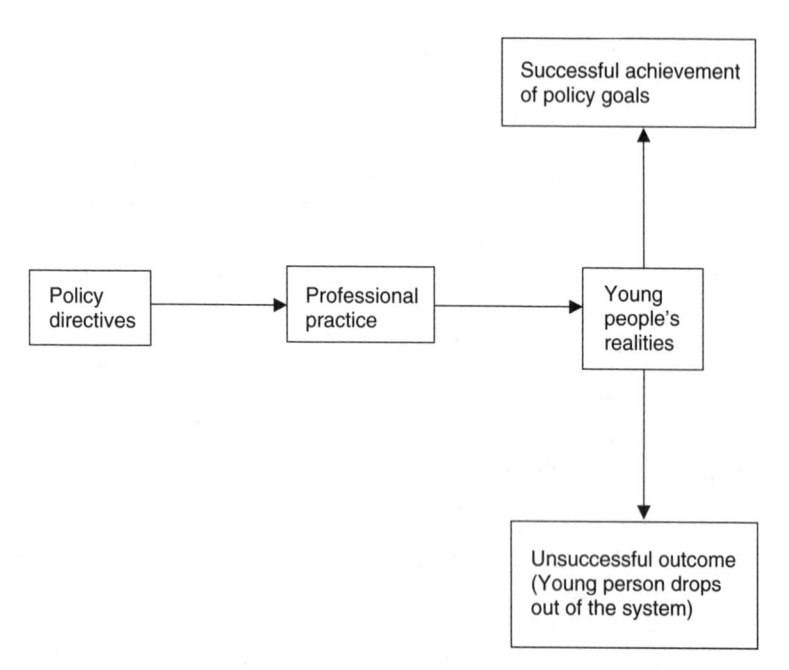

Figure 4.1 Conceptualisation of linear approaches to youth policy interventions

Third Way politics requires interpretation at a more grounded level and as a 'critically reflexive endeavour' involving tacit learning and negotiation of rights and responsibilities. In this vein, they draw attention to the potential for learning from youth work. Yet, in spite of Blair's talk of 'mutuality and solidarity' (1993, pp. 3–4, cited in Heron and Dwyer), in terms of the way policy is configured, enacted and experienced, the interaction between youth and society appears to be assumed to be one way. That is, if youth act and behave in a particular way they can be integrated into society and so-called youth problems will be solved. The 'encounter space' (Percy-Smith and Weil, 2002) in this case is hence characterised by the implementation of policy objectives which may give rise to friction if the agenda of the young person does not fit in with that of the original policy intentions. This appears inconsistent with Third Way politics and undermines the integrity of young people as cultural producers in their own right engaged in the construction of their own lifestyle projects (see, for example, Reimer, 1995; Bennett, 2000; Miles, 2000). Instead it seems more useful to understand youth problems as co-constituted outcomes resulting from the dynamic interaction of different young people with social processes and structures in particular contexts and with different stakeholders (Rudd and Evans, 1998; see also Wenger, 1998).

Scenario 2 Success through empowerment: encounters between young people and staff at The YMCA Northampton (TYN)

The YMCA Northampton have a different ethos in their approach to work with young people. Rather than seek an outcome on the basis of policy goals, TYN work more responsively to the agendas set by young people and differentially with notions of social responsibility and empowerment. Unlike many initiatives or organisations that purport to be client-centred, sustained inquiry over six months indicated that TYN actively struggle to practice what they preach throughout the organisation. With the New Deal Advisors there are disjunctions between policy intentions and the dilemmas advisors are dealing with, which undermine and disempower both advisors and young people. With TYN we have not just individuals supporting young people but a whole series of layers of the organisation knitted together by a common ethos and philosophy, made meaningful through continuous cycles of critical reflexivity that involves young people as co-inquirers.

I had come to TYN in a bid to find out more about how those who appeared to remain 'beyond New Deal', experienced and made sense of training and guidance opportunities as a means for enhancing social and economic participation. As I walked into one of the supported accommodation centres there was a completely different atmosphere to what I had experienced with mainstream practices. These people were working 24/7 with young people with multiple problems, whom the mainstream system was struggling to know what to do with. On walking into the drop in centre, it felt like a young person's place, like it was really there for young people and that young people were valued and respected (unlike the more formalised setting of the New Deal office with an all pervasive air of state bureaucracy) – a smoked filled room with graffiti walls, pool tables and loud music – and amidst this 'light' workers doing some real work with young people in the course of their everyday social interactions and on terms that the young people had control over. The centre co-ordinator introduced me to Bob, an apparent gentle giant carrying the burden of a lost childhood. We all sat around as a table of equals as Bob started to recount his life story – in and out of care home, a mother that couldn't cope, a father he didn't get on with, an unsuccessful schooling and low self-esteem. It became apparent that something had changed since he had been at TYN. He was more stable, felt better about himself and was gaining in confidence through coming to terms with his life and as a result felt ready to think about independent living and work to go with it. Like many others in his situation Bob is not without ability, but has been held back in getting on in his life by severe emotional disturbance.

In contrast to New Deal, repeated visits to TYN revealed a 'safe space', characterised as a soft cushion, in which young people are supported to gain stability and take steps, as and when they are ready, into the labour market and independent living. TYN's culture and ethos of 'success through empowerment' and being non-judgemental does not only guide their relationships with young people but with everyone throughout the organisation. The principle is that in seeking to empower young people, workers also need to be empowered. This is achieved through the creation of a coherent organisational culture of support in which young people participate in all aspects of the organisation's work from house rules, to deciding what they need help with to representation on the management board. The difference with the TYN approach is that it is holistic, flexible and genuinely person-centred and based on a recognition that the needs of young people are complex, variable and may be unknown to the worker. It allows for issues and dilemmas to be explored and addressed jointly by the young person and the worker. The nature of TYN encounter spaces is then adapted to accommodate the particular needs of the young person and necessary support mechanisms set in place. TYN is thus engaged in ongoing social and organisational learning – open and reflexive – seeking to learn from practice how it can best empower young people, each of whom are seen as individuals. Young people are not only empowered in terms of the services *provided and the outcomes they achieve, but are also empowered as agents in the solution of their own problems.* As one 16-year-old stated:

What makes it work is staff... compromising, working with you, helping you out... but it's got to be vice verse as well. It's a two-way thing really. It's just the staff working with the individual and the individual working with the staff.

These two contrasting case studies illustrate the strengths and limitations of different types of youth interventions. Notably, they highlight the need for critical reflexivity in the way organisations respond to young people and the need for research to combine learning, in and from action, with the development of policy and practice in response to the complex and multi-layered realities alive in youth intervention encounters. The difference with TYN is that the system is able to change and grow in a state of perpetual dynamism and responsiveness in ways that empower young people and professionals involved. In contrast, with the New Deal, if the process is not successful the first time, the system does not necessarily learn and change, but instead re-engages that young person in the system that has already failed him or her. If organisational learning and change does take place this is often after the event, with little benefit for the young person or professional.

Making sense of 'new paradigm' research and co-inquiry-based practice in youth interventions

Instead of seeing the relationship between professional and young person as a one way process of policy implementation, as was the case with the New Deal scenario, in the YMCA situation the encounter space is characterised as a process of dynamic interaction in which professional and young person seek to achieve a better understanding of the issue(s) at hand from which possible choices and actions can be considered. TYN workers try to embrace holistically the complexity of what it means to make a difference in the young person's life whilst working within organisational and policy constraints. Through openness, humility and a desire to be responsive TYN are able to bring research into practice by creating spaces for joint learning and change. Such a situation pre-supposes a more 'democratic relationship' characterised in the TYN's case by a non-judgemental and empowering approach based on equality and respect, in which meaning and in turn action is negotiated through a dynamic process of mutual engagement, learning and reflexivity (see Figure 4.2). Wenger (1998) refers to this joint enterprise as the complementarity of participation and reification. This type of situation also requires a degree of 'critical reflexivity' as workers seek to jointly construct interventions (or actions) on the basis of the informal situated learning (or inquiry) that occurs. Weil (1997, 1999) refers to this type of inquiry-based practice as 'critically reflexive action research' (CRAR).

We can summarise some key principles of CRAR in the following way. CRAR begins and ends with real situations. It does not aim to create one representation of reality, but rather the unravelling (and documentation) of multiple realities and rhetorics that are in mutual and simultaneous interaction. CRAR aims to build and validate systemic capacity for noticing what is appropriately or inappropriately present and absent in dominant epistemologies of practice, and for recognising and learning from disabling disjunctions, patterns and contradictions. CRAR aims to generate and document more critically reflexive choices of responsible action and inquiry in complex and ever-shifting situations that involve multiple bottom lines. CRAR involves inter-related processes of collaborative diagnosis, action planning, action taking, evaluation and the communicating and testing of learning outcomes. CRAR aims to bring

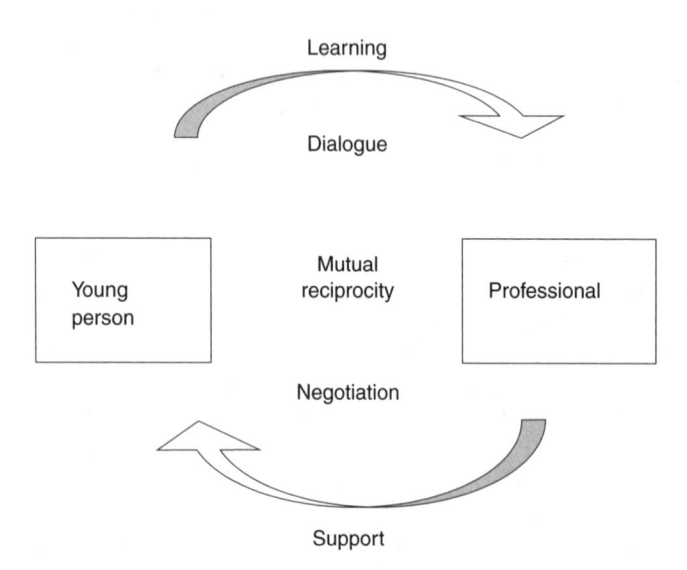

Figure 4.2 A conceptualisation of co-inquiry-based approaches to youth professional encounters: bringing research into practice

about shifts in the underlying assumptions and world-views of those involved, across a system, in ways that are often unexpected and cannot be predetermined, and which can guide further cycles of inquiry. CRAR brings theory and practice, reflection and action, thinking and doing, and different ways of knowing (for example, experiential, imaginal, conceptual) into dialectical relation as the basis for surfacing disabling and enabling dimensions of systemic interaction and revealing possibilities for more responsible action, choice and inquiry.

Working with a 'whole systems' approach it is possible to identify three levels at which critically reflexive action research can enhance the quality of youth interventions. First, at the levels of *interaction between the professional and the young person*. At this level the degree to which the professional is responsive to the young person, and to which the two parties can work together to explore the nature of the problem and find solutions which are mutually beneficial, appears critical to effective practice. Second, at the level of *organisational practice* the capacity of the professional to work in this way depends on the extent to which the organisation is able to be responsive and facilitate change based on learning in and from action. Recurring patterns thus become a focus for co-inquiry. Third, by being responsive to young people's diverse and changing needs, learning can inform the *development of policy* which in turn can add cohesion to the structure and functioning of the organisation or programme.

Central to this approach is a need to transcend the need to control or pre-determine the outcomes of the inquiry process rather to open up opportunities to see differently and question established thinking. Specifically the task is to understand better the complexities at play, for example in terms of the disjunctions and paradoxes between what is espoused at policy level, what is enacted in practice and what is experienced by young people. By working creatively with such tensions, these can serve as fruitful lines of inquiry to support the development of practice by critically reflecting on the values and assumptions that underlie behaviours and actions.

In the research project on which this chapter is based, we sought not to simply learn about what was happening, but to actively engage young people and professionals with these issues in a way that challenged them to reflect critically and change their own orientations to such encounters and what was possible. At one level we did this by setting up workshops with young people and professionals to share, explore and reflect on values, assumptions and outcomes and consider what would make a difference within what was possible, to enhance the participation of young people in the labour market and in society at large. What we found was that TYN already had in place an organisational culture and way of working to allow this to happen quite naturally. On the other hand, despite monthly meetings to discuss problems, NDPAs were limited in what they could do as a result of the rigidity of the system and their own powerlessness in the system.

However, in seeking to reconstruct the nature of youth intervention encounters, we also acknowledge that such interactions are characterised by power, diversity and resistance. It is important therefore to attend to power inequalities as a basis for collaborative social learning and action inquiry. There are three important criteria here.

First, there is a need to provide a *secure, supportive and empowering (communicative action) space* (Kemmis, n.d.; Wenger, 1998) for young people to engage (see also Barber, 2001), be active in the solution of problems and develop their capacities, but also to challenge and change the nature of that space. Within such a space, disjunctions between young people's realities and orientations and the intentions and assumptions of policy and practice can be explored and new possibilities for choices and actions created. However, the nature of what constitutes such a space itself should be the focus for critical reflection and action-based co-inquiry between professionals and young people.

Second, the *critical role of professionals and the nature of the systems* in facilitating this type of communicative action space necessitate that a dialogical process is established whereby both young people and professionals can be part of a process of critical reflection in and on action around the assumptions, values and motives underlying individuals and the systems and structures they are a part of. This challenges professionals to reconstruct their role as 'expert' professionals in the form of 'interpretive' professionals (Edwards, 1998; Jans and Percy-Smith, 1999; Janssens *et al.*, 2000), that is, someone who seeks to understand the life of the individual and through recursive dialogue is able to work with individuals to reach an appropriate outcome through ongoing modification to practice.

Third that *communicative action should initiate learning*, should be action orientated and should provide the space for critical reflexivity in responding to emerging outcomes. Instead of a confrontational space in which boundaries are drawn between professional and young person and options for change closed down, a 'communicative action space' is created in which interventions, learning and action for change are intertwined in a dynamic critically reflexive process of social learning and reanimation. This means that both professional and young person are intertwined in a shared process of collaborative learning and inquiry around the problem at hand in a way that is interpretive and generative as new understandings of the problem are developed and alternative possibilities for change are jointly created. Action becomes the basis for joint experiential learning (Weil, 1989). In this situation, the professional does not seek to peddle standardised responses. Instead, (s)he accepts that they do not necessarily know the answer but are open to jointly exploring and developing solutions appropriate to the individual. Wildemeersch (1996) refers to this as 'social learning' which he understands as:

> The learning or groups, organisations and communities... aimed at the solution of... context problems, and is characterised by an optimal use of the problem solving potential of which a group, institution or community disposes. Social learning is action and experience oriented, it is critically reflective, in other words it is based on the questioning of assumptions and taken for granted problem definitions: it is interactive and communicative, which means that the dialogue between people is of foremost importance. And... it is interdisciplinary, as the solution of relatively complex issues presupposes the collaboration of a diversity of actors [*and perspectives*].

In the case above of the NDPA enacting the 'expert' professional role, we see that opportunities for learning and generation of more relevant and socially responsible options for change are closed down by bracketing out issues which standardised views of young people and 'packages' of provision are not able to deal with. In contrast, a practice-based learning approach to policy implementation involving social learning seems to offer a space to reconcile the frequent disparities between policy intentions and the diverse and complex realities of young people's lifeworlds.

Conclusions

The scenarios presented in this chapter have highlighted some of the dilemmas in current youth interventions, but also suggest there is value in developing professional and social relationships in such a way that the intervention becomes an interpretive and co-inquiring activity within the context of a multi-layered communicative action space. In such a space the answers are not always clear at the outset, but are created through a dialogical process of co-learning and critical reflexivity in which the assumptions of both parties are challenged and outcomes collaboratively negotiated. However, in the real time of target-driven and policy-constrained practice, competing agendas accentuate tensions, which may undermine original policy intentions. Within such contexts, encounter spaces sit precariously on the boundaries between what remains fixed and what is movable in terms of creating the space to make a difference.

Yet on the margins of mainstream practice, there are numerous examples of successful practice in youth interventions at grass roots level, involving not-for-profit and project-based organisations and initiatives, conducted within tight budgetary constraints (for example as exemplified by the case study of The YMCA Northampton). However, in order to survive, voluntary sector organisations such as TYN are having to become more mainstream to secure funding. This runs the risk of undermining autonomy by creating new strands of accountability through standardised assessment, evaluation and monitoring of outcomes. What might be lost here?

In summary, there appear to be three key dilemmas which problematise attempts to enhance young people's participation in social processes as equal citizens and which underlie the rationale for new forms of CRAR not just in academic work, but in the development of policy and practice. First, the structure, functioning and prioritising of government bodies place emphasis on economic and financial considerations, operate on the basis of being 'experts' working on behalf of young people's (and other's) best interests but according to the singular assumptions and agenda of politicians, funders and bureaucrats. As such, the assumptions underlying youth policy may be at odds with the lifeworlds of many young people. Emphasis on simplistic and mechanistically conceived institutional responses to 'youth problems' undermines the possibility for more creative solutions to complex social problems, and in ways that empower rather than disempower young people themselves.

Second, young people are commonly seen as in some way inferior to adults, as lacking the capacity to participate as citizens with equal rights in local decision-making processes and in the determination of their own lives. There also appears to be a fear of allowing young people more of an opportunity to input their own values and perspectives in case it destabilises the status quo. Such a view appears to be based on negative conceptions of youth and ignorance of their cultures, values and capacities. There are two paradoxes here. First that the status quo that young people are expected to participate in is far from satisfactory; yet young people are often denied the opportunity to be meaningfully part of the process of creating new systems. Second that despite political rhetoric of social responsibility and individual agency, social systems tend to undermine rather than encourage the development of the capacities for socially responsible and active citizenship. There appears to be an expectation that young people should conform to, and be integrated into, society, organisations and systems on adult terms rather than in ways that allow young people to challenge, change and innovate social systems through the contributions of their own values and perspectives. New Deal for 18–24-year-olds is a classic example of 'the system' providing opportunities in the assumed best interest of young people which are intended to address problems of unemployment and social exclusion. But despite the rhetoric of the New Deal as being flexible and client centred, the pressure of targets contributes to a situation where inadequate account is taken of young people's life circumstances (problems of multiple disadvantage, individual biographies and so on). Without young people having the chance to influence the conditions and ways in which they participate in labour market transition processes, their commitment may not be maintained and the original policy intentions of New Deal may be undermined.

The third key dilemma is in terms of the separation of research from the development of policy and practice based on differentiated roles and responsibilities according to specified expertise. However, increasingly there is an acknowledgement of the need for partnerships, multi-agency collaboration, and of community participation in local development processes. Yet, the processes of research and development which are used often diminish the contribution of young people as subjects rather than participants in the research and development process. If closer links between youth research, policy and practice are to be achieved then there is a need for developing a different type of research based on practice, grounded in the real time of projects and lived realities, but simultaneously systemic in bringing about leaning for change in organisations, projects and for ongoing policy development. As Hart (1995, p. 41) states:

> We cannot rely on the traditional approach of social science which observes (young people's) lives and reports it to policy makers in the hope that they will improve (their) conditions. We now need a more radical social science research with (young people) in which (they) themselves learn to reflect on their own conditions, so that they can gradually begin to take greater responsibility in creating communities different from the ones they have inherited.

It is with respect to these three dilemmas that we argue the need for new forms of research, policy and practice which reconstruct young people as co-constitutors of change in their communities, in addressing social problems and as agents in their own lives. This requires a different approach to developing policy and practice based on the cooperation of relevant stakeholders including young people, in processes of critical reflection and social learning around contextually based problems, which take account of issues of power and diversity (for example in terms of competing values, agenda and multiple bottom lines) and which allow for individuals, systems and processes to learn and develop. The Local Government Management Board (LGMB, 1996, p. 4) state that there is a need to:

> Establish a process to promote a dialogue between the youth community and government at all levels... establish procedures allowing for consultation and participation, promote dialogue with youth organisations... incorporate into relevant polices youth perspectives on social and economic development and resources management.

There are some local authorities and projects that have taken steps to involve young people in research and development. Yet in spite of the increasing availability of good practice guidance (Willow, 1997; Johnson *et al.*, 1998; Kirby, 1999; The Routes Project Team, 2001; Wade *et al.*, 2001; Kirby and Bryson, 2002), the way local partnership, projects and authorities approach research and development has been slow to change. It is our hope that the experiences and ideas provided in this chapter provide stimulus for reflection on the way research, policy and practice are undertaken and at the same time, make a contribution to new approaches to collaborative, practice-based youth research and development. To this end we feel that the principles underlying CRAR offer a way forward.

Notes

1. This research, funded by the EU Targeted Social and Economic Research Fourth Framework Programme, was a two-year project undertaken between 1998 and 2000 involving six European countries.
2. See previous endnote.

5
Onions and Apples: Problems with Comparative European Youth Research

Fred Cartmel

Introduction

Since the 1990s there has been a substantial expansion in funded comparative European youth research projects and an increase in academic papers relating to cross-national sociological research. This is mainly due to an increase in the European Commission funding of comparative research to investigate social problems across Europe and in particular around the issues of social exclusion and educational under-achievement (Coffield, 1999). In this chapter I investigate several methodological and practical problems related to cross-national research and examine the contribution that European research projects can make to our knowledge about the experiences of young people. The title of apples and onions is used to emphasise that in many comparative research projects very different youth experiences are being compared, which is like attempting to compare a vegetable with a fruit. Comparative research across different countries is not a new phenomenon within sociology. Marx, Durkheim and Weber's sociological investigations all involved theoretical comparisons across countries on subjects such as suicide rates, religions and production relationships. Durkheim (1970) for example examined rates of suicide across seven different countries using official data to establish contrasting patterns across different societies. This methodological trend has continued with the majority of comparative research projects using cross-sectional data (that is data collected at one point in time) to investigate a specific phenomenon.

The reasons why sociologists engage in comparative youth research vary according to the research question. Although comparative research involves two or more countries, the unit of analysis can be different

85

within each study. In cross-national research the country can be the object of study, the context of the study or the unit of analysis. Therefore, defining the research question prior to starting the research is of primary importance. Comparative studies have succeeded in comparing the labour market experiences of young people from two countries, with the results highlighting major institutional differences in the pathways from school to work, which impinge upon the experiences of young people in contrasting labour market systems. This is especially true of research which has compared the labour market experiences of young people in Germany and Great Britain. The labour market systems within the two countries are structurally different with the rigid dual system in Germany providing different experiences for young people in contrast to the more flexible labour market policies adopted in Britain (Bynner and Roberts, 1991; Evans and Heinz, 1993). Though such research is useful for comparing the differences in the experiences of young people, it is more difficult to interrogate theoretical models with such research. A key reason for the lack of theoretical development, as I go onto suggest in this chapter, is that it is problematic to make reliable comparisons between societies because of the many structural differences between the societies in the research. Nevertheless, comparative youth research which for example draws comparisons between labour market systems operating in the two or more countries can contribute to the development of social policy (Furlong and Cartmel, 2001).

The funding of social research by the European Commission has increased since the 1990s with the various Framework and Leonardo programmes enabling a greater number of researchers to undertake comparative research. The overall resources committed by the European Commission to the Sixth Framework that runs from 2002 to 2006 is 16,270 million Euros[1] (European Commission, 2002, p. 2). However, this agenda has prioritised the examination of social policy issues relating to young people rather than wider theoretical concerns in youth studies in for example models of youth transition. The funding therefore of comparative research projects has been predicated upon the use of research methodologies that are best suited to the analysis and development of social policies rather than theory-orientated projects (Higgins, 1986). Also, political imperatives often inform research projects which involve comparisons between social systems, as politicians across Europe are concerned to develop best practice on policies related to vocational training, the educational system and labour market programmes (see Furlong and McNeish, 2002). The political goal of reducing youth unemployment in the European Union has been a key factor which has driven the social science research agenda in recent years.

Another crucial reason why countries fund comparative research is to assess their standing in the world economy and to examine how social policy programmes contribute to their economic output. Coffield (1999) contends that increased economic competitiveness between countries forced the British Government to reassess their performance against France, Germany, the United States and Singapore. The Department for Education and Employment argued that:

...with the increased international mobility of other factors of production, so that capital and management skills can now be brought in more easily from abroad, a country's economic performance arguably now depends more on the (relatively immobile) human capital of its population than it has done in the past...As a result, education, and training may now be becoming more important determinants of a country's rate of economic growth. (DfEE/Cabinet Office, quoted in Coffield, 1999, pp. 3–4)

One consequence of this use of comparative research is that it enables individual states to impose stricter economic sanctions upon young people in order to increase wider economic productivity. Hence, the findings from comparative research can be used to assist those in power rather than be used to empower young people through the development of flexible training systems.

A key question raised when conducting comparative research across Europe relates to whether youth researchers are investigating uniformity between countries or searching for uniqueness within or between countries. The majority of research projects seek to identify common experiences among young people across countries, which can verify theories and research results posited at a national level. For example, several comparative research projects have highlighted that greater educational achievement can reduce the risk of young people experiencing long-term unemployment in European Union countries (Gallie and Paugam, 2000), though at the same time the research also notes that some countries are distinctive, as patterns of long-term unemployment among young people are not consistent with any other country. The long-term unemployed young people in Finland for example have different social characteristics compared to other countries within Europe (see Gallie and Paugam, 2000; Furlong and Cartmel, 2001). One consequence of these sorts of findings is that the unique experiences of young people in one societal context make it difficult to generate general conclusions which can then be easily disseminated to research, policy and practice communities. Accordingly, Sztompka (1988) has contended that researchers should shift their emphasis from seeking uniform patterns across societies to investigating 'enclaves of uniqueness' among growing homogeneity. However, unique experiences in particular countries can be difficult to explain, as differences between countries could be due to a multiplicity of processes such as contrasting cultures and traditions as well as young people's access to economic resources (Gipps, 1996). The historical development of institutional systems (such as education, welfare and the family) also needs to be taken into account during the data analysis stage and during the dissemination of information. It should not be underestimated that one needs a good background knowledge of the history of welfare regimes, education and training system in order to undertake good comparative research.

Comparative European research has provided youth researchers with a vast array of empirical evidence which can highlight differences in young people's experiences across western industrial societies, but very few new theoretical ideas have been forthcoming. Thus the challenge for youth researchers is how best to use this empirical evidence to develop new theoretical ideas, which can then be used to interrogate existing theoretical models of youth cultures and youth transitions. Despite the fact that in some sub-fields of youth research theoretical discussion has been prioritised over empirical evidence (Cohen and Ainley, 2000), researchers must be prepared to ground such discussion in empirical observations or theories become worthless. As Kohn (1989, p. 4) points out:

> Empirical observations must be related to some kind of theoretical construction, and no theoretical construction has any value unless it bears some relation to empirical observations.

Although Evans (2002) in her comparative work on young people in England and Germany has attempted to rework notions of structure and agency in her model of youth transition on the whole, there has been little sustained development of new theories in youth studies.

With increased globalisation, country comparisons have to consider the wider world economy and the consequences this has on national and local labour markets. New theoretical ideas within sociology argue that countries and nations are no longer as relevant for analysis, as the states' decision-making powers are decreasing through the rise of global capitalism (Giddens, 1990, 1991). A downturn in the global economy for example caused the recession in Britain in the early 1980s which then contributed to the restructuring of the youth labour market. Hence the internationalisation or globalisation of the world economy has heralded an upsurge in research investigating the different social and cultural differences across national borders. While global economic activity effects the experiences of young people, the dismantling of legislative frameworks developed in the Fordist era can also shape the demand for youth labour. As we have seen most markedly in the UK since the 1980s, political decisions can be made which either strengthen or weaken the social protection for young people which in turn dramatically effects their life chances. Therefore, the interplay between globalisation and the reaction of the nation-state to the internationalisation of the labour market is a key consideration which is taken into account when undertaking comparative youth research.

Different methodologies in comparative youth research

There have been numerous different quantitative methodologies used in comparative European research and some of these are set out in Table 5.1. We can classify these into four main types, all of which have various strengths and weaknesses.

The quantitative methodologies range from bi-lateral analysis that involves comparing two countries to multi-lateral analysis which involves a collaborative project where member countries collect new data through

Table 5.1 Methodological differences in EU research

Methodology	Example	Strengths	Weaknesses
1. Bi-lateral analysis (primary)	Karovnen *et al.* (2001)	Internal knowledge	Incompatibility
2. Multi-lateral analysis (primary)	Julkunen and Malmberg-Heimonen (1998)	Control over questions	Increased complexity, difficulty in interpretation
3. Secondary analysis	OECD	High quality data	No control over questions
(a) National datasets (b) A European dataset	European Household Panel		
4. Thematic networks	EGRIS (2001)	Inexpensive	No empirical data

a questionnaire using compatible questions. There are also several collaborative qualitative studies that have been conducted in Europe, which raise different methodological problems to these quantitative studies, which will not be discussed in this chapter. The sort of quantitative research methodology adopted by researchers will shape the nature of problems such research will face and how these can then be addressed (or not in many cases). Although some common problems arise whatever research methodology is used, these can be addressed in different ways by researchers. Oyen (1990) identified four different types of researchers who engage in cross-national research: purists, ignorants, totalists and comparativists. Purists believe that conducting sociological research across different countries is no different to other sociological research. Ignorants tend to deny the fact that comparative research can lead to greater complexity when analysing results. Totalists ignore stumbling blocks in comparative research and neglect the scientific requirements of the discipline. Comparativists raise issues about the distinctive nature of cross-national research but argue that obstacles have to be overcome to enhance our knowledge. The four typologies provide different solutions to problems that arise in comparative research and the stance taken can have a marked effect on the results produced by the research.

In the following section I discuss the problems with each different research methodology, and begin with bi-lateral analysis which uses independently collected datasets that are matched with comparable data from one other country.

Bi-lateral analysis

An example of bi-lateral analysis is that of Karovnen *et al.* (2001) who analysed the leisure and lifestyles of young people living in Helsinki and Glasgow, using two independently collected datasets within these two cities. The authors contended that although the two surveys were matched for equivalence on age, stage of life, there remained a crucial question regarding the equivalence of the key measures of social class, lifestyles and health behaviours. The authors went on to argue that:

> The goal of comparative studies is to find a balance between the measurement precision and the meaningfulness of the comparison; a perfectly identical measure may still mean different things in different cultures (Karovnen *et al.*, 2001, p. 41).

This quote highlights the problems with comparative research and raises the question about the rationale for undertaking cross-national research. On the one hand, there is the temptation among researchers to strive for methodological perfection and develop perfect comparisons of measures. On the other, they could aim to match broad categories in order for them to produce more meaningful results. After all, the comparison of two independent sets of data is undertaken in order to identify different experiences of young people in two different societal contexts. Methodologically, the depth of comparison within matched datasets is its great strength if compatibility between questions can be achieved. Nevertheless, one major weakness with this method is the laborious task of matching two datasets to ensure compatibility which can also be very expensive.

The Karovnen study employed established researchers within the countries involved though some research projects have attempted to collect data from overseas countries from the researcher's base in their native countries. This strategy is used to overcome the epistemological problems of sub-contracting the data collection to researchers who are not part of the core research team as there may be

>...the loss of external insight and fresh perspectives on social phenomena which is surely one of the very purposes of the undertaking social science research (Cockrill et al., 1999, p. 21).

Using the same group of researchers to conduct research in overseas countries can have both advantages and disadvantages. The main advantages are that individual researchers can maintain strict control over the fieldwork, ensuring that data collection methods are identical in both countries. Another advantage relates to dissemination and analysis being conducted by one research team in one country which allows for greater consistency in the production of key outcomes from the research. A key disadvantage of such an approach as highlighted by Cockrill et al. (1999) is that research is conducted at 'arms length' to the actual experiences of the research subjects. There is then an issue of managing the problem of different institutional structures and the misunderstanding of meanings which young people attach to their experiences.

Multi-lateral analysis

Multi-lateral analysis can offer solutions to the problems of bilateral analysis, as researchers in their respective countries collect new data from collaborating colleagues in other countries. However, there are major methodological problems that have to be overcome when engaging in cross-national research, such as sample design, equivalence of measures and dissemination. On a practical level, one of the most pressing problems is the securing of research partners from different countries who are able to participate in the research. Drawing on recent experiences of such research there are some ways to avoid the more common pitfalls. Firstly, ensure that the research group is fluent in one common language (English, French or German), otherwise endless hours can be wasted with participants who cannot speak the common language. On one large European Union project, for example, the participants dispersed into language groups of three to discuss relevant issues in different languages and then report back to the group in English, which was spoken fluently by only six people in a group of 16. This not only wastes valuable time at meetings, but also important theoretical and methodological issues can be overlooked.

Another problem facing such collaborative research is that the sampling procedure in one country can be difficult to achieve in other countries and this can lead to compromises in data collection. For example, when selecting respondents from an official sampling frame ensure that the criteria for individuals joining the sampling frame are compatible. Although it is expected that a national unemployment register should only contain those who are experiencing unemployment, but this is not always the case (as with Italy for example). Compromises therefore in such instances have to be made.

Translation of questionnaires should be undertaken professionally to minimise mistakes, then translated back to their original language to check for errors. The cultural differences between countries must be taken into consideration when compiling the questionnaire. Cockrill *et al.* (1999) raise the issue about using a schedule or questionnaire in several countries and illustrate the problem that some concepts are 'untranslatable'. There is also the issue of literal translation and psychological equivalence. Robinson (1984, p. 163) raises an important point about using measurements in two languages:

> Instruments [for research] should offer psychological equivalence to respondents and not apparent objective equivalence to the investigator. To pose the same form of question to two people who are different may require posing that question in two different forms.

This issue of the content of questions and their use in comparative research is exacerbated by the fact that in some countries (such as France) government regulations prohibit the use of questions which ask respondents about topics such as their political involvement and illegal activities, though these questions would be permitted in the UK. Hence the researcher has to ensure at the beginning of the research project whether such prohibitions exist in the countries under investigation. There are many advantages to undertaking comparative research. Projects funded by the EU have enabled researchers to exercise more control over sampling and data collection. Another advantage is that experts from the respective countries participating in the project are available to provide details of the institutional arrangements of those countries. Nevertheless, some difficulties arise as the funders of EU research play a major role in the actual shaping of the research foci which are often based around pressing social issues such as social exclusion, marginalisation and unemployment (Levitas, 1996). However, social exclusion is a contested term within sociology in Britain and debates continue about whether the term refers to a static social position or is an ongoing social process (MacDonald, 1997). Littlewood and Herkommer (1999) for instance discuss how social exclusion has been extensively used by research funders in Britain and how the problem of definition has increasingly emerged when this research agenda has been translated into a European context.

Secondary analysis: national datasets

The secondary analysis of two national datasets is undertaken in order to investigate differences or similarities within the nations under study. The methodology employed to compare the experiences of youth in two countries involves comparing nationally collected data that is compatible across both countries and ideally where respondents were asked similar questions in both societal contexts. Holdsworth and Elliott (2001) used this method when comparing the experiences of young people's timing of family formation in Spain and Britain and compared the British National Child Development Study with the Spanish 1991 Sociodemographic Survey. The results highlighted a range of differences in the patterns of family formation but the authors warned that:

> Explanations for recent delays in fertility may be linked with familistic characteristics of Southern European societies (but these may be) associated with delays throughout youth to adult transitions, starting with leaving home (Holdsworth and Elliott, 2001, p. 18).

The authors appear therefore to be unclear about the sociological reasons for extended family formation in Spain and Britain. These trends may be the result of distinctive family formation or due to the wider transformation of youth transitions. Nevertheless the strength of this method is that it draws on high quality national datasets that are currently available and aims to offer valuable insights from the secondary analysis of this material.

Secondary analysis: independent national surveys

In a recent European Union funded project (for example, The CATEWE Project[2]), the collaborators attempted to link together national surveys of school leavers from three different countries. The main problem with matching nationally collected data is achieving equivalence between variables within the sets of data. Brannen and Smyth (2000, p. 2) highlighted the methodological problems faced by the group stating:

> While every effort was made to select the most comparable datasets, it was evident that there were significant differences in the sample designs used, partly reflecting differences in the institutional systems themselves and partly reflecting the purposes for which the national transition surveys were originally designed. In addition, the surveys differed in relation to the time elapsed between leaving school and the survey.

If primary research is subsequently used in a comparative analysis problems can arise when matching the two independently collected national datasets. These problems emerge as the original data was collected to identify national trends and is not specifically designed for comparison with other countries. This creates difficulties when matching with other countries across Europe, but has also created problems with comparisons across Britain. The Scottish Young People's Survey cannot be matched to the England and Wales Youth Cohort Study due to methodological differences. Although the data can be analysed separately, then presented in a coherent way which provides a measure of harmonisation, there are difficulties in making comparisons due to the distinct nature of the education systems within England and Wales and Scotland. Hence Raffe (2000) argues that future surveys of school leavers should only be undertaken once agreement has been reached on how harmonisation may be achieved.

The main problem that existed in the secondary analysis of survey data (such as on school leavers) was that it was difficult to find equivalence between educational systems and welfare systems across Europe. These problems have been partially solved with the introduction of the

Casmin scale (see Müller and Shavit, 1998) and the creation of typologies of benefit welfare regimes by Esping-Andersen (1990). The typologies are widely used for grouping of different countries with the same welfare regime (see Gallie and Paugam, 2000).

Secondary analysis: European datasets

The existing European data (such as the European Household Panel Survey and the Labour Force Survey) which are collected at national level provide opportunities for researchers to compare the labour market experiences of young people across different European countries. The advantage of this approach is that it is relatively inexpensive for researchers to obtain copies of European datasets that have compatible variables across countries. Indeed, there is much research which has documented the transition experiences of young people across numerous numbers of countries. Couppié and Mansuy (2001) examine the school-to-work transition across 15 different countries though they offer a more descriptive account of these experiences rather than develop sociological or social policy explanations for these experiences. Similarly, Brauns et al. (2001) provided descriptive information on the link between education and the risk of unemployment in France, United Kingdom and Germany, but offer little insight into why the links were different across the contrasting countries. There are therefore several weaknesses with employing secondary analysis of established European datasets. Firstly, the researchers have no control over the questions which were originally asked. Thus, the research questions in subsequent research projects are often framed around the original variables. Secondly, in some officially collected National data only small numbers of young people are sampled at each age group; hence, with such small cell sizes it can be difficult to establish statistical inferences and these may not be conclusive due to the low sample numbers. Thirdly, researchers often have little contextual knowledge of the countries they are analysing, which often then leads to an overly descriptive treatment of the data and the inability to develop theoretically informed conclusions about the experiences of young people (de Broucker et al., 2000; Gangl, 2000). Raffe (2000, pp. 8–9) has highlighted other weaknesses of European surveys which have been subsequently used in secondary analysis projects:

> Other limitations of the LFS for the analysis of transition are that it collects relatively little information on education, on itineraries within the education/training system, on youth training and employment schemes, or on transition processes... It does not collect

subjective data, or data on the social background of new entrants to the labour market. It is a household survey and the quality of response is dependent on how the respondent interprets the question. It includes relatively few sample members making the initial transition to employment in a given year in a given country, although this problem can be dealt with by combining consecutive years. Above all the main LFS is based on a cross-sectional survey, and thus records stocks rather than flows.

For Raffe the lack of subjective data in European surveys is a major constraint to conducting meaningful analysis of young people's experiences.

Finally, though these technical problems[3] with data are important, a major concern to sociologists is how national data is collected and presented. Very often nationally collected datasets are incorporated into larger datasets (for example, OECD, Labour Force Survey and so on) and then used by politicians to highlight its social profile to its population and the world at large. Therefore, political decisions lie behind such social profiles, which can lead to bias in the ways in which countries collect and present their data. Political influence therefore can weaken statistical comparisons based upon existing data collected from a particular state.

Thematic networks

Thematic networks are based around researchers from several countries discussing theoretical ideas around a particular theme (such as youth transitions, consumption or educational experiences) and this approach involves no data collection. EGRIS (2001) used a thematic network approach to generate sociological and theoretical informed insights into the experiences of young people in Europe, but no empirical research was undertaken to confirm their hypotheses. The network provides academics with the opportunity to discuss sociological theories about youth that are emerging within other societies. The thematic networks contend that different experiences among young people do exist but as no empirical evidence exists to verify these claims, some have argued that such an approach represents a case of 'galloping theory' (Roberts, 1997). This inductive research methodology is unusual for comparative research projects, as a deductive method is usually employed in order to begin to develop sociological theory. Although the EGRIS network did bypass one of the main sociological problems with comparative research as:

All the eternal and unsolved problems inherent in sociological research are unfolded when engaging in cross national studies (Oyen, 1990, p. 1).

This statement implies that comparative researchers encounter sociological problems that would be non-existent in nationally based projects. The strength of thematic networks is that they provide the opportunity to discuss new theoretical advances in different countries. The methodological problems associated with sociological research in one country can provide researchers with many problems, but when research is across different countries, new difficulties arise that are challenging to researchers.

The new theoretical ideas emerging from Europe include new categories of young people who are deemed as 'trendsetters', which refers to young people making individual choices within their life biographies. The notion of 'trendsetters' has emerged in several European countries, where young people are pursuing a biography that is based upon personal enhancement, rather than economic gain (that is, a young person who spends two years travelling around the world before settling into the labour market). Although deemed as 'trendsetters' in some European societies, youth researchers in other countries would characterise these young people as 'an affluent minority' and not worthy of investigation. A concern about such concepts as 'trendsetters' is that they largely abstract from notions of gender, social class and ethnicity. Ken Robert's (1997) has recently suggested that such research has not struck an appropriate balance between theory and empirical investigation.

Conclusions

In this chapter, I have attempted to outline some of the strengths and weaknesses of different methodological approaches in European research when using existing data or collecting new empirical data. Many of the difficulties associated with undertaking comparative research are linked to the 'problem of meaning' and the issues of meaning and interpretation in sociological research. Weber defined meaning being arrived at 'when the overt action and the motives have both been correctly apprehended and at the same time their relation has become meaningfully comprehensible'. The meanings attached to different questions and categories in comparative research can vary in relation to the societal background of each researcher participating in the research. Thus, we have the example of a Greek and a Finnish academic who were debating the social position of women farmers in their respective countries. The Greek academic argued that all women farmers were excluded and repressed in Europe; her argument was based upon qualitative research conducted in five European countries. The Finnish academic argued that this was not the case in Finland where women held high esteem in a rural community if they were 'mather's'. The social position of 'mather' is distinctive to Finnish society where women in a village are held in high esteem and sit on committees, own the rights to the farm and do all the work on the farm while their husbands work outside agriculture. Throughout comparative research, one major concern for researchers is that equivalence of meaning is achieved across countries.

The sociological theory behind comparative research is that comparisons can be made between contrasting countries and new theories can then eventually be developed. There are two conflicting arguments concerning sociological theory and cross-national research. The first contends that macro-sociology may be used to focus on sub-fields of sociology where theories can be tested and macro-sociology provides the best arena for sociologists to examine their skills as sociologists (Eisentadt and Curelaru, 1977). The second argument suggests that cross-national research can lead to developments of sociological theories. The generality of findings from a single country can be validated through comparisons with other countries (Kohn, 1989). In comparative research, observations must be related to the theoretical construction and the theory has no value unless it is related to empirical observations.

The trends in collaborative research have been towards empirical research into different situations among young people in different European countries, usually based upon existing surveys or new empirical work. Sophisticated statistical models producing numerous correlations highlight individual country differences among the experiences of young people in the transition from school to work. Although these studies provide useful information about young people's different experiences, they are void of theoretical insights into the social change occurring in individual countries to substantiate the country differences. The other side of the coin is 'galloping theory' where researchers are being driven by theoretical ideas but have no empirical evidence to substantiate their ideas.

Comparative research can reveal startling results that can inhibit academics from disseminating their findings to academic communities. Furlong and Cartmel (2001) found that on an objective level, long-term unemployment was prominent in Scotland and Finland and led to marginalisation and social exclusion. On a subjective level, the Scots were marginalised but the Finns were integrated into society. We presented these findings at two different conferences being convinced that our analysis was correct. However we were then approached by a leading academic who stated that she had uncovered similar results, but was concerned about presenting them as she was worried about their validity. What then is the sociological imagination about if it is not about the uncovering of social processes across different nations and cultures and striving to generate hypotheses that can be tested and critiqued in the academic community? As Coffield (1999, p. 5) has remarked, the value of cross-national comparative research is that:

> At their best it challenges, and perhaps even punctures, national myths which tend to feed on confirmatory, but which seek to ignore contradictory evidence.

If the role of sociology is to challenge 'common-sense' assumptions about youth through providing alternative explanations of young people's behaviour, comparative youth research must be a way forward to achieve this goal. Youth researchers have a valuable role to play in influencing debates about the situation of young people across Europe, but they must also exercise caution in ensuring that methodological problems encountered in the early stages do not undermine the research process. Therefore, methodological vigour should be complemented with new theoretical perspectives. The large number of cross-national research projects being funded by the European Union provides youth researchers with the opportunity to investigate changing social policies that impact upon young people's lives across different European countries. Youth researchers should ensure that they do not become 'handmaidens' of European governments that use research to merely develop their own narrow social policy agenda. Youth researchers therefore are vulnerable to political influence and developing research which is more descriptive than critical and theoretical. This descriptive research tends to juxtapose phenomena in one country with another undermining the real strength of comparative research:

> Juxtaposition is not comparison, and no matter how many descriptions, of even the highest interest, we may record, they still remain descriptions unless we are able to reveal patterns which exhibit similarities and differences, identify their cause and effects, and relate them to other patterns which exhibit similar features in a similar context (1979, p. 4, quoted in Cockrill *et al.*, 1999).

Youth researchers should always remember that their main aim is to construct new theoretical ideas or build on existing theories of young people and challenge 'common-sense' assumptions about youth as a problem. Successful European research is based upon a balanced approach where researchers can balance empirical findings with their developed theoretical ideas. A concern about European research is that new theoretical ideas regarding young people are underdeveloped at country level and therefore cannot be explored in a cross-national context. If there is a lack of theory in youth studies in Britain, it is not possible to move into a wider European research agenda until these theoretical issues are more clearly developed in domestic youth research.

Notes

1. This covers all areas of funding not just social science.
2. The CATEWE Project attempted to match School Leavers Surveys with three different countries and encourage other countries to implement a school leavers survey, then the school-to-work transition could be analysed across Europe. With the increased participation of young people within post-compulsory education, the first sweep of the surveys is not informative, except for highlighting who is most likely to leave school at the minimum school age.
3. See Gangl (2000) who highlights other technical problems with the Labour Force Survey.

Part 3
Reflections on Fieldwork

6
Ethnography in Practice: A Case Study Illustration

Ruth Emond

Introduction

This chapter outlines the experience of undertaking a participant observation study with young people living in two children's homes in the North-East of Scotland. In doing so, it will reflect on the *process* of conducting ethnographic research with young people. The methods used to gain access and acceptance to the group will be presented, focusing on the particular ways in which young people sought to protect their group space and culture. The ways in which this acceptance was achieved are considered through a discussion of the author's journey into the field which itself is compared with a young person's journey into residential care.

This chapter has at its heart, an attempt to provide an honest and reflective account of conducting ethnographic research with young people. It argues that ethnographic researchers are required to do more than merely state the methodological approach taken. Rather, there should be a commitment to outlining to the reader the process of the research, how access and relationships were granted and built and the impact that the research has on those taking part. Those who conduct ethnographic research with young people need to make explicit the way in which they addressed issues of age, gender ethnicity, class and so on. It is a dangerous trap to believe that as we were once young so we have insight and experience of what those we are studying enjoy and endure. The proceeding chapter is written in this spirit and exposes both the strengths and the weaknesses of my own ethnographic experience.

Researching young people in 'looked after' care

The sociology of youth has historically been concerned with two key elements of young people's lives. The first has focused on the transitions young people make between 'youth' and 'adulthood'. Such research has been dominated by studies of school-to-work transitions although in more recent times there has been some interesting work undertaken into situations where this transition may be restricted or extended (see, for example, Furlong and Cartmel, 1997; Roche and Tucker, 1997). Crucially this 'transitional' approach has been criticised for its history of exploring the experiences of those deemed to be 'out with' mainstream society in an attempt to explain the mainstream experience (Tait, 1993). The second approach is that which is concerned with the study of particularly subordinate youth groups. Subordinated groups are regarded as striving for mechanisms to resist their oppressed status and 'win space'. These attempts are reflected and manifested in cultural behaviour. Thus, such studies have the class struggle as a central tenet of their analysis.

Ethnography has been most markedly used with this second approach to the study of youth. In order to understand and explore the complex practices and views of these groups of young people, it was felt that they were best researched from the 'inside' or certainly from 'alongside'. As such, many of the 'spectacular' youth groups were approached from the perspective of being anthropologically 'strange' with whole sets of dress, customs and language which through ethnographic research could be identified and learned. In more recent times, this methodological stance has been successfully used with a number of youth-related issues or groups (see, for example, Thornton's (1995) work on club culture). However, there remains a sociological association between the use of ethnography and marginalised or non-mainstream young people.

The methodological approach taken in the research does not rest purely on a philosophical stance. In order for the research question or problem to be addressed, some consideration must be given to which approach will elicit the greatest level of insight or quality of data. In relation to the case study used in this chapter, a participant observation approach was taken. However, the decision to use this method was not initially taken by myself as a researcher. I had considered that, as a means of gaining insight into the ways in which young people in residential care gained status within their groups and managed group structure, qualitative interviews with a number of young people in a variety of settings would reap the greatest reward. After I had piloted my interview schedule, I met with the young people who had agreed to take part in the study. From this discussion, it became clear that the young people did not agree with my approach arguing that the ways in which the groups functioned and how they felt about living alongside other young people were subject to significant change. It was they who suggested that I conduct an ethnographic study or as one young man put it: 'If you want tae ken (know) what its like to bide (live) here I mean really ken then you'd have to come and bide' (Neil).[1]

As a result of these pilot stage discussions, I spent a year living alongside young people in the two residential units used for the pilot study. The young people involved in the pilot were clear that their views concerning the group changed over time and that this was closely linked to what was occurring within the group or indeed in their individual lives.

On reflection, however, there are a number of other reasons why an ethnographic approach was best suited to the study of these groups. One of the primary reasons was the history young people in the care system have of being asked questions by 'adults' and often adult strangers. Young people in residential care are most likely to have also experienced other forms of looked after care, most notably foster care (Bilson and Barker, 1995). They will have had to respond to questions from social workers, foster parents, residential staff, parents and in the case of Scotland, children's panel members. The result of this is that many of these young people associate being asked questions with a change in their circumstances ranging from fairly innocuous issues such as favourite food to a change in placement or levels of family contact.

Ethnography by its very nature requires the pursuit of 'depth' data and as a result, the boundaries around confidentiality must be clearly negotiated and adhered to (Burgess, 1985). In order for participants to begin to allow a researcher into their 'world', they must be clear as to how this world will be exposed. Consideration needs to be given to how ethnographic data is recorded and stored. This has significant implications for participants now and in the future. With the growing expectation that data be archived and available for future reference, ethnographers must feel confident that participants confidentiality is not compromised (Ackeroyd, 1984).

Young people in 'looked after' care will have been informed of the notion of confidentiality. However within social work this is a somewhat moveable feast. Whilst no one outside the care system may be told of any information, given many within it will have this information shared with them. In relation to confidentiality in the research process young people may have a level of suspicion and have particular concerns about what happens to the information given. Further, young people may develop a scripted response to questions which serves to protect their sense of self and limit the potential impact of the information shared.

The point therefore is that young people are not a homogeneous group, and consideration must be given to what participation in research might mean for them. Ideally to empower young people to take control over how information is shared goes some way to address such issues. Crucially ethnography provides a catch all term for a range of methodological tools that have the flexibility to adapt to the existing culture of the participants and their social world (Skeggs, 2001).

In any ethnographic study it does not suffice to say that young people were observed and their social practices and communications analysed. Rather, it is the ways in which relationships with the young people were established and the resultant degree of access to their everyday lives which is vital if participant observation is to be accepted as a worthwhile research tool. As an approach ethnography requires that research is conducted within the social context of the participants lives. Thus researchers must take into account, and account for, the relationships that existed within the research process, the impact that the researcher has on the data being generated and the social context itself (Oakley, 1998; Skeggs, 2001). As Gouldner (1971, p. 490) recommends:

> [By adopting a reflexive sociology] we would increasingly recognise the depth of our kinship with those whom we study. They would no longer be viewable as alien others or as mere objects for our superior technique and insight; they could instead be seen as a brother [sic] sociologist, each attempting, with his [sic] varying degree of skill, energy and talent to understand social reality.

There is a sense of process to this type of research, which in its presentation illustrates issues relating to the level of understanding achieved by the researcher and the perceptions held by the participants of the researcher him/herself. Indeed, Strauss and Corbin (1998) consider the process to be not of a linear nature but of a spiral of understanding; understanding during the process becoming increasingly refined. The following section explores this process within my research and draws out some of the key stages and dilemmas that were experienced.

Moving in

It is crucial that researchers take cognisance of their first impressions of the research setting. These initial perspectives form the beginning of understanding the young person's social world (Corsaro and Molinari, 1990). Often these reflections can give insight into the experiences of the young people involved in the study. They provide the initial 'stranger' experience that is central to an ethnographic approach (Hammersley and Atkinson, 1983). Indeed, Becker (1971) in his discussion of his sequential approach to analysis identifies the initial period of fieldwork as being concerned with gaining an understanding of the social context and identifying how that understanding has come about is the first stage of analysis. First impressions are a crucial record of the beginning of the research relationship and therefore of understanding how we become part of the social group under study.

I was filled with trepidation prior to entering the units. I was uncertain as to how the young people would regard me. I was also concerned about the experience of living in the units without the safety and protection that being a member of staff can provide, not least because they get to go home at the end of their shifts! This sense of anxiety was shared by young people:

> You know, I thought it would be like a big castle or something, you know, a prison or something. It is big like, bigger than a normal hoose but when everyone speaks about a 'home' they think about a big castle or something with millions of mental kids running about. I did think I would get a hiding [assaulted] like, ye ken, that it would be full of nutters (Hilary).

Being admitted

Gaining access to a research site is only the beginning of being admitted to and accepted by the group under study (Calvey, 2000). Arguably young people are active social agents who, despite being formally 'controlled' by adult practices and structures, create strategies to create a sense of control over their own environments (Harden and Scott, 1998). The job of the ethnographic researcher is therefore to negotiate access to these social spaces. It is essential that good ethnographers move beyond the 'front stage' behaviours that young people under study elect to present to the world and instead enter into the 'back stage' (Goffman, 1959).

I quickly discovered that, despite the numerous bedrooms, the comfortable lounge and the welcoming kitchen, the young people had colonised what was referred to as the 'Quiet Room'. This was the only room in the building in which the young people could smoke. It was perceived by all as the young people's space, the staff rarely frequenting it and as such it became the setting for the collection of the most indepth data. The young people accepted that, as a resident, I had access to this space. This was not, however, a universal welcome. In the initial few months of fieldwork, one young man would leave the room as soon as I entered whilst at other times conversations would end as soon as I opened the door. In so doing, the young people quickly made me aware that although accepted and welcomed at one level I was clearly not yet one of their group. At times, this was difficult and upsetting and made spending time with the staff group even more attractive. In hindsight, however, by resisting this temptation my position as a non-staff member was enforced.

During this stage of the research, ethnographers begin to try to gain some sense of how acceptance by the group may be facilitated (Hughes, 1976). Consideration must also be given to the part the researcher's age, gender, class and ethnicity may play in this (Fine and Sandstrom, 1988). The danger in undertaking research with young people is that researchers believe that they have a pre-existing level of understanding because they were young themselves once. Even more concerning is that many researchers believe they are still young and have to therefore make little effort to be the 'stranger'. Social proximity can be as much of a hindrance as a help and is not necessarily a short cut to establishing research relationships. The role of the ethnographer is to learn about the group under study from a position of cultural stranger. Researchers must be vigilant therefore as to how much everyday 'knowledge' they assume is something known and shared with their participants.

During the initial months of my fieldwork, I found that it was the young women who appeared to take a more active role in welcoming me to the unit. It was they who would invite me to join them and who would include me in discussions. I considered that this was as a result of my gender, but I was later to discover that young women always took control of welcoming new admissions (Emond, 2000). At this time, I felt conscious not only of my gender but also of my age and regularly expressed my feelings of anxiety and fear around living in the unit and of being accepted by residents. I found that this 'accidental' honesty facilitated discussion and added to the construction of me as 'student', in need of help. I quickly became less of a threat and more of an object of pity, which in the longer term became a role that was difficult to shake off. Hammersley and Atkinson (1983) argue that the management of self-disclosure is a crucial factor in negotiating access and establishing research relationships. They argue that this may have increased significance when researching vulnerable or marginalised groups. Self-disclosure may be an informal way of demonstrating respect or empathy with participants thus making clear that the purpose of research is not to judge or further stigmatise.

It is also at this early point in fieldwork that researchers are required to set boundaries to their relationships and role. Fine and Sandstrom (1988) suggest that 'gifts', both material and financial, can help establish research relationships with young people and in some ways address the power imbalance. It may be argued that this can have quite the opposite effect and may lead to confusion over roles and create a sense of being 'bought'. I made clear that I would not distribute cigarettes or money nor would I accompany young people outside the building. The young people accepted my position and, although it set me apart from them and their behaviour with each other, it served to clarify my role and arguably limit the 'performance for pay' behaviour which may have occurred. Confidentiality and data collection techniques were frequently discussed in this initial period. Lee (1993) states that access is a process of continual negotiation and that such negotiation can make a key contribution to the development of trusting relationships. For example, the young people were uncomfortable with my taking notes, either in front of them or leaving the room to do so. They felt that it made them too self-conscious and that they were anxious about what I was choosing to record. As a result I changed from taking notes to using a tape recorder which the young people controlled in terms of switching it off and on. I regarded this as positive, in that it seemed to refine my role as researcher and continue the participatory approach to the research itself. In my view, this was a far more helpful way of addressing the power imbalance than material gain would have been.

In many ways this initial period of fieldwork may create a sense of loneliness or vulnerability for researchers (Lee-Treweek, 2000). They are no longer in the role they are used to and at the same time have not been accepted by the young people under study. It may be that observing and striving to participate within this new environment can leave researchers feeling overwhelmed by new sounds, smells, language and routines. These experiences can, however, provide interesting insights into the experiences of young people:

> When I first came here...I hated it...I couldn't sleep in my bed at night. I wasnae in my mam and dad's hoose...I felt like no one wanted me...like no one here kent [knew] me. I suppose I just felt lonely...aye, lonely (Bryony).

Gaining trust

Before research relationships can be built, a level of trust must be established (May, 1993). Within my research young people made clear the value that they placed on being able to trust not only me, but also other new admissions. As a researcher, however, it is essential that effort is made to gain insight into what such terms might mean for the young people under study. Indeed, failure to understand language and meaning provides a clear example of where 'adult centred' notions can serve to undermine the research process (Williamson and Butler, 1995). The participants in my study constructed trust as a level of safety and of mutual understanding about the group's expectations and demands of social practices and beliefs. It was therefore viewed as essential to 'suss out' the suitability of any new prospective group member. Crucially there appeared to be an acceptance that the young people could, in no way control *whom* they lived with but could control, or at least have influence on *how* they lived with them.

Testing out

Ethnographic researchers have reported feeling 'tested' by their participants (Lee-Treweek, 2000). Westmarland (2000) in her discussion of conducting ethnographic research in the police force states that many of the 'tests' she experienced existed as an opportunity to prove to the police that she could cope and that she would not interrupt police proceedings. She goes on to suggest that these tests were also linked to her gender and to the unspoken expectation that as a woman she would be less likely to manage violence and stress. This position is also true of work with young people. In many groups, clubs or institutions there may also be a general period of testing which exists for all new members of the group. The ethnographic researcher is therefore required to not only identify that they are being tested and what such tests consist of but also to explore the meanings attached to such tests.

The young people in my research understood such tests as a means of protecting the group and of restricting access until safety and understanding could be assured. Indeed, during my fieldwork some residents appeared never to get beyond this testing out stage; their calibre was never fully confirmed. The degree to which new admissions were tested varied, and this variation appeared to rely on the initial presentation of the young person, the group's previous knowledge of him/her and his/her care biography.

Tests were developed by the young people to maintain or make permeable the group's protective boundaries. I was aware, during the initial three months, of being monitored and discussed and at times of being placed in positions where my relationships with the young people could be assessed. One of the most significant 'tests' placed before other new residents and me was the test of loyalty, of not being a 'grass'. To 'grass' on fellow residents was disliked by all the young people. I was later to see that this apparently straightforward philosophy was in fact much more complex and was concerned more with the way in which information was passed on rather than to whom. However, such subtlety was not immediately apparent to other new admissions, or myself. Instead it appeared we were being judged solely on the ability to hold counsel.

This element of the test was particularly relevant to me, as confidentiality was a central component of my research. Furthermore, I regarded the young people's recognition of this to be crucial to my acceptance by the group. If I was to be approved in my role as participant observer rather than, as my age and employment history would suggest, another social worker, I was required to demonstrate my loyalty to the group. Significantly, I did not realise at the time that I was being tested beyond the regular 'you won't tell anyone will you?' comments that I had received from the young people. In fact it transpired that the young people had together decided to construct a situation whereby I would be given a piece of information regarding a member of the group. After this information was passed to me I was monitored to see whom, if anyone, I discussed it with. After a period of three months I was told by a group member that they had 'set me up' but that it was good that I hadn't grassed; either about the information given to me or at being 'set up'!

Having agency

Researchers, as previously mentioned, can experience feelings of being overwhelmed or of being tested by the group under study. However, it is essential to recognise that, as researchers, we do have agency and an ability to control ourselves if not to control our environment. Williamson and Butler (1995) argue that young people make quick judgements as to the character of researchers and that this judgement can be difficult to shake off. It is crucial, therefore, that the researcher considers the impact that they have in their wider social world and how this may be translated and transported into the world under study.

One significant factor, which aids the ethnographic process, is the pace of the research. Allen (2001) in his study of the Foyer model of housing states that the opportunity to 'hang around' for long periods was essential to collecting depth data, freeing individuals up to behave without being cognisant of being actively 'researched'. In relation to my study I viewed the fieldwork as taking 6–8 months and therefore felt that I had time to slowly become accepted by the group. As such in the initial two to three months I spent time away from the young people, trying not to follow them around as they moved from room to room. As far as possible, I waited for invitations to participate although always having smoking as a legitimate means of being with them in the 'quiet room'. In retrospect, this pace worked in my favour and as the weeks went by I found myself increasingly being invited to be more active in the group. This notion of pace was not exclusive to me. I saw a number of new admissions behaving in similarly 'sensitive' ways:

> ...anyone that comes in this place, well anyone with a brain, is always quiet, they dinnae speak a lot, you've got to speak to them... you dinnae want just someone coming in and wrecking the place that's the thing aboot emergencies and that, they forget...well dinnae ken that this is our home (Duncan).

I was not universally welcomed nor trusted and those that felt unsure were often the ones who would either remove themselves from my company or who would 'act up' as the stereotypical (in their view) child in care. I would therefore be the audience to what were 'displays' of aggression, self-injury and vandalism. This is not to say that at times in my fieldwork such practices were not apparent. However, in my initial period of fieldwork I did believe that such displays were put on for me. It may be argued that, by behaving in this way, the young people were able to test out whether my claims to not be a member of staff were valid:

> ...[laughs] mind that time that we burnt holes in the table... I couldnae believe Ruth just sitting there, nae daeing anything... [sarcastically] 'one o' us' right enough (Fraser).

Researchers are often in the uncomfortable position of wishing to be accepted at any cost and yet maintaining the young people's awareness that they are being researched. For me, I did attempt to address this by continuing my discussions on data collection, allowing young people control over the dictaphones and debating my analytical ideas. I was also helped enormously by the staff. They bought into the notion that I wanted to become as close as possible to the reality of group living and would, in the same way as the young people, be publicly reprimand for my misdemeanours. The staff also helped in maintaining awareness that I was conducting research, which I regarded as a positive step. By making this humorous, it further removed the threat that such endeavours may evoke. I was, for the bulk of my fieldwork, known as the 'invisible researcher' and could therefore be ignored, walked into and so on in the name of humour.

Having agency also includes the way that researchers dress, talk and the extent to which they joke and join in (Williamson and Butler, 1995). Much of this relates to the way in which young people construct researchers, and indeed the expectations held of 'someone from a university':

> I thought you'd be posh like...I didnae think when they said you were fae a university that you would be like us, ken I thought you'd be auld [old] and snobby (Duncan).

Young people tended to be informal in their interactions and would regularly use slang and swear words. I communicated with them in a similar way but to a level with which I was comfortable. As Cottle (1973) suggests, young people are resistant to researchers who try to 'be like them'; they appear false and patronising. My clothing was informal and, as I was in the units most of the time and unlike the staff was not required to leave the building or act 'professionally', I rarely wore shoes. These small differences marked me out from the other adult staff and also signalled a level of relaxation which, in turn relates back to the notions of accepting as much as acceptance. The young women in particular were positive about my dress sense to the extent that they would borrow items of clothes or make-up. Such props helped me in moving to the next level of building relationships.

Building relationships

Part of the ethnographic process includes recording and reflecting upon the ways in which the experience of being part of the group under study changes over time (Lofland and Lofland, 1984). Central to this development is the extent to which relationships are built (Polsky, 1962). There has been a great deal of debate amongst qualitative researchers as to the nature and extent of the research relationship. Oakley (1981), for example, encourages the notion of striving for a friendship relationship and believes that such relationships can be achieved through self-disclosure on the part of the researcher. This approach she argues minimises the level of exploitation endemic in the research relationship. By contrast, other feminist researchers, for example Stanley and Wise (1983), argue that researchers must be vigilant to the fact that they are in a position of power and that it is a 'working' relationship and not an egalitarian friendship.

As the fieldwork continued into its third month, the young people became increasingly accepting of my involvement in their resident group. I spent extended amounts of time in their company, becoming an active participant in the group. As such, I was expected to offer opinions, challenge speakers and join in the 'fun'. This was a somewhat gradual change and appeared to begin with two of the young women's approach to borrow clothes. The three of us spent time in my room as they selected the items that they wished to wear. The discussion then moved on to my selection of make-up products and how they compared to their own.

From this apparently insignificant exchange, I was allowed to interact as a young woman rather than as 'student' or 'researcher'. On this occasion, we stayed in my room chatting for most of the afternoon and afterwards I was invited down to the quiet room to smoke. Almost immediately the degree to which I was included appeared to increase. Although by this point the young people had begun to be more open in their discussions whilst I was present, I had taken a somewhat silent role. Instead I was asked for my opinion and enjoyed the debate that followed.

As the fieldwork progressed, my 'role' as a non-staff member was aided by phone calls that I received from my friends and family as well as the use of 'home leave'. On returning to the unit or from receiving a phone call I, like other residents, would be asked what I had done whilst I had been away and in turn I would be anxious to catch up on the events in the units in my absence. I became increasingly trusted with information and would be sought out for advice, often being regarded as someone between a young person and a member of staff. In retrospect, I was being allowed to belong. The young people demonstrated this sense of belonging in a number of ways. As a group, we would talk about past events or memories and as time passed my part in these 'stories' became more pronounced. We now had shared memories and experiences that set us together. The young people would further demonstrate my belonging by physical acts. For example, when writing out lists of players for a game they would include me, or when discussing who would be attending a young person's birthday tea.

Ethnography undertaken using a participant observation approach makes much of the style and level of relationships built with participants. The early sociologists of the Chicago School provided 'thick descriptions' of the individualised nature of these relationships (Whyte, 1955; Becker et al., 1961). It is important if one is to accept that young people are not homogeneous that one also accepts that ethnographers will not build relationships of equal depth with all young people. Rather it is the task of the ethnographer to explore the extent of the relationships and examine why this variation may be occurring.

Within my own research, the level to which relationships were built varied amongst the group. My relationship with the two young women became increasingly similar to that of a 'friendship' and as such they were more willing to share secrets and private thoughts. In turn I was also expected to be more open about my 'personal' life. It appeared that as a direct consequence of my age and experience, I was given the role of 'older sister' (Fine and Sandstrom, 1988). Throughout such discussions, I would remind the women that I was conducting research, often by asking if I could record our exchanges. The young men were more challenging in respect of building relationships. In both units they appeared to place me alongside the other female members of the group yet maintained a reserve that was not so apparent with the young women. There were three exceptions to this. These young men appeared to accept me as someone that they could talk to. Again this 'sisterly' role was enacted. What seemed to add to the building of relationships was the willingness on my part to answer questions relating to my 'private' life and my unexpected non-adult behaviour (that is, lack of sanctioning, lack of authority and telling jokes).

A further aid to the acceptance by the group was the appearance of new admissions. The group's attention would turn to 'sussing out' these new members and therefore there was less time to devote to me. As a mark of my acceptance into the group, I was accorded involvement in this testing out process and my opinion was sought on the behaviours and practices of the new resident. Like the provision of advice, I felt concerned about supplying my opinion. As far as possible, I sat on the fence being rather non-committal in my judgements. Interestingly this seemed to work in my favour. The young people regarded me as someone who listened and who encouraged them to make up their own minds.

However, with my new found group acceptance I discovered that I was placed in a number of difficult situations. One incident occurred when I was watching television in the living room. One of the young women came in to join me and sat on the arm of my chair. As we chatted, a young man entered and proceeded to sit on top of the young woman. He reached his arm around her and began to stroke my hair. I was uncertain how to manage this, concerned that any extreme reaction would be seen as my acting as a member of staff. Instead I waited for a while and then said that I hated having my hair played with and did he mind stopping. I tried to laugh as I said this and hoped that my more general dislike would limit a perceived attack on him. He laughed and left the room, and the incident appeared to have little effect on him. Interestingly, the young women who had been with us praised me for 'standing up to him'.

Being a participant member of the resident group resulted in my having an acknowledged impact on the group members' practices. To remain separate, however, would arguably have restricted their behaviours further. As far as possible, I attempted to behave in similar ways to the young people. Like any new admission, I attempted to become accepted by being like the group, often waiting for other members to respond. In many ways I let others define my role.

> I just waited ken, watched what ab'dy else done... It's a'right here. Once they suss you oot and you suss them oot then you just get on wi it. No ab'dy's gonna be your best pal but... well chances are you will find a good pal amongst them. It's a laugh most of the time (Jack).

Leaving

One of the most significant issues for ethnographers is how best to leave the field. Predominately such researchers provide great insight into how they entered the field and how relationships were established (see, for example, Polsky, 1962; Lee-Treweek, 1996). However, what is less well described is the way in which these relationships are ended and the impact that leaving has on those being researched. For example, on her return to the village that she had chosen as a research site for her study of mental illness in rural Ireland, Scheper-Hughes (2000) was surprised to be met with hostility and outrage. Central to this reaction appeared to be the lack of adequate ending to her relationships with the villagers and the lack of communication about the analytical position taken.

As I neared the end of my fieldwork, I felt that I had achieved a level of acceptance with both the young people and the staff. I had maintained and developed the relationships established during the middle section of my fieldwork and felt that I was an active participant in the decision-making and activities of the group. The level of acceptance and the sense of belonging that I achieved served as a reminder that, although ethnography does allow researchers to 'get alongside' those that they research, the experience will always be different. In this case, ethnography gave me the opportunity to live in a children's home. However, I did so as a result of choice and with none of the ongoing family and personal problems that the young people had to face. In terms of 'pulling out' I knew from the beginning when I was going to leave, knowledge that very few young people in residential care have. Leaving became quite a personal issue for both the young people and myself.

Like many of the young people leaving the units my disengagement took place gradually over a period of months. It was assisted by a number of factors. After the six-month full-time block period at Strathmore,[2] I visited each month for a block of four days. The reduction in time allowed my leaving to be slowly accepted by the group and myself. It was aided also by my loss of bedroom, which had had to be given to a new admission. From the end of my six-month stay I slept in different rooms each time I visited, increasing my role as student visitor rather than as resident.

Changes within the group also made my disengagement more manageable. Many of the young people with whom I had lived had moved on or were moving into their own flats or returning to their families. Two of the young people were being moved to a residential school. In this way, despite the units appearing to be the same in terms of physical appearance and routine, they were in fact very different with new members comprising what were becoming quite different resident groups:

> ...it just insnae hame anymare...Every time I come back, ken tae visit, it's different...new staff, new kids, new cups and a'thing...but then I still come do I? (Bryony)

As these monthly visits continued, my time was increasingly spent testing out my analytical ideas and discussing them with the young people and staff. Due to the perceived changing nature of my task, I was increasingly less 'one of us' and more an outside researcher. I visited each of the residents who had moved on from the units and discussed my findings. This provided a formal ending which both the young people and myself found useful. This level of formality was later to be transferred to those who continued to be residents. I returned to both units to give a formal presentation of my findings and to facilitate further discussion. Again this formal procedure allowed for a distinct conclusion.

Conclusions

Ethnographic research with young people relies on the ways in which the researcher not only gains access to the research site but negotiates the extent of access to the group itself. The individual circumstances of young people must be taken account of in order for a methodological stance to be developed which is appropriate to them. It is clear from previous research that, like any group under study, young people are quick to make assessment of the researcher. I would argue that this assessment is underpinned by a questioning of the motives of the research and the extent to which the voices and experiences of young people are not only being listened to but heard.

Lacking in many research reports is an honest and reflexive account of the research process itself. In order for ethnographic techniques to be seen as a worthwhile approach to data collection, the researcher must demonstrate the ways in which he/she gained entry to the group under study and how he/she assessed and managed the impact that his/her presence had on the behaviours of those young people being researched. Researchers must take account of the potential impact of participant observation on young people. Indeed, for this approach to be successful a relationship needs to be established. We must therefore take cognisance of the effect of forming as well as ending this relationship. Again in order to do so they must have a clear understanding of the individual circumstances of those that they seek to study. Fundamentally researchers must not fall into the trap of assuming that because they are young or have experienced 'youth' that they have an immediate affinity to those they seek to research. The differences and indeed similarities between the researcher and the researched need to be made explicit as do the ways in which these are overcome.

Ethnographic approaches have the potential to empower young people in the research process. If undertaken in the proper spirit young people are given the power to control the pace of the research, the extent of access and therefore the extent of insight gained. If we are to see ethnography as the study of 'strangers in a strange land' we must be respectful and grateful guests.

Notes

1. All names of young people involved in this study have been changed. They asked that any quotes be written using their local dialect.
2. The names of the two residential units involved in the research have been changed.

7
Researching Young Women's Bodies: Values, Dilemmas and Contradictions

Liz Frost

Background

The contemporary emphasis in Western consumer societies on the visual display of perfected bodies seems to have a more damaging impact on some social groups than others. Concerns are being expressed at all levels from the Government 'body summit' initiative in 2001 to parent groups, that young women are at war with their bodies. There are fears that they starve them, punish them by over-exercising, have them professionally altered, and even cut and burn them in self-harming activities. Such is the level of social concern that at the extremes of such behaviour young women may be subject to psychiatric diagnosis and, sometimes compulsory, treatment. However for many young women engaging in similar activities, 'weight watching' and other forms of 'making the best of yourself' are socially endorsed behaviours. The research on which this chapter draws attempted to explore the ambivalent and, frequently, negative attitudes young women themselves develop towards their bodies. It also attempted to demonstrate that such 'body-hatred' was similarly experienced by young women labelled 'ill' and 'ordinary' young women in the community.

The extensive academic focus on key themes such as the body, identity, consumer capitalism and the structural inequalities of gender and youth offers a rich discursive field in which to examine the problematic. Perspectives on body-hatred which prove fruitful encompass broad social phenomena such as consumerism, poverty and identity (Bartky, 1990; Featherstone, 1991; Giddens, 1991), young people's group identifications (Langman, 1992; Furlong and Cartmel, 1997), psychological enquiries into such issues as self-esteem (Grogan, 1999), and (feminist) psychoanalytical perspectives on the link between body disorders and unconscious desire, identification and attachment (Orbach, 1978; Chernin, 1983, 1985). A notable absence from the literature seems to be a simultaneous focus on both the external context and the internal experience of body and appearance. Some social constructionist texts on body issues are helpful in their ability to dissolve the subjective/objective dichotomy (Bordo, 1993; Malson, 1998). However, the particular and specific strengths of a psychosocial feminist approach to young women and body hatred (which might, for example, engage with the constitutive effects of young women's social–structural position, their specific biographies and individual agency), seem to be mostly unavailable in the literature, though with some noticeable exceptions (for example, Hollway, 1984).

The fieldwork which this chapter considers was, then, primarily to address a missing dimension in the literature, by attempting to engage with teenage girls' personal interpretation of their physicality; their lived experience of embodiment. Given that previous studies theorised this as a potentially difficult and damaging relationship, it seemed likely that great care would be needed in constructing and executing this direct work. Some of the dilemmas – both value questions and epistemological dilemmas – which arose in interviewing young women about body-hatred form the basis of this chapter.

The research context: the body projects

Speaking to young women about the range of meanings that engaging with their appearances had for them could potentially touch negative feelings. Considerable care and creativity was necessary in the selection and deployment of research tools. Two populations of young women were needed as points of reference to and comparisons with each other: girls for whom body issues had been identified/diagnosed as problematic and girls for whom there were no particular known issues relating to this. Existing literature suggested that the age range 14–18 years was that in which body problems emerged (Rutter and Smith, 1995), and in relation to a complex nexus of issues to do with informed consent, power, comprehension and so on, it was decided to focus on the top end of this range: 17–18-year-olds.

Initial contacts were made with a semi-rural comprehensive school sixth form and the same age range of young women in an adolescent psychiatric unit. Discussion and reflection with teaching staff and psychiatric staff formed the next essential part of the research process. Invaluable knowledge and experience was offered in relation to the subject of body hatred, as well as ideas for creative approaches and support for the research project. Additionally, reviews of existing methods and consultation with experienced researchers all led to the conclusion that very specific methods needed to be formulated and deployed in relation to this enquiry. These various experts encouraged the formulation of an innovative project approach, which specifically elided to the existing work already being undertaken in each institution – the lower sixth art 'A' level group at the school and the health group at the psychiatric inpatient facility.

The school

The least direct and therefore potentially the least threatening place to begin to engage with the issue of 'in what way do I see myself?' seemed to be in relation to art and self-portraiture. As part of the 'A' level art curriculum of this medium-sized, semi-rural school, students must produce self-portraits, by building up a portfolio of details of self and surroundings using various forms, and culminating in painting a self-portrait. There is some formal teaching around the art-history of self-portraiture, and this whole section of the course was reported by the teacher as the most disliked of the syllabus, an issue which will be returned to.

It was agreed with the school that the lessons immediately prior to this could be annexed for a loose focus group on how people see and portray themselves. The pupils (both boys and girls) raised many of the general issues which the research then went on to develop; for example, the issue of how possible it is to resist the contemporary pressure on young people to produce a certain sort of homogenised appearance. Students commented thus:

> There is constant pressure to look a certain way, so personal appearance falls between quite strict boundaries, just like behaviour does.

> There's the pressure of society (media especially) and peers – "if you fail to conform then..." young people feel being individual isn't worth the hassle.

> It's necessary to spend time on appearances whether you want to fool people into thinking you're a certain "type" and try to deliberately influence the way they see you, or whether you try to defy

categorisation and express yourself. Whatever anyone says, first "physical" impressions make a huge difference to how people behave towards/see you and what they think about you.

Society is able to reject you on the basis of your appearance and everyone, especially young people (who tend to be more insecure) want/need to be accepted.

These ideas were used to inform the content of later interview material.

In the next stage of the project, students were asked to produce self-portraits. Students happy to be interviewed individually brought along their work which was used as a focus of discussion. Additional information was obtained from questionnaires completed by ten respondents. An in-depth case study was undertaken with one girl, from which came probably the most insightful material, for example:

I feel like it is always something I worry about, that people can hurt me with, like if someone was to... well it doesn't happen now, people aren't immature enough to call you ugly, but that could have happened, I think to most people it has happened in their life, but if I thought that could happen now, I would be really upset.

I think if you have an experience like that [being called ugly] it is something you will never forget, and it is always there – that somebody is going to say something like that to you, and it is, it is just so humiliating.

The adolescent psychiatric unit

Working within the health service context proved to be a far more complex process for bureaucratic and ethical reasons. Even with the approval of the consultant and the interest of the nursing staff, gaining the Ethical Committee approval was a lengthy process. And having gained permission to talk to young people they were only prepared to talk individually not in a group. This meant that comparability with the school, by using an already existing study group (in this case on health) similar to the art class, was immediately lost.

Lacking a group of young people in this context, a discussion with a staff group provided some perspectives on how the young people with whom they work experience themselves. This was useful, though clearly representing a different kind of 'voice' – an adult and professional one – to the school pupils' group.

Although at the time the unit was approached half of the residents agreed to be interviewed, the necessary consents from parents and doctors were not always forthcoming. A further complicating factor was the young women's psychological state. Arrangements for interviews had to be cancelled if the subject was experiencing high levels of distress that day.

Only a small number of interviews could be obtained with young women at the unit within the correct time-frame, though more have been undertaken since then. A case study was undertaken with one young woman, including a protracted exploratory interview, to 'match' the school contribution.

All of the young women involved in these projects in both contexts became absorbed in exploring the issues in relation to their age group in general and to themselves. All were prepared to talk at length on the subject. The final stage of the project was to undertake the two case study style interviews, both of which produced thoughtful and reflective personal observations which greatly enhanced the 'subjective experience of body-hatred' dimension of the enquiry.

Experience as circulated meanings

Although the direct contributions of the young women did offer some fresh insights into the experience of body dissonance, particularly in relation to its emotional impact, many of their expressed views paralleled the literature. For example, the girls who had diagnosed body problems often reflected contemporary clinical and academic debates in relation to eating disorders. One set of explanations focus on women's need for power and control where little is available (Bordo, 1993), an explanation which was used by one girl who was experiencing such difficulties:

> If your parents are in control of what you do, like when you go out, and like when you sit down and do your homework, and what they want you to do, and it gets to the point that you think 'I'm not in control of anything I do', apart from you are in control of your feelings and what you do to your body... and that just gets completely over the top.

Other explanations consider the media's role in circulating messages which normalise thin body shapes (Garfinkel and Garner, 1982), an argument which many of the girls were familiar with:

It's a horrible time because you are experiencing all sorts of changes physically as well as mentally. The extra pressure to look perfect can obsess teenagers and the attempts to look better can get blown out of all proportion – we can't see that we won't look this way for ever – everyone's still changing. I think people will always be critical of themselves but it may help if less importance was placed on appearance in the media.

and

I think young people have a lot of images and stories around them all the time. I also think fashion is changing all the time and young people are always pushed towards keeping up with the times, which costs a lot of money. Some young people are more influenced than others because they want to be like others. I always feel sorry for people who try and change themselves to look like others.

The individual explanations offered by the young women, then, often reflected the complex arguments advanced in the relevant literature. This can be understood as more than simply a process of copying. The ideas have become personally 'owned' as part of the girl's belief system in relation to their subjective biographies. As social constructionists might argue, meanings circulate within a given culture at any point in time, and it is those meanings which offer people/girls versions of who they are. Those meanings (discourses, ideologies) become the tools from which gendered identities are differentially constructed and reconstructed (Davies, 1993). The questions of 'who am I' and 'why am I like this' can and perhaps must be answered within socially available systems of meaning (Burr, 1995). Thus, the young women in the psychiatric facility offered versions of their body (and identity) which reflected medical and psychological fields of knowledge, in other words a 'patholigised' self. The young women in school, who had less access to expert discussion of eating disorders were more likely to reflect the general purpose individualistic 'pop psychology' available in women's magazines and television shows, which suggests general insecurity or lack of personal adjustment as the core problem.

In response to what dictates whether young people are happy or miserable about their looks, the discontented were described as: 'Depressed or lonely people with bad backgrounds, for examples, parents who have split up'; whereas the contented were: 'Those with a positive self-image who accept themselves for what they are' and 'People who base their ideal image on a flexible and realistic image.'

The young women in the psychiatric unit were then far more knowledgeable about the range of possible explanations of body problems, and made sense of their own feelings and actions through 'expert' discourses, whereas the school girls showed a tendency to draw on more popular, simplistic and volunteristic accounts.

Accessing sensitive material – some values and dilemmas

Creative methods

There is a tradition of research by and on women using creative processes drawn loosely from the arts to engage with groups of subjects (Reinhartz, 1992). Photography, for example, was being used as a major research tool from the 1930s in America (Hagood, 1939), and drama has more recently been used with work with adolescent girls in school (Griffiths, 1984). Art seemed to offer a similar but more connected medium for the issue of body dislike. Given the potentially emotional nature of the material, a method was being sought which was hoped might start a process whereby 'private, inarticulated feelings which might remain concealed in an interview or group discussion can...find expression' (Griffiths, 1984, p. 515). This is referring to the 'hidden' dimension of identity which raises the issue of the role of unconscious material in the interview process, and indeed of the question of the non-unitary, non-rational subject of the interview process, which will be returned to below.

The approach through art, and specifically through self-portraiture, also offered girls the potential to distance themselves – even objectify themselves – in a way which seemed to offer a place to retreat to in what could be very personal interviews. Rather in the way that writing in the third person allows a more detached engagement, then talking about 'the young woman in the portrait' gave the girls a chance to discuss 'her' appearance, rather than directly their own.

Several girls expressed very negative feelings towards *the portrait*, and it had already been acknowledged by the art teacher that self-portraiture was consistently the least popular part of the course. Drawing on interpretative approaches to unconscious material discussed below, one understanding of this phenomena would suggest that such a close and prolonged scrutiny of self may raise difficult identity issues for young people who are in the process of negotiating the new identity of 'adult'. Mainly the students either painted highly idealised versions of themselves, or versions of themselves which were hidden, and/or they expressed frustration at not being able to 'say' what they had wanted to about themselves:

> She's looking in the mirror and her face isn't too happy; looking in the mirror doesn't usually make me smile! But she doesn't show insecurity or a desperate side. I would have put lots of cosmetics round her and showed her crying into them if I had the skills.

None of the young women expressed positive feelings towards their self-portraits, and the range of emotional responses encompassed discomfort and dissatisfaction through to depression and despair.

Psychosocial frameworks

Some of the young women involved in this project were deemed in need of residential treatment for mental distress, and all were being asked to think about a topic which might pinpoint some insecurities or dissatisfactions with themselves. In both contexts, institutional protective mechanisms existed, appropriately, to prevent their charges from being harmed in any way.

In the context of both the nature of this and similar fieldwork enquiries (into a potential site of human unhappiness) and the nature of the institutional location of the work (the human welfare sector, loosely), the role of the researcher may need to encompass some of the values and skills traditionally associated with the 'caring professions'.

Professions such as counselling, social work and psychotherapy have over many years evolved a set of values, principles and versions of identity which have several common core features which may provide a model for research which aims to extrapolate complex and personal human experience. Perhaps the most useful facets of these can be summarised as a practice which:

- is respectful, anti-oppressive and/or emancipatory;
- utilises a primarily psychodynamic framework of understanding the subject as possessing an emotionally complex inner life, and offers an understanding of identity as contradictory, non-rational, complex and to some extent hidden;
- acknowledges the importance of the relationship between the practitioner and the subject of that practice;

- is able to constructively reflect on both process and content of the interaction between the 'client' and the practitioner and to bring interpretative skills to understanding and analysing the content and process.

At its most basic, then, adopting a psychosocial practice framework (in research and other forms of practice) has traditionally incorporated an expectation of values which demonstrate respect, understanding and acceptance (Brown and Peddar, 1991). This fundamental value base has been broadened out in the last two decades particularly, to address the issues of unequal power at a structural and interpersonal level, and how this may be addressed in interactions between professionals and those with whom they work (Dalrymple and Burke, 1995). Research has raised comparable issues.

Power between the researcher and the researched

The issue of power relations between the researcher and the researched has received substantial academic discussion over the last decades, with feminist research contributing much which questions the usefulness and inevitability of the expert-to-object dynamic (Oakley, 1981). These feminist certainties may be muddier now (Kelly *et al.*, 1994). Certainly in the research under discussion in this chapter, there was little point even pretending that the researcher could transcend the power divide. Not only were the structural dimensions of *female* and *youth* operating as categories of potential powerlessness, but the fieldwork was conducted within, and visibly aligned to, highly authoritarian institutions. Access to the research subject's lives was via the institutions they were legally compelled or medically pressured to attend. Being entirely mindful of this empowerment, in any meaningful sense, was not really a possible aim. However, that which is not empowering need not be oppressive: 'A distinction needs to be made between not exploiting participants,...and more grandiose ambitions' (Kelly *et al.*, 1994, p. 37).

The young people were treated respectfully and listened to attentively. Their consent was sought for each piece of the work and no pressure was put on them to be, or stay, involved. Other choices, where possible, were offered in some attempt to avoid total disempowerment, for example, whether they wished to be part of the group or to have their key-worker present at the psychiatric unit, and whether and where would they like the longer interviews to be held. Wherever possible, participants were able to self determine their level of involvement in the research. Even if consent had previously been given at the adolescent unit, on the day of the interview, the young women were given another chance to decide if they wanted to participate. But mostly the young women did want to talk; they did offer to come for one-to-one interviews and discuss what appearance meant to contemporary young people and to themselves. They reported enjoying talking about the subject (although this was not always congruent with the interpretation of the interviewer). It may be that, as Skeggs found in relation to research with young people, it offered benefits: 'The students sense of self-worth was enhanced by being given the opportunity to be valued, knowledgeable and interesting' (Skeggs, 1994, p. 81).

Or it may be, using a more practice-based understanding, that the experience of sharing problems or difficult issues, and of expressing contradictory or hurtful feelings within a sympathetic dynamic offered some actual therapeutic benefit. The notion of cathartic unloading does not necessarily pre-suppose long-term professional therapy (Brown and Peddar, 1991).

What was taken from the young women, then, was their views and their time, and from two of the young women their stories of their unhappy relationships with their bodies. What they may have gained was validation, and a chance to reflect on and make sense of their views. Certainly, this was within an unequal power dynamic, though group interviews may go some way to addressing this problem. This issue is discussed in more detail below.

Psychosocial subjects

Psychoanalytic theorising also informed the notion of the subject of research as non-rational and subject to unconscious conflict. Whether made explicit or not, some version of human subjectivity is invariably part of the research process. Ontological paradigms impact throughout the process, effecting even the minute detail of methods used. For example, the decision as to whether more 'authentic' material can be accessed by individual or group interviews, discussed below, connects to 'modern' or 'post-modern' beliefs, respectively, about the nature of subjectivity as independent or relational. Significant issues to the whole process of research are raised by fundamental psychoanalytical tenets that, for example, unconscious forces and processes may drive human behaviour, implying as it does then that the subject may be unable to offer coherent or comprehensive explanations or interpretations of their situation because they do not recognise it. As Hoggett (2001, p. 42) points out:

...our capacity to be a rational agent is often constrained by the difficulties we have in facing our own fears and anxieties...all of us in different ways find some ideas unbearable.

Although differing from social constructionist frameworks discussed earlier, in that the emphasis in identity construction is less on socially constructed meaning and more on the impact of internal frames of reference, the two paradigms have been usefully brought together as a working model of personhood which allows for agency, and internal conflicts on the one hand and social influence on the other. Thus, as Volger (2000, p. 24) observes:

...far from being determined by society, individuals are seen as absorbing and processing social forces such as discourses, ideologies, structural positions or whatever through a complex inner process located in internal psychic space.

This understanding of identity offered a conceptual framework for understanding the young women in this research. It also invariably connects to the practice of valuing and interpreting the dynamics of the relationship between the worker and the client – for example in relation to the notion of transference and counter-transference, inherited from psychoanalysis – and similarly, values the ability in the worker to exhume and interpret unconscious phenomena.

Psychodynamics in practice

Attempts to deploy a psychoanalytical framework in relation to research are now becoming more established (Hollway and Jefferson, 2000). Rejecting the overall influence of some of the more positivist approaches in research related to the human services professions (in which can be included education and psychiatry for example), Hollway argues for the importance of acknowledging the relationship between the researcher and the researched, and emphasises 'the need for a relational research paradigm, specifically a concept of unconscious intersubjectivity' (Hollway, 2001, p. 14).

The research under discussion in this chapter did acknowledge the importance of the relationship between the researcher and the researched. The methods described above consciously dictated gradual and increasing contact between the researcher and the researched, offering the chance to establish a trusting relationship into which personal material could be explored. Deployed here, this did seem to be helpful for allowing the young people to feel more open and communicative than they might have done with no prior contact. They were able to access some of their contradictory feelings with someone they knew at least a little. Welfare services practice would reinforce this. In case work theory in social work, for example, it has long been accepted that forming a relationship with the service user is a pre-requisite to discussing their difficulties with them, or looking at their lives in any depth (Oliver et al., 1989). Hollway's work revalues this in research practice.

The implications of the discussion above, then, may be that research interviewers need some similar casework or therapeutic skills to those undertaking interviews and assessments in welfare practice professions, in order to be able to offer what Frosh usefully describes as 'attention to the gaps in discourse, the contradictions, silences and other absences' (Frosh et al., 2002, p. 5).

Hearing between the words has a value. When, for example, the girls in the current research expressed frustration that they could not get their face in their self-portrait to be how they wanted, the noticeable incoherence a small number displayed when attempting to explicate technical explanations could be interpreted as demonstrating unconscious contradictions and dissonance. Their dislike of their portraits, and of self-portraiture as a form may, as suggested above, be very revealing of the psychic discomfort produced by their 'view' of their own faces and images at this transitional period of life. This could be explored further, though not necessarily directly, within the interviews themselves.

Hollway and Jefferson's (2000) work on incorporating psychoanalytical thinking into the research process led to them developing a specific research method based on these principles called The Free Association Narrative Interview (Hollway, 2001). The research on young women being discussed here did not adopt this method intact, for example transference and counter-transference dynamics were not specifically interpreted, but instead drew on the overall psychodynamic framework, as exemplified above, to construct the process and content of the semi-structured interview and case study method. However, further work in this area will incorporate methods similar to Hollway's F.A.N.I.

To return to the issue of the researcher, if a psychosocial model for research is adopted, then is it only a specifically trained interviewer, qualified to include such psychodynamic values, knowledge and methods into the research process who can apply this? In other words, if they are going to interview people about potentially worrying or distressing or even just 'personal' issues, do researchers need both an anti-oppressive value base and some training in psychosocial counselling or therapy? This is difficult to substantiate.

Research by those with considerable experience in psychotherapeutic practice, such as Frosh or Hollway, unequivocally demonstrates the advantages of these skills. Their recent qualitative research projects show a depth and interpretative sophistication which produces an unusually thorough picture of the complex layers of meaning and being of the research subject. Their conscious engagement with the unconscious, adds a powerful and enlightening dimension (Hollway and Jefferson, 2000; Frosh *et al.*, 2002).

However, it also must be noted that positivism has not disappeared, and in many fields of research is still *the* powerful paradigm. This perpetrates an ongoing debate about the credibility of many forms of interpretative research, compared to positivist frameworks, which this chapter can only acknowledge. Psychoanalytically grounded methodologies, which, for example, draw on transference phenomena as a source of data, may be considered by the 'scientific' school of research as having almost no claim to validity at all.

However, on a more pragmatic level, demonstrable interpersonal skills of various kinds may be essential for access reasons in some research. The project under discussion in this chapter, for example, simply would not have been permitted if the researcher did not have a substantial background in psychodynamic mental health practice. And such experience protects the researcher and the researched; interviews with people who are quite distressed or disturbed make specific demands on both.

Sessions may be or may become whilst in progress inappropriate because a subject is too upset. The ability to 'hear the silences' can predict and divert this. Judgements as to tolerable and intolerable levels of anxiety must be made; the subject may need reassurance or support, or even a metaphorical or literal escape route. These kinds of skills, of course, would apply to interviewing any populations about 'difficult' issues.

For quite legitimate ethical reasons, then, it is unlikely that anyone without convincing credentials in mental health work and/or counselling access would be allowed to teenage adolescent units, and even in relation to the school population, experience of counselling may reassure heads of pastoral care that their charges would be 'safe'. Even if access were allowed, researchers without this experience may not feel competent or confident to undertake such research into sensitive material.

Experience in psychosocial and/or casework methods no doubt would offer support for such work. Overall, the skills of the research team in relation to certain subject areas, and certain methods, may be just as important a value consideration as that of power imbalances and structural inequalities.

Group interviews, power and meaning

Young people's membership of friendship groups or gangs has represented to the adult world of the researcher both a source of rich material and considerable suspicion. The behaviour of young people when in collective situations with chosen others has provided the ground for arguably the most creative seam of youth research in the last few decades (Willis, 1977; Lees, 1986; Blackman, 1995). For research, it has also seemed to offer one way of equalising the inevitable power imbalance referred to earlier in this chapter, between adult researchers and young people. Being part of a group may make the young person feel less vulnerable, more able to assert themselves or even reject the interview process if it becomes too intrusive. As Wilkinson (1998, p. 114) comments:

> ...groups tend, in practice – and simply by virtue of the numbers of research participants involved – to shift the balance of power during data collection, such that research participants have more control over the interaction than does the researcher'.

Group research participation may also have the advantage of offering the members other interactive benefits, for example the potential for re-evaluating experience or a sense of solidarity.

However, researchers working within modernist paradigms of identity have tended to privilege the views of the individual, who is seen as both the site and the guarantor of authentic meaning. The group is seen as potentially distorting of individual 'truth', especially in those who might be seen as young and therefore subject to influence. The peer group has frequently been viewed, for example in some psychological studies, as a powerful and corrupting force. Adopted by some youth studies material, peer groups are seen as factors on which young people may become dependent, which may influence youths to act or think against their 'real nature', for example in relation to drug or alcohol abuse (Hendry *et al.*, 1993). In research terms, this might lead to concluding that the opinions reported or views stated are less likely to be the interviewee's own in a group context and a less than 'honest' picture will emerge, especially now when it has been argued that the influence of peer groups may be seen to be becoming stronger (Furlong and Cartmel, 1997).

Using a social constructionist framework shifts the emphasis in research towards a methodology in which the collective construction of meaning is valued. As mentioned above, if identity is viewed from a post-modern perspective, and therefore seen to be fluid, discursive and/or interactive, then the independent, individual subject is no longer the exclusive site of the authentic voice, or the authoritative voice, as they are in modernist versions. The meanings produced in dialogue or conversation are just as 'real' and worthy of research. In Raabe's research, for example, on young people's views of power and social relations, she undertook group interviews as well as questionnaires precisely to: 'examine the dynamic negotiation of the meanings of responsibility, autonomy and decision making' (Raabe, 1993, p. 374).

The social constructionist/psychosocial framework of the fieldwork under discussion attempted to draw on group and individual methods. For reasons of empowerment, and the ongoing construction of the voice of the young people, as well as the issue of getting to know the interviewer safely, the group interviews provided a useful site. Rather as ethnographic research does, this had some elements of attempting to talk to people in their 'natural habitat', in other words in groups with their mates. It has been argued, for example, that opinions are formed and revised in social contact between people, and hence the group situation is the most naturalistic setting to look at peoples' views (Wilkinson, 1998, p. 20).

Social constructionist versions of the nature of identity, then, can distil into group research methods. Still allowing that individual gendered subjectivity may well be the perceived location of opinions as expressed, the process of collective, fluid and endless ideas formation is acknowledged as fundamental. However, to explore the unconscious material and/or the emotional content of the research subject's meanings may, as discussed above, require a dynamic relationship between the researcher and the researched in a one-to-one context (though whether this is necessarily the case is an interesting and so far relatively unexplored research dilemma in itself). The 'body hatred' interviews, then, used both these settings.

But having developed an interviewing rational that reflected both social constructionist and psychosocial practice agendas, the overriding value commitment to the research subject's self-determination and choice dictated that individual interviews commanded most of the interaction with the subjects. The school sample, although initially surveyed as a group, only consented to very general and hypothetical discussion of the topic in the group contexts, all preferring individual interviews for focused, personal and/or in-depth discussions. The young women at the psychiatric unit wanted no group participation at all. As is the case in all psychodynamic practice, including research, the fact that values can be sources of conflict and contradiction, rather than simply neat guidelines for resolution of difficulties, should be acknowledged.

Respect for individual knowledge – a further value conflict

It is also perhaps worth noting that not only did many of the young women privilege the individual interview over the group, but also, as noted earlier, privileged individualistic, psychological explanations for young people's unhappy relationships with their bodies. Young people's own insecurities, or inadequacies in their families, or the way in which they were too influenced by the views of the media were the narratives offered, mostly devoid of political context or a wider societal view. And again, given a post-structuralist perspective, this would be a likely view: the most prevalent explanations for human distress in popular cultural products with which young women engage such as television 'soaps' and girls magazines offer just those explanations. Raabe (1993, pp. 372–3), for example, found just this in her research with young women:

> Individualistic analyses which focus on the importance of personal responsibility and choice are widely used by the majority of young people in making sense of their social worlds. This is not surprising, given the dominant discourse that 'there is no such thing as society'.

But although this may be predictable within a post-modern epistemology, it does raise a value contradiction in relation to respecting young people's standpoints. To what extent is the subject their own 'expert' if their consciousness remixes and recirculates dominant discourses? Even given the notion of unconscious forces and agency at work which psychoanalytical versions of identity might elide to, there still remains a question around how 'knowing' is the knowing subject if they are 16 years old and have limited experience and limited access to a range of explanations of social and subjective phenomena? Or is this so-called 'limited experience' a valid youth perspective, which is demeaned by adultist patronage? 'Mother knows best' is not a helpful attitude, and it may well be that they are engaging with a whole range of subversive and resistant discourses in other areas of their lives which they *choose* not to accept. And perhaps if very prolonged, gradual and interpretative methods are used, as discussed above, some unconscious material might emerge which would offer different versions of the interviewee's 'truth', whilst clearly still being theirs, not the interviewer's.

There are, then, issues to do with the status of personal experience in the research process with young people, which are, arguably, similar to working with any group. Yes, their views are to be treated with respect; their understandings are important because they are the framework within which they operate; but the notion of personal experience as 'proof' of, for example, causality has to be treated with care. As has been well debated in feminist research, personal experience is a potent and powerful source of information, but the interpretative role of the researcher, applied in a number of ways, is vital in producing valid conclusions (Holland and Ramazanoglu, 1994).

Conclusion

Overall the small research project relating to how young women experience their bodies and appearances analysed here produced thoughtful material without, it would seem, exploiting or devaluing the subject. Certainly the young women involved – who, in keeping with notions of individual respect, were given a format to express their feelings about being researched – found the process both interesting and helpful. However, the fieldwork also raised a range of issues, explored in this chapter, relating to fundamental debates in contemporary research. Epistemological and even ontological paradigms, and their ultimate implications for the fine details of research practice have been foregrounded for reflection and discussion, and perhaps for fellow researchers to mull over when planning their own fieldwork with vulnerable people and/or issues closely related to the subject's identity.

Some points of clarity did seem to emerge, at least for the author, in relation to the study. A strong case can be made, for example, for the need to ensure that if psychosocial epistemologies are to be translated into practice (which may include elements such as offering free association techniques, building trusting relationships between the researcher and the researched, and interpreting transference phenomena) then not just the methods but the values and skills of the researcher become a highly significant issue. Whereas there is now a body of knowledge, some of which has been drawn on above, examining what constitutes psychosocial research, there is little reference to what might define the practitioner of this form. Existing 'therapeutic' practice frameworks, for example those incorporated into psychodynamic social work, counselling and psychotherapy could be drawn on to develop and define the notion of the psychosocial researcher.

Some issues in the chapter are highlighted, and remain uncertain and in need of further debate. But perhaps the most important discussion it undertakes ultimately reinforces what social scientists of a post-modern, interpretative and/or psychoanalytical learning have already understood in relation to research subjects and their worlds: that they contain much that is ambivalent, ambiguous and riven with internal and external conflicts.

'Simply' asking people to recount their experience or views is not at all simple, nor probably accurate, authentic or reliable. 'The naive approach that treats as factual what people say', as Hollway describes it, can and should be abandoned and replaced by the struggle towards engaging with what Hoggett calls 'the passionate, tragic and contradictory dimensions of human existence' (Hoggett, 2001, p. 37; Hollway, 2001, p. 13). The research produced may well then show less clarity and more doubt, uncertainty and contradiction, but this could be indicative of more, not less explanatory strength. Whether it is really possible to take this approach without reintroducing professional mystification and the interpretative power to define others' lives, and therefore denying the relatively recently established emancipatory project of ensuring the research subject can speak with their own voice, remains to be seen.

8
E-heads Versus Beer Monsters: Researching Young People's Music and Drug Consumption in Dance Club Settings

Karenza Moore

Introduction

In a hundred clubs and parties, molecules will wrench apart and recombine in now familiar ways, as chemically upgraded minds vibrate with the rich harmonies of desire. As hearts quicken under hard muscles eager to dance, recalibrated eyes will register the richly velvet texture of skin and capture the bright certainties in fresh-beaded sweat. Ears tuned to new frequencies, harsher truths will cease their whispering and all that we feel is everything (Hawes, 1998, p. 110).

'Club culture', sometimes referred to as 'Dance culture', is a heady combination of dance music in all its many and varied forms and drugs, ranging from the licit, alcohol and tobacco, to the illicit, amphetamines (speed), cocaine (coke), MDMA[1] (ecstasy or 'E') and cannabis (dope, gear, grass) among others. As Malbon notes, some substances are perceived as 'old favourites', including cocaine and cannabis, whilst others are newer 'synthetics' such as 3,4-methylenedioxyamphetamine (MDA), 3,4-methylenedioxyethylamphetamine (MDEA) and Ketamine (Special K or Vitamin K) (1999, p. 116). The leisure pursuit of going to a 'dance event', be it a free party in a field or warehouse, an illegal 'rave', an organised festival such as The Big Chill, or a 'commercial' club, has been a key phenomenon in British 'youth culture' for over two decades. The focus of my research is on clubbers, clubbing experiences and substance use within 'club culture' in Norwich and London. There are no Norwich-specific studies of club culture as an industry. The same dearth of information about the growth and recent developments of club culture applies, perhaps more surprisingly, to London. However, the market research company Mintel (1996) has published several reports on the UK-wide 'nightclub and discotheque industry'. Of the UK's general population, 42 per cent visit a club at least once a year, whilst 43 per cent of 15–24-year-olds visit a club once a month or more often (Mintel, 1996, p. 5). Release (1997) has also published a large-scale survey of clubbing in the UK. They interviewed 520 clubbers, 78 per cent of whom started clubbing during their teenage years. Release found that the motivations for going clubbing were (1) music (45 per cent), (2) socialising (38 per cent), (3) the atmosphere (35 per cent), (4) dancing (27 per cent) and (5) drug use (22 per cent). In terms of substance use, studies indicate that between 68 and 76 per cent of clubbers regularly take ecstasy (MDMA), with many others consuming amphetamines, lysergic acid diethylamide (LSD) and cannabis (Mullan et al., 1997; Release, 1997). The Release (1997) survey, for example, found that 81 per cent of their 520 participants (clubbers aged between 16 and 29 years) had tried ecstasy (MDMA) and 91 per cent had tried cannabis, although this can be contrasted with the British Crime Survey (BCS) which found that, of the population of 16–29-year-olds as a whole, 6 per cent had tried ecstasy and only 34 per cent had ever tried cannabis (BCS, 1994). Release states 'in essence, people who go out take more drugs than those who stay in' (Release, 1997, p. 12), a rather obvious but crucial point. In order to research substance use by young people, I decided that it was important to 'go out' to the places where young people were consuming legal and illegal drugs to better understand processes of justification, legitimation, authentication and differentiation. Research in such settings brings with it all sorts of unique methodological and ethical issues which, in effect, highlight the specific demands placed on, and skills required of, youth researchers, particularly those deemed 'young' themselves. Throughout the following discussion of the findings of my research, I highlight these dilemmas and end this chapter with a more detailed examination of what they mean for youth research more generally.

Club culture and youth research: enigmatic beasts

Contemporary club culture's definition is open to a myriad of interpretations and can be studied from a variety of perspectives. Recent work within broadly speaking the 'social' or 'human sciences' include Richard and Kruger's (1998) paper on the German 'rave' scene, Thornton's (1995) *Club Cultures: Music, Media and Sub-Cultural Capital* and Malbon's (1999) excellent qualitative study of London clubbers. Contemporary 'club culture' could be about the enjoyment of dancing, environmental awareness, and 'race' and/or 'class' relations. It could also be about the social repercussions of the drug economy, changing gender relations, corporeal experiences or the construction of notions of community. In a sense, there are as many interpretations as there are distinctions within club culture. These 'ravers' or 'clubbers' are not a homogenous group positioned against the 'mainstream' or the 'establishment' in their consumption patterns. Rather this 'imagined community' can be thought of as a kaleidoscope of shifting distinctions, 'ideologies' and 'sentiments', all of which feed into cultural, medical and social discourses about the 'authenticity' of drug use and 'abuse', about risk, and about health, illness, healing and the human body.

For the youth researcher, the complicated nature of club cultures can be intimidating at first glance. It can be hard for a qualitative researcher with little or no experience of club culture to find a 'way in' to this ever-shifting world. I argue that familiarisation with a geographical area's club culture is a crucial aspect of research orientation on this topic. This can take a considerable amount of time and money. Moving to a different town (Guildford) has emphasised to me just how problematic it can be for a newcomer to be accepted by groups of young people who are regular clubbers and consider themselves to be *au fait* with the local 'scene'. In all of the places my research focuses upon, Guilford included, it has taken me close to three months of club attendance to reach a position where I can talk to regular attendees without fear of being 'unmasked' as an 'outsider'. With entrance fees ranging from around 4 (for a night at a student union) to 40 (for 24 hours of music at the Creamfields festival in Liverpool), research in these settings can be a costly exercise. An awareness of the different events that occur at different venues, the DJs that are playing, the dress codes that are and are not enforced, the 'drug talk' that it is appropriate or otherwise to engage in, are all facets of a localised club culture that it is important for the youth researcher to become habitualised to. Having had difficulty in getting clubbers in Guildford to 'open up' about their substance use and corporeal experiences, I recently changed tactic and gained employment in a local club as a dancer in order to pursue my research on substance use in club settings. Whilst this has made it much easier to gain access to, and earn the respect and trust of, clubbers in Guildford, it has brought with it its own set of dilemmas which I discuss later on in this chapter. Drawing on recent work into contemporary club culture (Thornton, 1995; Malbon, 1999) and my own empirical research into club cultures in Norwich and London, I conducted the empirical work used in this chapter during 1999 and 2000 in both Norwich and London, although I was living in London at the time. I have since extended my empirical work to include clubs in Guildford, Surrey where I am currently in the process of establishing contacts with five 'regular' clubbers and five paid club dancers in the area. Altogether I spoke in-depth to ten clubbers in London and five in Norwich. I have also drawn on my own experiences of clubbing in these three cities for this chapter.

Given the extent of clubbing as a leisure pursuit amongst young people in Britain, I think it is reasonable to assert that the activity of clubbing has an impact on a person's sense of self, their identity and identifications, and their 'belongings' (Malbon, 1999, p. 68). As Thornton (1995, p. 3) asserts: 'The sense of place afforded by these events is such that regular attendees take on the spaces they frequent, becoming "clubbers" or "ravers".' Indeed for some young people, 'clubbing' is the lynchpin of their identity, and relates to each aspect of their everyday lives. Luke, a participant in Malbon's study of London clubbers, talks of identity in relation to the cultural and social experience of living in London:

... clubbing gives you a sort of identity. You belong to a relatively small group of people, with very different interests and skills but there is something that connects you. I like being in a city because its quite anonymous, but it feels very good to find steadying points in the city (Luke, in Malbon, 1999, p. 49).

Part of my empirical work involved posting a request for participants for a 'study of clubbing in London for university' on the UK-Dance website. Paul, an ardent clubber who contacted me via the UK-dance website in May 2000 told me how:

Clubbing is my life, my life-blood if U (you) like. What wld (would) it b (be) like if I didn't go clubbing? Boring I reckon ... yeah, I don't even know what I'd b (be) like (Paul, research participant, UK-Dance chat room, 28/05/00).

Here Paul finds it difficult to imagine what life, or he, would be like without clubbing. Luke (Malbon, 1999, p. 49) speaks about the 'identifications' he makes with fellow clubbers. Malbon asserts:

Identifications might be understood as *elective forms of identity* (Scheler, 1954) ... Identifications are affectual in nature, usually small in scale, and might be premised upon affiliation with a charismatic leader, a totemic or tribal symbol and/or a shared emotional experience (for example, a shared appreciation of music) and a shared site (Hetherington, 1996; Malbon, 1999, p. 49, emphasis in original).

Key to understanding the interrelationship between substance use, club culture, identifications and identity is the notion of distinction (Bourdieu, 1984). We must remind ourselves that identifications do not replace identities. Difference is not demolished by an identification (Malbon, 1999, p. 50).

I have three principal aims in my research. Firstly, I seek to (re)construct the histories of dance music genres as they are relevant to contemporary British club cultures. I concentrate on the ways in which dance music genres are utilised by clubbers as a means of distinction. These distinctions centre on the values of 'authenticity', 'originality', and ultimately involve appeals of 'objective' aesthetic value. These issues impact upon a given clubber's sense of 'self', 'belonging' and embodiment. I ask how the *re-constructed history* of 'club culture' has a 'real' (as in felt-as-real) impact upon clubbers' notions of the 'good' or 'bad' night and the 'healthy' or 'unhealthy' body. Secondly, I aim to highlight sociocultural clashes between users of different substances within clubbing contexts. Here the use of substances is manifest in bodily demeanours, demeanours perceived as 'bad' or 'unhealthy' by certain factions of club culture, or displayed with pride by others. Dialogues surrounding the appropriateness of using a given substance can be said to reveal a 'deeper' set of distinctions within club culture, running along the lines of 'race', 'class', gender and sexuality. Finally, I aim to temper this concern with discursive practices by looking at how music and substance distinctions impact upon the clubber's sense of embodiment within the specific situated activity of attending a 'dance event'. I argue that the mysterious 'vibe', the sense of 'community' and 'unity' that urban clubbers speak of in this context is in part based on the 'body amnesia' that is possible when one perceives oneself to be 'among one's own'. Whilst my research does not attempt to explore the metaphysics of existence, I try to embrace 'matter' by asking how it is that the cultural context that surrounds and 'produces' a body, can also come to inhabit 'it' in the sense of changing corporeal experiences. Clubbers' perceptions of illness caused by substance consumption may draw on embodied 'self-knowledge', but this 'self-knowledge' can be said to be discursively constructed. Hence I avoid privileging personal corporeal experiences as 'true' or 'natural' knowledge, but instead view them as indicators of the impact of sociocultural distinction practices.

'My kind of music'

People can be said to love *their* 'kind of music', be it House, Jungle, Indie or Opera, and often *hate* 'that noise', that is the music of 'Others'. Lewis (1992, p. 137) proposes that we 'pretty much listen to, and enjoy, the same music that is listened to by other people we like or with whom we can identify'. Bourdieu (1984) argues that tastes in food and tastes in music are deeply ingrained. Whilst socially constituted, tastes in music are experienced as 'second nature'. They are *felt* in the body as an almost overwhelming admiration for *your* kind of beat, *your* kind of artist. We often experience repulsion for what is perceived to be the music of 'Others'.

Have you ever asked yourself 'How could he or she like *that*?' Music preferences are often felt to be involuntary, instinctive, *natural*. 'Your kind of music' is sometimes felt to be 'objectively' better than that of others. Jack, a research participant for example, says: 'The music seems to be getting harder and harder each time I go out. Lovely. That handbag house shit does my head in... like what's with all those stupid vocals eh?' (Jack, UK-Dance, 06/05/00). Thornton (1995, p. 113) asserts: 'As a deep-seated taste dependent on background, music preference is therefore a reasonably reliable indicator of social affinity'. Her point helps to explain the resilience of 'categories' of 'black' and 'white' music despite their conspicuous cross-fertilisation. Many dance music styles, house being the optimum example, have shifted from being perceived as 'black' to being perceived as 'white' as the years have passed. Of course there is no essentialist basis for why one style should be 'black', another 'white'. Yet as long as the social distinction of 'black' and 'white' continue to pervade culture, aesthetic distinctions along these lines will be held on to. Radio One Rap DJ Tim Westwood, for example, is white, and although he has an enduring popularity amongst Radio One listeners, he has frequently been berated for 'faking' his knowledge of and interest in Rap, historically constituted as 'black' music.

Processes of distinction are intricate in their mundane details; what record stores, bars and clubs are deemed to be 'places to be seen' by the various social groupings involved not only vary considerably between these groupings but also shift and mutate over time. These shifting research settings demand methodological and theoretical flexibility. Thornton (1995, p. 5) describes distinctions such as these made by clubbers as that between the 'hip' or 'cool' world of the dance crowd and its perpetually absent, denigrated *other* – the 'mainstream'. This contrast between 'Us' and the 'mainstream' is directly related to the fluid process of envisioning life-worlds and discriminating between social groups, particularly along gender, 'class' and racial lines. Thornton states that:

> ...veiled elitism and separatism enlist and reaffirm binary oppositions such as the alternative and the straight, the diverse and the homogenous, the radical and the conformist, the distinguished and the common (ibid.).

This 'Them and Us' dichotomy is manifest in many areas of 'club culture', from the music that is listened to, the clothes that are worn, the drugs that are taken to the magazines and books that are read. All are part of dynamic discourses that construct what is 'cool' and what is not. Malbon (1999, p. 58) notes:

> Where one clubber sees cool, another will see non-cool...The 'mainstream' is usually used to refer to what the clubber is not, whatever their preferences and resources of cultural capital.

It can thus be asserted that the 'mainstream' is not a static, monolithic entity, but rather a malleable concept that various groupings within club culture employ to authenticate their 'world-view'. Issues of temporality are vital here as accusations that an 'original' and 'alternative' scene has 'gone mainstream' or 'commercial' can amount to a cool kiss of death for the target of 'abuse'.

Music plays a key role as a marker of distinction within and across club culture, with certain musical genres believed to signify the 'type' of clubber who listens to them. This leads to inferences about the drugs certain clubbers take, whether they are likely to be violent, or at the very least unfriendly, and what their 'world-view' is likely to be. To give a pertinent example, DJ Vibes, talking about 'Happy Hardcore' (HH), maintains, 'HH is energy for people with energy and that's why more young people are into it. HH is for people who want to have a good time in a club. It creates a happy vibe' (DJ Vibes, quoted in Saunders, 1995, p. 202). As a genre, and rave in general, HH is associated with the use of amphetamines and MDMA (ecstasy). Collins (1997, p. 258), in his description of the first 'Junglists',[2] asserts:

> They wore pricey casual-wear, flashy designer excesses of Versace and Moschino – the girls in flesh-revealing lace, lycra and gold...Jungle's primary stimulants of choice were weed (cannabis) and champagne,

although the heavy bittersweet fumes of burning rocks (crack cocaine) had been detected on dance floors as early as 1991.

The intricacies of what clothing is associated with disparate groups of clubbers can be essential to the process of gaining access to certain dance club settings. Negotiation of 'the door' of a club and with the bouncers who police it rests to a certain extent on the 'rightness' of one's attire. I discuss this issue in more detail at a later point. However, I now move onto a discussion of the ways in which substance use and music are interlinked in discourses of distinction which are manifest within British club culture, which serves to further contextualise the research dilemmas raised by substance use in the setting one is interested in.

Social distinction and substance use

I'm quite wary of places where you see coke around. I prefer this gaff as you know pretty much everyone is E'd-up, it makes for a friendly vibe (Tasha, research participant, regular clubber in Norwich, Ipswich and London, 14/08/98).

The 'drugs problem'

Firstly I think it is important to stress that with regards to 'drugs', at a conceptual level at least, we are dealing with a profoundly *cultural* matter. This is so whether we talk about the perception of a substance and its use as a problem or not, or whether we talk about the 'realities' of the substance for users or abstainers, dealers or police, patients, doctors or pharmacologists.[3] McDonald (1994, p. 17), writing as a 'critical medical anthropologist', notes how a substance such as cannabis, which can evoke a self-conscious, laid-back, peace-on-earth counterculture in many parts of the West, can mean tough manliness and the daily rigours of manual labour among male work gangs in South America. Thus the importance of cultural context looms large when it comes to 'drugs'. This may seem an obvious point but I think that it is often taken for granted that there exists a social danger inherent in the substances themselves, or risk located *within* certain individuals. In a sense, without the notion of a substance being a social, moral and/or political threat, there can be no comprehensive or persuasive pharmacology of harm, or alternatively no persuasive talk of a substance's benefits.

These processes, whereby different groupings in society employ a number of power resources to put forward their versions of the 'truth' about substances, have often led to vehement conflicts within and across club culture. If a researcher wishes to investigate these different social and substance groupings and conflicts within club cultures in any depth, attendance at dance events appears to be highly necessary. However, the discourses of and on club cultures and substance use circulate in a number of different settings. Analyses of texts from and about club culture, articles from the national press, the visuals of flyers and posters, magazines such as DJ and Mixmag, and the layout and content of clubs' websites (see www.gatecrasher.com for example), can hugely enrich research into club cultures. Awareness of, and familiarity with, these texts and materials can also help the researcher to become more of an 'insider' in the eyes of his or her research participants.

E-heads and beer monsters

> They sip on Lucozade and water, sneering at 'beer monsters' who don't know how to enjoy themselves and who sadly parade in the meat market discos, throwing up after a curry in the back of a taxi and fumbling with some stranger they cannot recall the morning after (Henderson, 1997, p. 49).

Release's 1997 research used face-to-face interviews which aimed to elicit the experiences of some 250 people attending 'dance events' between March and September 1997. It provides evidence that at that point, ecstasy remained integral to club culture. From my informal interviews with five Norwich clubbers and ten London clubbers, and from the dance events I have attended in Norwich and London, the Release findings appear to hold, although there is tentative evidence that so-called 'poly-drugging', where several different substances are consumed simultaneously, has become either more prevalent in club culture, or at least more widely acknowledged by clubbers themselves. However, ecstasy and alcohol remain a combination which clubbers tend to avoid. Ian, a clubber from my London sample says:

> I much prefer to avoid drinking and drinkers when pilled up (taking ecstasy). I'm not averse to polydrugging, but booze doesn't work as mixer for E AFAIK (ecstasy). Also, of you're drinking you can't take GBH, which is God's own combo with E! (Ian, research participant, UK-Dance chat room, 02/05/00)

The Release survey found that 85 per cent of males and 83 per cent of females claimed to have taken ecstasy at the dance events they had attended; 53 per cent of males and 52 per cent of females had taken, or had planned to take ecstasy the night the interview took place; 68 per cent named ecstasy as their favourite drug to take at such events, and this preference held across all age groups and both sexes. Release found that although respondents did not experience ecstasy use as unproblematic, in their view they had experienced more positive effects than negative effects. Ecstasy has had an impact upon many young people's perceptions of substance use. 'Drugs' perceived by wider society to be relatively acceptable, at least in the eyes of the law, are greeted with disdain by some young people. Particularly during what Henderson (1997, p. 47) calls the 'Ecstasy honeymoon period' of the late 1980s, especially the 1989 'Summer of Love', many users perceived ecstasy to be not only a viable alternative to alcohol, but also a *less harmful* alternative. Henderson maintains that: 'Users singled it (ecstasy) out from others (substances) as being different. They were anti-alcohol' (1997, p. 49). My study confirms that many young people within club culture still hold this view, and continue to look down on 'Beer Monsters' (Henderson, 1997, p. 49) as lumbering, clumsy, potentially violent and likely to harass women on the dance floor. The perception amongst ecstasy users that alcohol is incompatible with a non-threatening club atmosphere is borne out by the findings of Lifeline's Manchester survey (Henderson, 1993) which noted that amongst women, sexual safety was an attraction at 'raves' in contrast with alcohol-based clubs, which were seen as 'cattle-markets'. Participants in my survey echoed the perception that alcohol is not conducive to 'having a good time'. Mash, a clubber in my London sample (gender unknown) says:

> It's weird, I used to love getting pissed but just can't be bothered anymore. Wow those booze clubs are funny, mouthy women in little black numbers and blokes in shoes/shirts wandering around practicing their pick-up lines and falling over each other (Mash, research participant, UK-Dance chat room, 16/05/00).

Here we see processes of cultural *distinction* in action, the very processes that the youth researcher must be mindful of when gaining access to clubs and securing clubbers' participation. These distinctions centre around which drugs are, or are not, deemed acceptable by those involved in club culture. Missy, a Norwich clubber, relates her experiences of clubbing in London to going out in her hometown of Caernarfon, Wales:

> That's what they all do where I'm from, come rain or shine, summer or winter there'll be a bunch of blokes who think it's hard to go out in T-shirts and girls who think it's sexy to have goose-bumps

all the way up their legs. Lovely. They all like to fight over each other come closing time too. Don't know if it's still true but on the weekend Caernarfon used to have a higher violent crime rate than Brixton (Missy, research participant, met at *The Fridge Bar*, Brixton, on 12/11/99).

The discourses producing 'drug appropriateness' focus on the desirable effects and bodily demeanours that ecstasy use promotes, for example a 'smiley' face, whilst simultaneously emphasising the 'out-of-control' bodies of aggressive drunken 'lads' going for a kebab after clubbing on a Friday night. Whilst 'hedonism' is strongly valued by ecstasy users within clubbing settings, it must be hedonism that does not interfere with the 'luved-up' vibe they seek to encourage, and any hedonism must still allow the person to dance frenetically for a long time, something which alcohol does not encourage. Mixing alcohol and ecstasy was to be avoided as much as possible according to the majority of participants in my survey:

> E and Alcohol...yuck! Done it a few times and it made me feel gormless on the night and the effects on the next day comedown/paranoia etc are multitude. Don't know if it's a real medical fact but I reckon it's pretty hard on the kidneys too. I've felt kidney pain when I've significantly mixed the two (Mash, research participant, UK-Dance website, 16/05/00).

> In my experience the combo (ecstasy and alcohol) is crap and can be unpleasant or dangerous. Booze can make the E more rushy/mongy but it blunts me to the more buzzy/uppy effects. On NYE (New Years Eve) I got very dehydrated after sinking a couple of Sea Breezes (an alcoholic drink) before I took my pills. I felt very ill and got a cystitis-like feeling in my urethra...er, too much detail perhaps. Also when the hangover hits it can ruin your e-buzz (Leisha, research participant, UK-Dance website and Ministry of Sound, London, 16/05/00, 23/05/00 and 27/05/00).

These ongoing surface wranglings between ecstasy users and alcohol drinkers may at first glance seem to be borne purely out of necessity, that is being able to dance for long periods of time at (often all-night) dance events, an activity not usually demanded of those who spend their leisure time at pubs. However, it is also possible that since public discourse surrounding ecstasy remains on the whole highly negative ('Fear'), ecstasy users 'react' by seeking to legitimise their drug consumption. They have singled out alcohol as 'health-damaging', and have stigmatised the bodily demeanours associated with drunkenness. The legitimisation strategies employed by ecstasy users have not sprung up randomly. Rather they are linked with the 'real' effects of ecstasy on the body, namely that it raises heart rate and blood pressure and can result in heat-stroke if water is not drunk regularly (Saunders, 1995, p. 74). Here is an example of how clubbers' embodied experiences are an essential element of their shared sociocultural understandings, upon which their systems of language and meanings are based. In research terms, bodily demeanours that 'fit with' the substance associated with each club setting are important in the process of becoming 'one of our own' to a group that the researcher wishes to engage with. Certain ways of dancing may be 'expected' at different venues and on different nights. For example, the frenetic and highly energetic dancing expected of clubbers at a drum and bass night in *Mass*, Brixton, where revellers take illegal substances regularly, would look distinctly out of place at a typical Friday commercial house night at *The Drink*, Guildford, where clubbers predominately, if not exclusively, drink alcohol.

Researching young people in club settings

Having contextualised some of my findings from my encounters with clubbers in London, Norwich and Guildford, I now want to discuss some of the main problems encountered doing research in club settings, and consider the ways in which these problems can be tackled. I first became interested in clubbing and its sociospatial relations as a student and regular clubber in Norwich. Observing and talking to clubbing friends offered a 'route-in' to the spaces associated with clubbing in the Norfolk town. The frames of reference I have built up to understand the clubbing phenomena are inextricably linked to my own personal experiences as a 'youthful' clubber. Without 'youth on my side' so to speak, I may not have had access to these clubbing spaces and my interest in studying them through a sociological lens may not have taken hold. This point highlights the ways in which youth researchers' personal biographies and socioeconomic circumstances impact upon their choice of 'topic' and the way they approach the phenomena that interests them.

The researcher interested in 'illegal' activities, in this case substance use and differentiation within clubbing spaces, is faced with a number of difficulties. Gaining access to the given 'world' is the most obvious obstacle. How far one is able, or for that matter wishes, to 'penetrate' into that world will impact upon the research's scope and claims to authority. For me, much of the background work researchers have to embark upon had already been achieved. However, there is a tension here between the practical usefulness of having 'knowledge' about the topic of interest and possessing the openness and inclination to have such 'knowledge' challenged. Social inquiry must involve critical self-scrutiny by the researcher, or active reflexivity. When doing research in a 'difficult' social setting such as a club, particularly when we also visit such places during our leisure time, we may find ourselves taking actions that we have not accounted for, or even imagined in our research plan.

I resolutely did not take ecstasy or speed when I knew I would have opportunities to speak to clubbers as part of my research. However, there is a tension here given the 'normalisation' of some substance use in club settings. When asked what I had taken I tended to nod vaguely and say 'You know, the usual', and tried to steer the conversation away from my own substance use. One tactic I used was to always drink bottles of water in front of my 'participants', since drinking water is associated with ecstasy consumption. Whilst this may seem like a somewhat grave deception, I could think of no other way to make myself appear to be completely 'part of the crowd' without going so far as to take drugs myself. My concern with looking 'part of the crowd' was linked to my personal experiences of clubbing in the past where I had felt part of the crowd. It was also related to my research aims as I thought an 'obvious outsider' would find it more difficult to get clubbers to talk about their experiences of substance use.

I had to take research opportunities as they came, such as attending 'after-parties', where many clubbers go to relax after dancing for hours on end. I often felt not only extremely tired, but also shy despite people's general friendliness. However, I think if such 'moments' in the research process can be reflexively used to better understand the phenomena at hand and our relations to it, then serendipity can be (re)worked to the researcher's advantage, particularly in terms of creating new routes of understanding and possible modes of interpretation. Being a club dancer has opened up a different realm of interpretation for me, leading as it has to an awareness of, and point of critical reference with regard to, issues of corporeal demeanour and body image that are involved in being 'on view' in a club, set apart from the crowd below. However, the experience has brought its own dilemmas, for example deciding whether to bow to pressure from the club's floor manager to wear 'skimpier' outfits. Yet even this dilemma created new research possibilities as I listened in to, and eventually became involved in, the debate fellow dancers had about this demand.

What are deemed to be difficulties by the researchers are dependent on their personal biography and socioeconomic circumstances. What may prove to be a moral dilemma for one researcher may go unexplored by another. However, within the context of institutionally endorsed research that is by a university and/or government funding body, there is a sense in which a researcher has to stay within a historically and culturally sanctioned remit. Other concerns such as not exploiting sensitive participants and not putting oneself in potentially dangerous situations can also come to the fore. In certain clubs, I have felt 'unsafe' and faced the quandary of wanting to conduct research whilst realising that it might be dangerous to continue. On such occasions I would stay for an hour or so, and through observation and reflexive thinking, try to surmise *why* I might feel 'unsafe' since clearly this is a sociologically interesting phenomenological experience. Built environment seemed to be an important factor in these experiences; one free party I went to in East London was in a warehouse with six floors and only one small staircase (packed with people) joining all of the floors, whilst another dance event was in a building surrounded by a barb wired fencing, with one entrance guarded by unfriendly bouncers with metal detectors. However, another dance event I attended also involved passing through metal detectors, but the bouncers and 'pickers' were friendly and joked with people as they entered the building. Despite the amount of visible drug dealing and the defending of 'patches' (where certain dealers can stand in prime spots to deal which are not to be used by other dealers) occurring in that club, I felt 'safe'. This demonstrates that the 'vibe' that clubbers speak of, and seek, is related to a multitude of factors (drug and music consumption, staff attitudes, built environment and so on) that impact upon whether they can feel ontologically secure in a dance event setting.

The young academic researcher: an advantage or disadvantage?

For a young academic researcher studying young people within a particular setting, similarity in age can be both a blessing and a bind. Club researcher Ben Malbon effectively employed his age as a resource in his work, given that he attended clubbing nights with his research participants. In order to gain access to these central London clubs, Malbon had to negotiate the 'bouncers' and 'pickers' who decide who is 'right' for the club, and/or a particular night. Getting past the door often provides the clubber with the first 'concrete' test of their claim to belong. It is one of the several 'tests' that the researcher into club cultures has to 'pass' if his/her research is to be successful. Malbon (1999, p. 64) notes how:

> Getting into a club-joining a clubbing crowd-can be a mere formality, yet it can also be an anxiety-provoking experience, with some clubbers comparing club entry to passing an exam.

If Malbon had been older, it may have been even more difficult to negotiate 'the door', since as well as having official lower age limits (which are not always observed), clubs often seem to operate an unofficial upper age limit. My nights out with my clubbing participants had an impact on the ways in which they could relax with me. I think that if I had been unable to garner entrance to these clubs, unable to 'pass the test' so to speak, then I may not have been able to elicit such frank replies to my sometimes rather 'nosy' questions. This was where my own youth became crucial, since I 'don't look like an academic researcher' as Rudi, one of the participants in my Norwich study, said, aiding the processes of trust-building required to talk about drugs. However, I did find that my youth detracted from any 'authority' I had with participants, although maybe given the topic of my research this could have also been a benefit.

It has proved tempting to social researchers to both idealise and, in some cases, demonise 'young people'. This is perhaps unsurprising given the social and academic history of 'youth research'. Valentine *et al.* (1998, p. 10) write how:

> Academic interest in teenagers was born within criminology, fuelled by moral panics about the nuisance value of young people on the urban streets of Western societies. Thus, the research into youth groups was marked by a preoccupation with delinquency and associated with the study of so-called 'condemned' and 'powerless' groups in society such as the working class, migrants and the criminal.

We remain susceptible to such tendencies today. A focus on the 'public' and the 'spectacular' aspects of youth culture can discourage explorations of more mundane everyday aspects of young people's lives, such as relations with siblings (McNamee, 1998). Yet I think that during my studies of clubbing and substance use, I have come to have a sense of how clubbing can be simultaneously mundane (an expected part of many young people's weekend activities) and highly 'spectacular' (the very public display of sociospatial practices and sites of differentiations and belongings that clubbing involves). It could be said that the spectacular and the mundane do not have to always be intellectually polarised. It is often the tensions and the overlapping of the 'mundane' and the 'spectacular' which can prove to be useful tools for understanding youth cultures. Indeed, what may be 'spectacular' to one researcher/research group may be considered 'mundane' firstly to another researcher (again dependent on personal and more specifically work-related biographies) and more importantly to the 'subjects' concerned. To conclude, investigating young people's substance use in dance club settings brings with it a set of issues, dilemmas and controversies that the researcher must face up to and overcome. Being a 'youthful' researcher may make access to world of clubbing easier, but it also brings with it a number of challenges, such as the expectations of other clubbers that you will have consumed the same or a similar substance as them, that this chapter has attempted to tackle.

Notes

1. MDMA (Methylene-dioxy-N-methyl-amphetamine) is the chemical name for what is known in wider public discourse as 'Ecstasy'. According to numerous surveys (Henderson, 1993; Release, 1996), ecstasy is no longer the only drug used in the club context, although it does remain extremely popular. 'Ecstasy' has come to be seen as synonymous with 'dance culture', particularly in England.
2. Jungle is a dance music genre characterised by an off-beat 'sub-sonic' kick-drum percussion running at around 160 bpm, whilst the bass and vocals are much slower. It draws on numerous 'black' music traditions including reggae, ragga, hip-hop and breakbeat.
3. However, this should not be taken as a denial that substance use, legal or illegal, can lead to great suffering for individuals, and their friends and families.

Part 4
Issues in Ethnography

9
Double Exposure: Exploring the Social and Political Relations of Ethnographic Youth Research

Robert Hollands

Introduction

In the last 10 to 15 years, the social sciences and cultural studies have experienced a renewed interest in investigating issues of power in the research relationship, and debates within ethnography, in particular, have played a key role in this revival. The purpose of this chapter is to explore and develop some ideas surrounding the politics of ethnographic research practice in relation to studying young people, specifically through an examination of what might be called the 'social relations of fieldwork'. In doing so, it will draw upon a range of general commentary on the researcher–researched relationship, as well as provide some concrete examples from my own ethnographic study of young people's transitions into work and training in the mid-1980s (see Hollands, 1990).

Research, like all social relationships, is fundamentally one of power. Power implies the capacity to define rules and command resources in social situations (Giddens, 1977). Power in this sense is viewed on a continuum and does not constitute a 'zero-sum' concept (that is, all or nothing). For example, the individuals one interviews and observes are not simply passive objects of analysis, but can be active definers of both the researcher and the research relationship. A short example involving studying young people in particular, will suffice to make this point and comes from an article concerning a number of examples of 'rebellious research objects' (Kriesi, 1992). In the case in point, an attempt to study a political youth movement in Zurich led to the researchers' office being broken into and documentary case material and questionnaires being taken. This was followed by the printing of a leaflet by the movement which accused the researchers involved as being 'alter-naive handymen to the authorities and their divisive politics, and careerists abusing the movement in a cynical way for our own personal advancement' (Kriesi, 1992, p. 194).

While somewhat of an extreme example of the power research subjects can collectively possess, it is perhaps more commonly recognised that power differences in research relationships have much to do with the political choice of what to study and how to study it. However, simply asserting the idea of differential power into the research process is insufficient. The researcher/researched dichotomy is only a general form of more specific power relations inherent in society. Indeed, one might argue that this generalised relationship has tended to dominate much of the debate around method at the expense of broader political forces and the complex arrangement of social relations (that is, gender, class, race, age and so on) that enter into conducting all forms of research, including ethnography. These broader social and political relations contour the overall intellectual division of labour, as well as inscribe themselves, in different combinations, in the research process and fieldwork situation.

In the field of cultural studies, there is an ongoing debate about a lack of a politics of method (Johnson, 1983). It has been argued that there is a basis for developing a new and different type of ethnography, which theoretically captures the relationship between structure and agency, while also advancing some new ideas surrounding a politics of method (Willis, 1980; McRobbie, 1982; Johnson, 1983; Hollands, 1985a; Griffin, 1986). The basic elements of a 'structural' or 'critical' ethnography are: (a) the situation of human experience, meaning and action within the context of power and material social relations and structures (without reducing the former to the latter); (b) the recognition of human subjects having multiple identities and being affected by a number of different social relations; (c) the theme of reflexivity and the rationalisation of action (for both the researched and the researcher); (d) the notion of a theorised and politicised ethnography informed by variants of neo-Marxist and feminist premises; (e) the potential of a dialogue or collaboration between theory/ethnography and researcher/researched. All of these elements, advance the point that a more adequate politics of method is desirable and that ethnographic research could provide an important type of political practice (see Hollands, 1985a). In this context, Hammersley (1992, p. 96) defines critical ethnography as 'a form of qualitative research that contrasts with more traditional approaches in being closely, perhaps one should say organically, linked to socialist and/or feminist politics.'

However, critical ethnographies do not come without their own methodological limitations. There is, for instance, a tendency for critical theorists to develop and utilise a 'unitary' notion of the researcher–researched identity and theoretical framework (that is, women studying girls via feminism equals a 'shared femininity'; working-class men studying working-class boys via Marxism equates to 'male class resistance'), rather than dealing with theories about multiple identities, relationships and theories. Second, while being acutely aware of how social identities and inequalities affect their subjects structurally out in the 'real' world, radical ethnographers have sometimes remained quite blinkered when it comes down to analysing their own position of power and how this might influence both fieldwork relations and their final (re)presentations of their subjects.

Failure to grapple with these issues has resulted in three disturbing tendencies within critical ethnographic research projects. First, a lack of concern over thinking through how social relations manifest themselves as relations of power in ethnographic work, can result in researchers taking a 'vanguard' position in relation to their subjects' accounts. Second, failure to come to terms with these relations can also lead to quite bizarre 'readings' of specific subsections of the group under study (that is, male researcher's misreading of young women's cultural forms). Finally, in ignoring how fieldwork relations and representations of another social group are political issues, ethnographic reporting can elide with a kind of naturalism in the presentation of another culture. These tendencies remain problems with almost all contemporary ethnography. Yet the way forward can only come from researchers beginning to explore the subtle ways in which the social relations of society are constitutive of their own research into and (re)presentation of other groups.

Power, interaction and politics in the social relations of fieldwork: a case study of youth

Background

The case study from which the following material and observations come from relates to my PhD work conducted at the Centre for Contemporary Cultural Studies (CCCS) at the University of Birmingham in the late 1980s, later published as *The Long Transition* (Hollands, 1990). The research was an ethnographic study of the cultural identities and transitional experiences of 50 working-class youths as they made their way from education into the world of adulthood through vocational training (that is, the Youth Training Scheme, YTS). More broadly, the study was concerned with evaluating the historical impact vocationalism was having on shifting and fragmenting working-class transitions, identities and experiences in modern Britain. The fieldwork took place over a three-year period and involved in-depth interviews and participant observation on schemes, at work placements, in the home and in various leisure/public venues.

To put the research into a wider context it is important to situate the study briefly within the organisation and broader concerns of the CCCS at the time. First, the work was part of an Education sub-group project designed to follow up their study of the failure of post-war social democratic education in Britain (Education Group, 1981), with a further examination and critique of 'New Right' educational policies (Education Group II, 1991). In addition to developing a theoretical critique of education, the sub-group was also interested in the growth of vocationalism and training, not to mention how the various actors and agents working within these fields were reacting to the new conditions imposed by Thatcherite policies. Additionally, the Centre's overall preoccupation with exploring the relationship between class, race, gender and new social movements, the concern with defining and outlining the theoretical and political basis of cultural studies (Johnson, 1983) and an increasing interest in methodology and cultural politics (Hollands, 1985a,b) all helped shape my research agenda. The point is that all research, of whatever type, has a political history and a social context.

The original focus of the research in question was to cover both the young unemployed and those on training schemes, but it quickly became apparent that its scope was too wide. Instead, I worked briefly on a project looking at youth unemployment in a neighbouring town (see Willis, 1985), while visiting a single scheme very intensely over a ten-month period, where I was enlisted to help trainees with communication skills and develop their leisure interests. Due to the fact that I had little prior knowledge of YTS, newly arrived from Canada, much of my initial introduction to the topic came from young people themselves, unfettered by either academic or political sources. This situation often fuelled my later feelings that such unstructured interviews revealed a hidden and often submerged set of concerns which were rarely addressed by public discourses on the 'youth question' at that time.

When this first phase of fieldwork ended, there were two main concerns and/or developments which resulted in a shift of emphasis in the project. In the first place, despite its qualitative richness, it became apparent that the study was not dealing with working-class youth and the new vocationalism in all its complexity. For example, interviews had largely been restricted to a small group of (primarily) male trainees, who have been typified in the school-to-work literature as the 'lads' (Willis, 1977). The second development came out of my involvement in a number of regional and national bodies concerned to monitor, research and campaign against present government training policy. These background factors were important in shifting the direction and organisation of the study in a number of ways. For instance, the limited ethnographic sample and additional knowledge gained about the national structure of YTS led to a much greater concern about 'ethnographic representativeness'. The study expanded to include not only a more balanced gender and racial focus, but also branched out by looking at distinctively different types of training schemes (that is, community projects, private training agencies, college-based schemes and so on). Second, I began to view the research as being located within a broader political debate about the changing nature of class and the response of the labour movement to young people and vocationalism. Additionally, the theoretical backdrop of the thesis increasingly moved away from a somewhat orthodox and productivist view of class by taking on board the idea that the new vocationalism was helping to produce a diverse set of youth transitions and identities (Cohen, 1984).

As this context shows, researching youth should be viewed as a dynamic and changing process that is constantly effected by a variety of forces, events and developments. Ethnographic methods, in particular, are adaptable to such changes of direction. This method should have the capability to 'surprise' the researcher, to move the theoretical debate forward, to allow scholars to reassess their initial interpretation of events. This is not an argument against rigour or a justification for research to be easily swayed by outside events. Yet the reality of these forces raises the question of how such broader processes and considerations impinge on the research process, and suggest that researchers need to consider how wider social relations may influence or structure their fieldwork in particular ways.

Power and the social relations of fieldwork

It has been argued that the politics of research is inherently revealed by the choice of one's research topic, the methods utilised and the social context in which the research takes place. Yet power and social relations are also inscribed into the fieldwork setting and research practice itself.

Specific combinations of social relations exist in the interview/participant observation situation and these ultimately work to structure our final '(re)presentation' of our subjects. Not only are our subjects often differentiated by cross-cutting social relations, especially young people, but so too are researchers, thereby throwing up a multitude of overlapping relations and situations (that is, differences in age, class, gender, race and in this case nationality). It will be important to analytically separate out these main social relations of fieldwork in order to investigate the various ways in which they structure interaction and (re)presentation of one's subjects.

The most sought-after textbook example of the research identity is a neutral one. Even in ethnographic work the nameless, faceless, 'fly on the wall' observer is at least one of the suggested guises. At best, in participant observation, the research may opt to go 'native' (adopt the style and manner of one's subjects) in order to blend in and cause the least disruption. I have already criticised this objectivist position whereby the researcher is assumed to have a neutral identity, while the second approach does not appear to call into question why the researcher wants to 'fit in' anyway. In fact, subjects may already have popular conceptions of what a researcher is and how she or he is supposed to act, and will react according to any discrepancies to this image.

In a number of ways in this case study, I simply could not fit into a neutral research role. In the first place, it was painfully obvious to anyone, from my accent, that I was not English and it was also clear that I neither acted nor indeed looked the part of a typical clipboard holding researcher. Many young people I interviewed asked me extensively about young people and life in Canada, and I often spoke freely and openly about this topic. My national identity had, of course, certain advantages and disadvantages. For example, I found that relationships of trust and confidentiality build up fairly quickly between myself and most young people, as I wasn't easily categorised into one of 'them' of 'them and us' (that is, adult and middle class, employed by the scheme), and perhaps they felt more open because I was supposedly returning to Canada. There were also clear disadvantages, similar to those experienced by many anthropologists visiting a foreign environment. For instance, at the beginning of the research there were a whole range of cultural nuances, behaviours and language differences that led to some fundamental misunderstandings. As my comprehension developed some of my initial ideas and theories around aspects of the interview material changed drastically. This demonstrates that interview data itself is highly open-ended and can be 'read' in multiple ways as researchers themselves develop.

Age differences also can help create certain relations between researchers and their subjects. In this study, I was 26 when I began interviewing 16- and 17-year-olds, although age may have been less of a factor than it might have been in this case. Youthfulness is a fairly elastic category anyway and most trainees guessed, because of the way I looked and dressed, that I was at least in the 'youthful' age bracket. In fact, both age and nationality may have worked to alter many young people's perceptions of me as a researcher. In the first place, I rarely invoked such an identity amongst trainees themselves. I was casual and frank, and my initial role was often one of learning rather than researching. Additionally, I also spent a significant amount of time with trainees outside the scheme, and became friends with a number of my subjects. Finally, I was often in the role of listener as initially I knew very little about their experiences on the training scheme and elsewhere. There was little sense in which I was explicitly more powerful than my interviewees, outside of the choices I would make in terms of using their words and making analytical sense of the interview material. Overall, I neither came across as 'neutral' nor as a 'researcher' in the traditional sense.

A concern with social class was not only a crucial theoretical part of the research – it also impinged upon the social relations and practice of fieldwork. I have already hinted that my own perspective on class shifted during the course of the project. First, many of my initial ideas on class relations were restricted to fairly orthodox notions of 'production' and 'structural position' rather than on cultural notions of 'transition' and 'identity' (see Cantelon and Hollands, 1988). Increasingly, I came to understand class as a lived relation, expressed over a wide range of social sites. Second, due to the diversity of identities and transitions into adult life expressed through the ethnography, it become obvious to me that class was an extremely heterogeneous phenomenon.

The key question is how did these changing concerns with class actually affect fieldwork relations and later (re)presentations of these young people? In short, it meant that I expressed a genuine interest in their class experiences in face-to-face situations. My own social background is not really transferable to the English situation and can only be awkwardly described as rural, upwardly mobile working-class Canadian, which roughly translates as I have both experienced growing up working class (albeit in a different cultural context), as well as had the opportunity to study class as a theoretical concept. There were of course class-based attitudes and behaviours that were expressed which I did not always agree with (that is, forms of nationalism or racism and sexism), but overall their forms of knowledge were viewed as legitimate and valued accordingly.

There were a number of ways in this dichotomy between class experience and my formal knowledge of class that was reflected in my fieldwork relations with young people. For example, while I may have had a theoretical and political grasp of class relations, I didn't want this to pre-empt their own specific experiences and sets of concerns. In many cases their political views were often at odds with my own views, and indeed with the thinking of much of the organised labour movement! In fact, many of their day-to-day problems stemmed from being treated as 'dogsbodies' and 'gofers', often by other workers as well as bosses. As such, I increasingly felt strongly about young people's specific exploitation as 'trainees' rather than 'workers' and as young people rather than as simply class agents. It became clear, however, that the very day-to-day issues that they were experiencing – being constructed as a subordinate workforce of trainees, separated from any democratic and collective structures and facing individualist and careerist ideologies about employment and training – were precisely the new class issues of the day (Hollands, 1991).

As such, I began to differentiate less between their specific daily experiences and the so-called real political issues associated with the new vocationalism, and instead increasingly saw myself as an intermediary between young people and elements within the labour movement. Alain Touraine has described this interchange as 'action research' or 'permanent sociology' (Touraine, 1979). On the one hand, I saw myself as a resource person for any young person whose set of problems might be advanced by collective action. This often manifested itself through the issue of youth rights rather than trade union membership. On the other hand, I sought, as often as I could, to make the voices, concerns and activities of young people on YTS as visible as possible to people within the trade union and labour movement. Like all researchers, I was in a mediating role between a first party (my interviewees) and a third party or parties (the public/the then Manpower Services Commission/ the labour movement).

Gender theory and relations were also crucial to the project's rationale, politics and fieldwork. To begin, it may seem too obvious a point to state that my interaction with working-class males on the scheme was influenced by a certain degree of similarity and familiarity. Despite some fundamental exceptions, there was at least an 'assumed' shared experience on many matters. This meant that there were things male trainees revealed to me simply because I was a man (that is, views about women, sex and so on). This is not to argue that there is a universal male rapport or that even amongst the group of male trainees interviewed that there was a shared experience or singular class cultural form. While it was clear that a cultural grouping one might call the 'lads' still exists (Willis, 1977), this subsection of males was far less uniform than previous ethnographic work would appear to suggest. For some, underneath the hard exterior shell of masculinity was a soft underbelly of fears and insecurity. Additionally, the lads formed only one type of working-class male. Some were upwardly mobile, others sensitive to gender relations and still others were overtly political in character (Hollands, 1990). In other words, the social relations of fieldwork revealed a wide range of male responses which went beyond much of the theoretical and public discourses surrounding male youth culture (Hall and Jefferson, 1976).

As such, I developed, without prioritising, quite different relations with different subsections of male youth. For example, I discussed many of my ideas and politics with various young men labelled 'politicos' and I often solicited their views on such issues. With one trainee in particular, I developed a close personal friendship which still continues today, and we discussed my research in some detail at various points. For others, I followed up their views around issues like racism and sexism by having them read and discuss a series of educational comics on these topics (this research is reported in Hollands, 1985b). I did this not to demonstrate that there was some 'naturalistic' way to present their thinking on these controversial issues, but to explore their attachments to particular ideologies and engage in some form of action research methodology.

The use of feminist theory, including issues around methodology (Stanley and Wise, 1983; Harding, 1987), also had an impact upon the social relations of fieldwork. It is, of course, tremendously difficult for men to conduct research on, understand and attempt to represent women's experiences. There is a double bind here. Either male researchers choose not to conduct research on women and go on reproducing the 'malestream' character of much of the literature on youth or other subjects or they begin the process of exploring different accounts and experiences informed by feminist theory, while accepting some of the limitations of their research (also see Blackman, 1998). In the main I reject the former position which suggests that only women can do research on women. Such a position errs equally in the opposite direction by assuming that 'womanhood' is a unitary category or subject position. While all women do have some common experiences, this does not explain the effect that multiple combinations of social relations and identities will have on fieldwork. Janet Finch's (1984) article 'Its Great to Have Someone to Talk To', is a good example of both the insights feminist thinking can have on interviewing and the limits of a notion of a 'shared femininity' (McRobbie, 1982).

In the wake of some of these problems, and not wanting to leave young women out of my analysis, I began to reflect seriously on my position as a male researcher and what that meant for both the fieldwork and my representation of women. This cross-examination took a number of forms. In the most basic way, this meant prioritising the experiences of young women and taking seriously what they had to say (additionally not just tacking them onto male experiences and theories, see Eichler, 1988). It is also important not to take a position which renders women powerless but rather one in which gender is viewed as a relationship of power. Related to this is coming to terms with the importance of male interpretations of women's experiences. It is the male researcher's responsibility to try and minimise the gendered relations of power in the ethnographic situation and to give a serious 'reading' to women's differential experiences.

There were, of course, certain subjects that were totally inappropriate for an older male researcher to broach to young women. Topics such as sexuality and domestic violence, for example, merely enhance the social relations of power inherent in the interview situation and hence there are absences in the study around certain issues central to young women's lives. At the same time, it was important to include topics and subjects into the conversations not 'normally' viewed as concerning women (that is, politics, work, careers and so on), as this 'taken for granted' assumption often have the effect of reinforcing gender stereotypes. In conclusion, it must be said that young women's experiences can be presented by male researchers who scrutinise their own assumptions and situate their research in the light of women's oppression in the wider society. There will of course always be absences and caveats. However, ethnographic work on women (by either women or men researchers) can help clarify feminist arguments and modify existing theoretical models based primarily on men's experiences. The point is to recognise some of the specific limitations men face interviewing women and avoid presenting accounts which are not contextualised within a theory of women's oppression in general.

Similarly, during the course of the research, I became increasingly conversant with some of the general arguments surrounding the problem of white researchers conducting studies of black culture. Particularly important in this regard was the 'new racism' perspective exemplified in the CCCS Race and Politics Group (1982) and Barker (1981). In the CCCS work, Lawrence (1982) forcefully argues that sociologists in the race relations field have been centrally involved in the construction of black cultural forms as 'pathological' or 'deviant'. This is again not to say that white researchers should not include black people as subjects in their research. In my own work on young people and YTS, over 20 per cent of the youth population in the locality were either Asian or African Caribbean, so it would have been wrong not to include their experiences in the study. Nor is it to say that many black youths don't face many of the same barriers and structures that their white working-class counterparts experience. Finally, neither should it be taken to mean that there is some kind of monolithic black identity or cultural form (this is ghettoising in its own right). However, their own specific class positions are clearly overlaid with racial identities and the impact of racial discrimination from white society. The main emphasis then was on the crucial structuring influence of 'white' racism (see Hollands, 1990, Chapter 8). Black cultural forms can only be fully understood within the confines of white racism from employers, trainers, career officers and amongst white working-class trainees themselves.

In a similar way to gender, white researchers must look closely at their practices and theories in the light of black people's responses and experiences in a racist society. White racism is a problem of white society, not of black cultural response or underachievement. A stress on forms of white racism and institutionalised discrimination is a start in shifting away from a 'black pathology'. White researchers then must be careful not to present untheorised statements or black cultural experiences outside of the context of white racist ideologies.

Conclusion: the politics of fieldwork relations and the problem of (re)presenting youth

In summary, it must be said that in the preceding discussion I have artificially pulled apart a multitude of social relations which exist in particular combinations, which influence fieldwork practice and research with young people. The implications of this show that there is some way to go in constructing a more adequate politics of the ethnographic method, especially in relation to studying young people. There remain questions as to how power and social difference here might be used to guide interaction in the field and hence transform the purpose and justification of much youth research. Additionally, it is clear that the social relations of fieldwork are crucial in the final (re)presentation we make of our subjects, again a point which should not be lost amongst youth researchers in particular.

In terms of the case study on youth reported here, it has been argued that there were a series of overlapping social relations that entered into the fieldwork situation and helped structure the research. Beyond the simple researcher/researched dichotomy, there were intersecting and multiple relations such as class, gender, race, age and nationality which overlapped in different combinations. By analytically separating them out I have necessarily simplified their complex interaction in practice. There is little likelihood that any researcher will perfectly reflect a group under study, unless it is a very specific subsection of a social grouping, or if the research is conducted by that group themselves (that is, a different kind of ethnography altogether). Instead, researchers must actively utilise the idea that neither themselves nor their subjects are homogeneous beings and instead social relations of difference must be recognised and used to structure their interaction with the group under study. It is precisely these relations of difference that produce varied readings of social groups, which should be used not to combat objectivity in research, but rather be utilised to explore the possibilities of different kinds of knowledge being produced, by whom and under what conditions.

These points are particularly pertinent when researching youth in particular. For instance, with the possible exception of young graduate students conducting PhDs on youth, it is surely the case that youth studies is an increasingly greying profession. In other words, those academics who continue to research youth issues have to be particularly aware of how generational and age differences impact on their approaches and fieldwork practices. At the same time, as many writers in the field have pointed out, youth is fairly unique in that it invariably is cross-cut by a range of social relations and divisions including social class, gender, race and sexual orientation (Griffin, 1993; Miles, 2000). This also means that youth researchers have to remain aware of the diversity of youth populations, and recognise how such internal divisions influence and structure both their fieldwork and their theoretical orientation. Finally, because youth is highly susceptible to bouts of 'moral panics' and various social problem paradigms, it is equally crucial that youth researchers are extremely careful how they chose to 'represent' their subjects and ethnographic findings.

This latter point become more focused when we begin to relate the politics and social relations of fieldwork to what has been coined a 'crisis of representation' in the cultural field (Marcus and Fisher, 1986). What implications does this have for my own work and others attempting to undertake critical ethnographic practice with young people? One crucial issue is how does one represent a social grouping like youth and explore the social relations of fieldwork all at the same time? It is often difficult enough trying to write up our subject's accounts and our interpretation of them. Ethnographic research methods make it difficult to let go of a naturalistic style and the tendency to invoke a kind of authenticity. This, however does not mean that there is nothing researchers can do. Writing and presenting papers on method or attaching a methodological appendix to books and theses is a start, even if it is a fairly standardised procedure these days. Of more consequence will be the development of methods and forms of representation whereby youth researchers can make themselves and their characteristics, activities and actions more visible in their work and in the text. Similarly, researchers could begin to experiment with opening research project up to subjects, by having them define issues, conduct interviews with fellow subjects or set up joint studies. Some researchers have placed their subject's accounts alongside of their own ethnographic interpretations or played with narrative structures to break down the naturalistic tendency of participant observation methods and interview data. Of course none of these developments, in and of themselves, address the real problem surrounding a wider politics of research and representation. The main issue is the way in which the current intellectual division of labour is organised in our contemporary society. If we are all to be 'intellectuals', in the truly Gramscian sense, then we need a system whereby all have equal access to the production and consumption of knowledge forms, including the young people we study and learn so much from.

10
Researching Young People as Consumers: Can and Should We Ask Them Why?

Steven Miles

We live at a time when the role of young people as consumers is apparently crucial to who it is they are. Social scientists and journalists are equally prone to speculate as to what it means to be a young person, and how being a young person is somehow symbolic of what it means to be at the cutting edge of social change. In this context, the question of consumption at least *appears* to be fundamental to young people's lives at the beginning of the twenty-first century. In this chapter, I want to argue that consumption does indeed play a key role in young people's lives, but not simply as a mode of self-expression or escape. An understanding of young people's experience as consumers may indeed give youth researchers a unique insight into what it actually means to be a young person at a time of apparently rapid social change. In what follows, I will suggest that young people's experience of consumption and their engagement with consumer culture presents the youth researcher with a particular set of challenges. If those challenges can be met, the benefits for youth research are potentially enormous.

I have long argued that the sociology of youth and youth research, more generally, is hamstrung by its inability to adequately conceptualise or indeed research young people's lives (Miles, 2000). The challenge of researching young people's lives as consumers lies in the fact that consumption says as much about their experience of structural constraints as it does about their cultural freedom or lack of it. But sadly, the multi-dimensional nature of this phenomenon represents unfamiliar territory for the sociology of youth. Most damagingly, the sociology of youth is characterised by a divide: a divide between those researchers interested in structural aspects of youth such as employment, education and youth training, and those concerned with the more cultural elements of young people's lives. It may seem an obvious point to make, but neither of these concerns are independent of each other. The structural impact reflects upon the cultural and *vice versa*. It is certainly true to say that a gulf exists between cultural and structural aspects of young people's lives. But that gulf exists in the minds and methods of social scientists, rather than in the lives of young people themselves.

Over the past 20 years, an orthodoxy has emerged in the sociology of youth in which structural constraints on young people's lives are prioritised. The sociological agenda has therefore largely been set by those sociologists interested in youth unemployment, housing, training and suchlike (for example, Coles, 1995; Roberts, 1995; Furlong and Cartmel, 1997). At the other end of the spectrum, many youth researchers are concerned with questions of sub-cultural style (for example, Muggleton, 2000), clubbing cultures (for example, Thornton, 1995) and music (for example, Bennett, 2000). But it's very rare for these two 'camps' to interact in any meaningful way. In fact, they tend on the whole, to treat each other with no little suspicion. The structural camp tend to see the cultural as too journalistic for their liking, whereas those undertaking more cultural work, tend to object to the rather structure-down nature of the work of their counterparts. The implication of this division of labour is that it is relatively easy to divide up young people's lives into discrete elements. In other words, the implication is that what young people do as consumers has nothing to do with their experience of broader structural influences on their lives. This is quite clearly not the case: young people's experience of consumption is an active expression of their broader structural experience. The degree to which they can consume is, for a start, dependant upon whether the circumstances in which they find themselves allow them to consume. For instance, a lack of resources may create a situation in which young people are under intense pressure to consume in particular ways, but in which they are simply unable to do so. The problem here is that while the structural approach tends to draw a picture of young people as vulnerable victims subject to the ups and downs of a market economy, the cultural approach all too often venerates young people as powerful consumers of music, fashion and sub-cultural life. The 'truth' lies somewhere in between; but the 'truth' is simply not accessible as long as the artificial divide outlined above persists, and as long as it continues to problematise young people in a way that does not adequately reflect the active and complex ways in which young people relate to the aspects of social change.

The current state of youth research as represented by the recent ESRC programme, 'Youth Citizenship and Social Change' which operates largely at one end of the spectrum discussed above, illustrates the problem here. Although the programme is committed to providing a holistic approach to young people's lives and despite some commendable and at times path-breaking research, the vision it presents of young people is one of a social group that *reacts* to social change. In other words, however unwittingly, young people are not portrayed as active players in the social world. It is, of course, natural to address the experience of young people from a problem-oriented point of view. The programme does exactly that with projects which look at broad range of issues including the 'underclass', drug use, young fathers and the vulnerabilities experienced by young deaf people. But all these projects seem to be concerned with the difficulties young people experience and how they react in specific contexts to those difficulties. Above all, they concentrate on young people's reactions to structural constraints on their lives. They are not so concerned with the cultural manifestation of such constraints. And yet, the whole point about young people is that their everyday experience is about balancing structural demands and doing so in cultural contexts. A lack of employment opportunities is not experienced solely as unemployment, but also has implications for the cultural capital that a young person may bring to his or her peer group. As far as a young person is concerned, the lack of resources they may be able to call upon might well constitute the most significant impact of unemployment upon their everyday lives at any given point in time. I have argued elsewhere that consumerism, in the above sense, represents a bridge between structure and agency (Miles, 1998). It is not simply an arena in which young people hedonistically indulge in trivial cultural practices. Rather, it represents an active reflection of how young people engage with what for them, can be, at least potentially a very traumatic life experience. This point is crucial insofar as it reflects the complexities associated with young people's consumption patterns and the fact that consumption isn't simply about consuming a service or product, but is actually about the sense of imagination and meaning that a young person invests in that process.

Consumerism is ideological in the sense that it both permeates every aspect of young people's social lives and insofar as we as consumers accept consumerism as a natural state of affairs. Any challenges to consumerism as a principle of social organisation, such as the anti-capitalist movement in which many young people are heavily involved, are largely peripheral in the sense that they have a limited impact upon the status quo. This is inevitable because we as consumers have, or at least think we have too much to gain from consumerism. Consumerism is perceived to be democratic, freedom-inducing and positive. Consumption is good because our society deems it to be so. Young people's consumption is particularly liable to be quoted as evidence of young people finding their adult feet and perhaps of them constructing their identities. In this light, consumption provides a resource; a realm within which young people can be themselves. If consumption is so ideologically loaded, how is it possible to research young people's experience of consumption? That research can arguably only be partial in nature. Young people themselves arguably do not know why they consume and why it is that consumption is or, indeed, isn't so important to them.

Given the ideological dimension of consumption, the developed world tends to treat consumer goods with a certain awe and reverence. By implication, the direct empirical study of consumption is one sacred step too far. If consumerism takes on what is almost a religious-like quality, what right do we have to critically examine it? Debates over post-modernism in particular have not only increased the sociological profile of consumption, but they have also, ironically, undermined the credibility of researching that topic in empirical settings. Langman (1992) identifies the move towards an 'amusement society', where everyday life actively offers the opportunity to interpret and contest meanings as one sees fit. Selfhood then represents a balance between spheres of domination and empowerment. Young people are apparently dominated by the hegemonic inclinations of mass-mediated popular culture and yet individually empowered by the very goods and cultural productions that serve to sustain the legitimacy of such domination. Shopping, as Shields (1992) also suggests, represents a form of solidarity, far from having a purely functional role. The shopping mall is essentially a public space where consumers can fulfil the communal needs that are not satisfied in other aspects of their lives. No attempt is made to validate this against the actual meaning that shopping malls have for the consumer. The 'loose' value-free theorising of post-modern discourse, therefore, underpins what amounts to a very generalised and unsubstantiated approach to the culture of consumption. Yet, this sort of lackadaisical approach to the role of consumption in contemporary society is justified by the philosophical foundations underpinning post-modernism which claim that there is no 'absolute truth' about such matters, only 'representations', thereby rendering empirical work redundant (Lash, 1990): we should not research the impact of consumer society on consumer's lives, because we can only aspire to an opinion or a perspective of an issue, rather than an authoritative account of that issue. The debate over the impact of consumption on contemporary society has therefore tended to operate on an abstract level, and as a result there seems to be assumption that consumption *must* be important. Good empirical examinations of young people's consumption are, at least partly, as a result of this process few and far between. But in actual fact, if we are prepared to critically engage with the meanings with which young people consume, if we are prepared to put ourselves out on a limb with our research, insofar as we conduct it in a critical, reflexive and differentiated fashion, then our understanding of young people's consumption may well tell us more than we might imagine about what it actually *means* to be a young person. The Economic and Social Research Council's introduction of a new research programme into Cultures of Consumption is a recognition of that fact. The consumer is in many senses a mystical being. Our society gives the consumer an unprecedented status. To consume is to belong; to consume is to justify yourself as a citizen of a contemporary society (Urry, 1990). Consumption is so important to young people precisely because their abiding concern is to belong to that society, and consumerism represents the primary means of doing so.

It is absolutely essential that any understanding of young people as consumers, pays particular attention to the broader structural processes which influence young people's lives. There is a strong argument to suggest that young people are living in a world that is increasingly individualised, and that consumption plays a role in their managing the experience of individualisation. In discussing the emergence of a so-called risk society, many authors have indicated that people of all ages are living in increasingly uncertain times. The early promises of modernity have apparently failed to materialise and we now live in a society that is pre-occupied with controlling risk (as opposed to pursuing progress) at both an environmental and a personal level.

> All of these changes are seen as contributing to a particular way of understanding the self and the world that differs dramatically from earlier eras. For the individual, it is argued, these changes are associated with an intensifying sense of uncertainty, complexity, ambivalence and disorder, a growing distrust of social institutions and traditional authorities and an increasing awareness of the threats inherent in everyday life (Lupton, 1999, pp. 11–12).

Human beings seem to be desperately trying to control the uncertainties that surround them, whilst simultaneously conceding the fact that such forces are in actual fact beyond their control. Thus, authors such as Frank Furedi (1997) talk about the existence of a 'culture of fear', insofar as though people live longer, and are healthier and wealthier than they may have been in the past, such advances have come at a cost and the social, economic and scientific advances which made these developments possible have actually created new and, in actual fact, bigger problems and fears. This apparently creates a distinctly inhuman environment in which human beings are having to learn to constrain themselves and their actions: an environment in which human beings are increasingly passive. Indeed, 'in a world awash with conditions and impending catastrophes, he or she is doing a job by just surviving' (Furedi, 1997, p. 12). The world has changed at such a dramatic rate and the global forces at work in ensuring such change are so far beyond individual comprehension, that both the present and the future have become scary, and stress-inducing possibilities manifest beyond the realms of human control.

For Beck (1992), a risk society creates a world in which the individual is less constrained by social structures and yet ironically, more constrained by his or her private whims. Despite processes of individualisation, human beings are increasingly subject to external forces, and arguably standardisation.

Young people may well feel the effects of the above changes, notably in the context of globalisation, more so than no other social group. In a world where traditional forms of social support appear to have broken down, Furlong and Cartmel argue that young people are facing a greater diversity of risks and opportunities than ever before. Family, work and school provide more unpredictable and less secure environments than they would have done in the past, and journeys into adulthood are therefore becoming increasingly precarious: 'Moreover, because there are a much greater range of pathways to choose from, young people may develop the impression that their own route is unique and that the risks they face are to be overcome as individuals rather than as members of a collectivity' (1997, p. 7). The irony of social change is that despite young people appearing to be at the forefront of such change in terms of maximising the advantages to be had in the communications and technology revolution, below the surface they are having to cope with all sorts of unprecedented tensions.

The question I am concerned with is how is it that young people actually cope with the above tensions? The suggestion I want to make in this regard is that consumption provides the arena within which young people play out the ups and downs of the more structural aspects of their lives. In effect, as Robins (1994, p. 455) argues: 'We must acknowledge how much consumption is linked to the protection of the emotional and bodily self.' Young people's patterns of consumption are not simply trivial, but provide youth researchers with a means by which they can actively begin to understand how young people engage with aspects of social change on a daily basis. This is a key point. By recognising consumption is more than simply a past-time, it should be possible to move away from a conception of young people as victims and towards an alternative model in which young people engage with the structural conditions that inevitably impinge upon their sense of freedom. In this sense, I am arguing that consumption represents what Holland (1977) describes as a mediation phenomena. What he means is that there are certain issues or concerns that have the potential benefit of filling the gaps between disciplines. Consumption provides such a possibility insofar as it represents the arena within which the individual negotiates the structural. What is important, in this respect, as Csikszentmihalyi and Rochberg-Halton (1981) note, is that consumer goods are not simply tools for making life easier or more comfortable. They actively embody personal goals and arguably reflect cultural identities. The material environment is not neutral, as such, but provides symbolic meanings which, arguably, go some way to giving order and purpose to our everyday lives. Consumption is an important focus for social scientific research, most especially because it engenders a variety of psychological, as well sociological, concerns. Yet as a direct result of the complexity of its psychological and sociological impact in cultural contexts, this focus has been lost amidst the vagaries of disciplinary tradition (see Archibald, 1976). Yet in the present circumstances as Csikszentmihalyi and Rochberg-Halton argued as early as 1981, 'despite the importance of objects, little is known about the reasons for attachment to them, about the ways in which they become incorporated in the goals and in the actual experiences of persons' (1981, p. x).

If we accept that young people's relationship with consumer culture is significant in the way I have outlined above, it is absolutely essential that youth researchers take the necessary steps to re-evaluate what they actually mean by 'youth', which at the moment constitutes little more than an imprecise and indeterminate label. Discussions of youth transitions imply that being a young person is about reaching or aspiring to a state of adulthood. I want to suggest here that youth is actually about aspiring to or at least maintaining an age of childhood. That being a young person is not distinguished by people of a particular age trying to be adults (as it may appear from the outside); but rather by people of a particular age trying to maintain some sense of stability, in a sense to offset the oncoming inevitability of adulthood. What I am trying to say here is that youth researchers tend to impose an adultist agenda on youth research. Living in an adult world, they are blinkered from the mundane realities of youth. Viewing youth from their critical problem-lead perspective, the assumption is that young people seek to reach a state of 'identity formation'. However much they might seek to deny it, youth researchers are all too often concerned with how young people reach a state of completion when actually, what young people are seeking to do is to offset the imposition of structure on their lives. Being young is about rejecting the paraphernalia of adulthood and not about aspiring to it.

Young people may aspire to the freedoms, and occasionally the responsibilities they associate with adulthood, but if youth is about anything it is about constructing a sense of self that is resigned to the fact that childhood is gone, but which simultaneously seeks to offset the inevitability of adulthood. In essence, youth is the purgatory of late modern life. It is a purgatory furnished by consumerism and all the partial freedoms a young person could ever want. In one sense, it is irrelevant whether or not young people can command the resources necessary to partake in this world. What matters is that they can imagine the world in which they live as a cocoon, in which they are in charge of their own destiny, and a life in which they are in control enough to make their choice of a new pair of trainers, apparently the most difficult decision they have to make.

Being young is about attempting to maintain the some sort of stability or equilibrium when everything around you appears to be changing. The opportunities young people have to consume provide young people with a certain degree of respite. Consumption is an ideal resource in this respect precisely because it is so transient. A good consumer is never satisfied and is always looking to or, indeed, imagining, the next opportunity to consume. Consumption in short is a malleable flexible resource within which young people can assert a sense of who they are. It is very important, however, that I do not give the impression that consumption provides young people with a *source* of identity. Rather, young people use consumption as a pro-active means of feeling they belong to a society which rarely makes them feel otherwise. By consuming particular styles of clothing, music and suchlike young people establish a sense of stability, however temporary in nature, in their lives. Their gender, ethnicity or class may well be far more significant factors in the construction of their identities; identities which are often expressed through forms of consumption. An unemployed young man may, for instance, display his working-class identity through his souped-up car, and his Burberry shirt and cap. A middle-class young woman may alternatively listen to NuMetal and wear long baggy jeans and a T-shirt indicating her allegiance to a particular band. These examples are in a sense stereotypical, but they demonstrate how young people use consumption as a resource which actively reflects their broader structural position. As such, young people no longer necessarily feel the need to wholeheartedly adopt the uniform of a particular all-embracing subculture. They rather interpret the subcultures available to them on an individual basis. Some will embrace the Burberry style, for instance, more wholeheartedly than others. But they are not controlled by such style, they use it as a language of stability. Perhaps the best example of how such language works is, of course, the mobile phone. Young people do not feel they are accepted as fully-fledged citizens of the society in which they live. The mobile phone provides a focus for a cultural world in which young people are at the cutting edge. Mobile conversations and text messaging constitute a form of consumption that put young people in charge. It is in this respect they constitute a highly visible means of expressing the fact that more generally young people are not given the respect they might feel they deserve.

In order to establish some of the broader benefits of looking into young people's relationship with consumption, it might be useful at this stage to discuss some examples of research in the area. A good place to start might well be Jones and Martin's (1999) discussion of the young consumer at home. Jones and Martin point out that due to an extended period of education and training, young people are becoming increasingly economically dependant on their parents. They therefore go on to comment, and rightly so, that the flirtation with post-modernism failed to recognise the role of consumption as a source of exclusion. Indeed, from this point of view, young people have been so socialised into 'commitment to the mainstream values of consumerist accumulation that even the long term jobless are locked into consumer markets' (Jones and Martin, 1999, p. 18). In this context, it is suggested that 'consumer citizenship' provides young people with a sense that they belong when their rights as citizens are so clearly threatened in other arenas of social life. In addressing these issues, Jones and Martin looked at the Family Expenditure Survey and as such they acknowledge the fact that a secondary piece of research of this kind can only tell us so much about the role of consumption in young people's lives. Indeed, they point out that young people's experience of consumption is multi-faceted. For instance, those young people living in transitional or non-familial homes may use consumption as a means of asserting their independence from their parents, while expenditure on leisure and lifestyle may present them with one means of coping with material deprivation in the home. Meanwhile, for young people living at 'home', the opportunity to consume may equally provide them with an avenue through which they can display the fact they are emancipated from their parents (even, if they, in fact, are not). Perhaps most importantly, Jones and Martin caution against the dangers inherent in assuming that evidence of conspicuous consumption can be taken to indicate a degree of wealth. Indeed, there is a growing wealth divide among young people. Some may be using short-term consumption strategies to cope with their lack of power in other spheres of their lives, but this does not make them "consumer citizens", with real economic power in the consumer markets' (1999, p. 39). As such, it is absolutely essential that the measures we use to research young people's consumption patterns and the impact of consumption upon their lives are multi-dimensional. This reflects an overriding concern that sociologists of consumption tend to generalise about the nature of young people's experience of consumption, whilst considering it in isolation from other equally significant aspects of young people's lives.

We live in a consumer society and we assume young people are in the best position to benefit from the opportunities that that society provides. As such, it is very easy to exaggerate the agentic possibilities of cultural consumption (see, for example, Willis, 1990). Young people clearly cannot consume entirely freely. The parameters in which they consume are, at least in one sense, decided for them, both by the producers and according to the degree of access they have to resources. Another common mistake amongst sociologists interested in the impact of consumption upon young people's lives is to generalise on a geographical level. For that reason, Merry White's (1994) comparative work on teenage consumption in Japan and America is of particular interest. White argues that becoming a consumer is a key aspect of growing up in both societies. In this context, her argument is that the relationship between consumer marketing and a teenage audience is an interactive one. However, in the Japanese case, a common peer culture is highly influential to the extent that in any one season a single style is likely to be dominant for a particular age group, simply because Japanese teenagers choose their styles in unison. Young people in the United States meanwhile, according to White, have more segmented taste and in contrast to the Japanese example, that segmentation is positively encouraged by marketers. In short, the teenage market in Japan reinforces tendencies to conform on a national scale; whereas in the United States the market reinforces differences. Cultural variations in the ways in which young people consume are clearly significant. White, for instance, discusses the phenomenon of young teenage girls in Japan who travel around in trains for the sole purpose of seeing what fashions are new and how these fashions are interpreted by fellow teenagers. Similarly, White quotes one of her Japanese respondents who has also lived in the United States: 'While in America people enjoy dressing with individuality, adapting styles to their own tastes, and calling attention to themselves, in Japan it is a bad thing to stand out from the crowd: you just stick out like a sore thumb' (1994, p. 131). In this context, it is very important that any assumptions made about the role of consumption in young people's lives are based upon empirical data, and that that data and the research tools used to collect that data are of a sophisticated nature, for reasons I will go on to discuss in due course.

One particularly interesting piece of research on young people's experience of consumption in localised settings is that undertaken by Chatterton and Hollands (2001) who look at youth, nightlife and urban change in Newcastle. Chatterton and Hollands argue that in recent decades, there has emerged evidence to suggest that young people are reacting against the constraints of the work ethic and are adopting more childlike patterns of behaviour due to a dissatisfaction with adult values and, indeed, as a means of escape from the risks associated with that adult world. In this context, the argument here is that nightlife plays a particularly significant role amongst those 'post-adolescents' experiencing the ups and downs of extended youth. They argue that the clubbing scene has become more sophisticated and responsive to what young consumers want, not least in the guise of an increasingly vibrant bar culture, which provides grounds for suggesting that young people's nightlife is more diverse and experimental than it was in the past, with the city centre of Newcastle providing a highly segmented and socially divided space reflecting a wide range of consumer preferences and tastes. In this light, Chatterton and Hollands (2001, p. 127) discuss the emergence of the post-modern 'social chameleon' who plays with his or her night-time identities as a means of escaping from the humdrum realities of the day-time:

> Going out in the 'toon' is often about becoming someone else, playing at someone you're not (through clothes, style, demeanour), or more simply just getting out of yourself (through drugs or alcohol) if only for an evening. In Newcastle, in particular, there is much

evidence of extended transitions of adolescence and a refusal to 'grow up' and accept some of the social and economic realities facing many young people in the North East. However, most people are acutely aware of the limitations of this individualist hedonism and its ability to bring about actual economic and social transformation of the self.

From this point of view, young people appear to be pursuing partial individualistic solutions to broader collectivist problems of social exclusion. Traditional social divisions may still be dominant, but at least consumption offers something of a way out. From a research point of view, Chatterton and Hollands were able to tap into the diverse nature of young people's consumption of nightlife precisely because they adopted the sort of multi-dimensional approach to their subject matter advocated by Jones and Martin (1999). As well as outlining a map of the changing configuration of nightlife 'production' in Newcastle, the authors also interviewed club managers, promoters, doormen, councillors and, most importantly, a diverse range of young people in order to get a rounded and contextualised understanding of the changing nature of youth nightlife consumption. But what is particularly effective about their work is the way in which they relate such changes to the broader pressures and structural constraints that exist in young people's lives. They note that any changes in the nature of young people's consumption habits reflect broader structural changes in what it actually means to be a young person.

What do the above examples tell us about how researchers should engage with young people's lives as consumers? The word 'engage' is important here. The above pieces of research illustrate the benefits to be had from a more grounded approach to young people's consumer lifestyles. As such, in this chapter I am advocating a move away from the more general pre-disposition for youth researchers to problematise young people. Because we conceive of the transition as something that a young person aspires to and 'achieves', youth researchers often neglect the experiential (and indeed experimental) nature of youth in favour of a structural goal-led perspective. This state of affairs is intensified by a situation in which youth researchers are obliged, perhaps justifiably, to pursue a policy agenda. Funders of research are only satisfied, perhaps understandably, if the research has clear policy relevance and benefits to end-users. Each of the three pieces of research I have discussed above tells us important things about young people's lives and the ways in which they seek to cope with the ups and downs of social change as expressed during the course of everyday life. But the significance that a more cultural perspective allows the youth researcher to create a set of circumstances which actively legislate against research with long-term goals, and promote a situation in which there is a genuine danger that similar kinds of research is reproduced year after year: research on youth 'transitions'. This creates a situation in which innovative kinds of research are actively discouraged and in which what on the surface appears to be research of a cultural bent (when in fact such research may adopt a cultural perspective as a more innovative and productive means of understanding aspects of young people's lives) gets pigeon-holed as such. The orthodoxy that therefore emerges is one in which the cultural dimensions of young people's lives – not least being their experience as consumers – are is not considered to be either policy-relevant or indeed worthy of funding.

I am not suggesting here that research should not by necessity, be policy relevant. But in the above circumstances, any researcher interested in young people's consumption patterns is obliged to work particularly hard to express the broader relevance of his or her work. Such work may well be more innovative and insightful than more traditional work on transitions, but unless a great leap of faith is taken by both researchers and funders alike in order to make the necessary investment in research that may appear to have less than immediate policy implications, its insights will never be fully realised and its successes will always be partial. In short, the suggestion here is that research into young people's needs has to be as flexible as young people's lives themselves.

It is crucial to the future of the sociology of youth that the sub-discipline persists from assuming that traditional methods and perspectives are sophisticated enough to cope with young people's ever-changing perspectives on life. Above all, this involves, as Jeffs and Smith (1998) note, closer attention to young people's actual experiences. Research needs to address young people's own meanings and therefore what Cohen and Ainley call 'local situated knowledge' constitutes a fundamental component of a reflexive youth research agenda. As such, it is essential that youth researchers are more prepared to take risks than they have in the past. In particular, as Macdonald (2001, pp. 232–3) puts it:

> We need to challenge the belief that our informants lack insight and awareness. We need to stop building these ideas into our research methods. And we need to stop overwriting their voices with our own. If we are able to produce accounts which we can actually learn from, accounts fleshed out and informed by insiders' lived meanings

and values, then we need to start granting them the ability and the opportunity to tell us their story.

It is all well and good to suggest that youth researchers take more risks in order to get to grips with aspects of young people's lives. But if 'taking risks' involves actively seeking to engage with the cultures through which young people conduct their everyday lives, a key concern here is the extent to which researchers are able to tap into the nature of youth experience, if as is quite possible, young people are not aware of the ramifications of that experience themselves. In the context of consumption, there is a particular concern that it simply is not possible to ask consumers how significant consumption is in their lives. Many sociologists of consumption are particularly fascinated by the role consumption plays in constructing young people's identities. Indeed, I myself have argued that consumption plays a key role in this respect, but as a vehicle upon which young people construct their identities as opposed to a source of identity in its own right. But how far is it possible for a researcher to tap into such issues? Can we ask consumers why they consume and the significance consumption plays in their lives? The problem here, as Marsh points out, is that human experience is not characterised solely by free will. There are all sorts of social structures and pressures acting on people's everyday lives. Indeed, as Marsh (1982, p. 100) points out, 'people may make history, they may exercise choice, but they cannot choose the conditions, the avenues of possibilities open to them'. In this respect, the work of Henry (1971) is important. Henry considers how far it is valid for marketers to ask consumers in a direct fashion about their motives for purchasing particular products. He argues, in fact, that the reasons consumers give for their actions tend to be post-hoc rationalisations: 'It is a human tendency for people to ascribe to the products they normally use, as to the countries, states or towns in which they live, any virtues which may be under discussion' (1971, p. 199). However, in arguing this point, Henry goes on to suggest that the word 'why' is multi-dimensional, and as such can cover consumer motivations induced by external factors, personal factors with a high level of generality, and more peculiarly unique personal factors. He argues, in particular, that this latter category of meaning is of no interest to the market researcher. However, it is precisely because consumer meanings express sociological, personal, yet generalisable *and* unique personal aspects of the individual's relationship to consumption that asking consumers why they purchase a good *is* a rich source of data for the sociologist. Henry (1971, p. 311) argues that, 'it is not possible to ascertain the motives which underlie an informant's behaviour by the simple process of asking him [sic]. He usually has no idea what his real motives are, and even when he has he is unable to assess them quantitatively.' The point here is that the needs of the market researcher or marketer are very different to those of the sociologist. My argument is that consumer meanings are an invaluable foundation upon which the significance of consumption in people's lives can begin to be assessed. As Marsh notes, actors do know a great deal about their own behaviour and we should not eschew their insights. Rather we need to treat those insights critically and with a pragmatic sense of circumspection. Ultimately, the pros to be gained by addressing personal meanings far outweigh the cons. As such, as Marsh (1982, p. 100) points out: 'The best sociological questions are those which aim to investigate the conscious, the subjective, the creative aspects of human action and to delimit the extent to which they are the key determinants of a given outcome.' It is therefore the responsibility of youth researchers to not only listen to what it is young consumers have to say, but also to contextualise such data as broadly and effectively as possible. In other words, it is not sufficient to simply interview young people about why and how they consume. Such data is only really useful if you consider it in relation to consumers' broader life experience. In a sense, then consumption is not worth studying simply for its own ends. To the question, 'Can we ask why' the answer can only be yes, but we cannot accept the answer uncritically. It can only inform our broader investigation.

The above investigation should take particular care to tap into peer group dynamics. As the above example from Japan so clearly illustrates, young people do not consume in isolation. In this respect, the freedom to consume is not a freedom at all for many young people. Rather it is the freedom to consume in the same ways as your peers. From a research perspective, it is therefore essential that the group dimension of consumption is incorporated into any such research project. Such an approach might incorporate group interviews or perhaps an observation of some kind. But it is absolutely essential that the researcher conceives of young people in a social and interactive context. What and how young people consume says something about them, but more importantly it says something about what it is they want to communicate to their peers. In effect, it is important for youth researchers to recognise the fact that young people's consumption patterns provide us with important data at a number of levels. At the very least such patterns inform us at the level of the individual, the immediate social group, the broader peer group, the age group, the level at which the media infiltrates young people's consumption patterns and it also tells us about how young people relate to the society at large. The single greatest failing of current youth research is its tendency to generalise. Young people come from a diverse range of backgrounds. Their relationship with consumer culture can vary enormously, not least according to class background and the opportunity or ability they have to access the necessary resources. In this respect, it is important to remember that a lack of opportunity to consume says as much about young people as the act of consumption itself. Having said that, the tendency to problematise young people should not encourage youth research researchers to fetishise working-class young people, whilst neglecting those from middle-class backgrounds.

Perhaps the key issue arising out of this chapter is that while young people's patterns of consumption are clearly experiential, so indeed, are young people's lives. The way in which young people consume is not always original or for that matter creative. As I argued above, young people engage with consumer cultures in ways that reflect the tensions they experience on a daily basis. Being a young person is not in any sense predictable. An approach to young people's lives that sees their experience as part of some kind of transition is far too inflexible to adequately comprehend the diverse range of meanings associated with youth. Youth is not a rite of passage, it is the right to live the moment and the latter is no more trivial than the former. The sooner youth researchers resist the temptation to pigeon-hole young people, the sooner they will begin to comprehend the pragmatic and at times rational ways with which young people cope with social change. The sooner youth researchers recognise the broader significance of young people's consumer lifestyles, the sooner we will recognise that young people's consumption patterns do not merely constitute a statement of escapist intent, but more importantly represent a graphic illustration of the sophisticated ways in which young people act in and react to them here and now.

11
The Use of 'Insider' Knowledge in Ethnographic Research on Contemporary Youth Music Scenes[1]

Andy Bennett

Following two decades of research on music and style-based youth cultures centred around narrative analysis, the 1990s saw a shift towards empirical work. This 'ethnographic turn' in youth and music research was in many ways a response to the predominantly theoretical accounts of previous work in which, as Stan Cohen (1987, p. iii) commented, 'the actors themselves just flitted across the screen'. At the same time, however, this interest in carrying out empirical work has also been motivated to some degree by the raw enthusiasm for the topic of the researchers themselves. Many of those pursuing field-based research on music-based youth cultures have backgrounds in those same youth cultural settings (see, for example, Malbon, 1999; Muggleton, 2000; Weinstein, 2000; Hodkinson, 2002), some retaining that connection and becoming, in effect, fan-researchers. As such, this new body of youth and music research generates its own epistemological problems. While, at one level, empirical studies have done much to address the absence of insider accounts for which earlier youth and music research has been criticised, little attempt has been made by researchers to critically assess how their own involvement in and/or tiedness to the subject of their work impacts on their research, both in terms of relations established with informants and nature of the data which is generated (Bennett, 2002). During the course of this chapter, I will critically evaluate the role and significance of insider knowledge in the research process and consider whether such knowledge serves as an advantage or an obstacle in the task of gathering social–scientifically informed fieldwork data on music-based youth cultures.

Pathways to research

A cursory look at contemporary studies of music and style-based youth cultures demonstrates that their starting point is very different from that of work conducted in this area during previous decades. Early studies of music and style-based subcultures, notably those conducted by the Birmingham Centre for Contemporary Cultural Studies (CCCS) (see Hall and Jefferson, 1976) and post-CCCS theorists such as Brake (1985), were largely guided by a discourse of cultural Marxism which argued that music, style and other aspects of popular culture had become resources in the struggle that underpins class relations in the capitalist society. This view was famously expounded by Clarke *et al.* (1976) in their notion of post-war youth subcultures as sites of working-class resistance. Moreover, according to the CCCS, the key to understanding and interpreting music and style as resources to be used in strategies of resistance came not through engaging with the accounts of youth stylists themselves but through theoretical abstraction. Such assumptions are rooted in the broader analytical approach of the CCCS cultural studies project. Thus, according to Hall (1980, p. 31)

> ... to think about or to analyse the complexity of the real, the act of practice of thinking is required; and this necessitates the use of the power of abstraction and analysis, the formation of concepts with which to cut into the complexity of the real, in order precisely to reveal and bring to light relationships and structures which cannot be visible to the naked eye, and which can neither present nor authenticate themselves.

More recent work on aspects of contemporary cultural life has challenged the assumptions implicit in the analytical approach of the CCCS and its debt to Gramscian cultural Marxism. Thus, it is argued, through its insistence on the groundedness of consumption practices in issues of hegemonic conflict between classes, such approaches overlook the potential for consumer reflexivity inherent in the act of consumption (Bennett, 1999). The widening availability of consumer goods in late modernity, it is argued, has given rise to new forms of consumer competence, with late modern individuals using their consumer choices in the construction of lifestyles (Chaney, 1996; Miles, 2000).

It is with this post-Marxist position that more recent studies of youth and music primarily engage; or perhaps it is more accurate to say that contemporary post-Marxist youth researchers relate more readily to the discourse of reflexive modernity (Giddens, 1990) associated with post-Marxist sociology. Thus, while music and style continue to be cast in a discourse of resistance and opposition by youth researchers, this is often interpreted at the level of micro-social, everyday struggles rather than an overarching theatre of class struggle (Clarke et al., 1976). Indeed, part of the objection to cultural-Marxist interpretations of youth on the part of younger youth researchers appears to emanate from their sense of having 'being there', of having experienced first hand the way in which musical and stylistic resources are taken up and used by young people in a highly complex system of resistant strategies and practices of negotiation in which youth itself has a high degree of reflexive involvement. This is evident, for example, in the introduction to Muggleton's (2000, p. 2) *Inside Subculture* where the author recalls his memory of reading Hebdige's (1979) seminal subcultural study *Subculture: The Meaning of Style* and relating his own experiences of being a punk to those described in the text:

> I fought my way through [the book]... and was left feeling that it had absolutely nothing to say about my life as I had once experienced it... The 'problem' lay not in myself and my failure to recognize what had ostensibly been the reality of my situation, but in the way the book appropriated its subject matter.

A similar view is expressed by Malbon (1999, p. 19), a dance music fan and clubber turned researcher, in relation to the CCCS's failure to empirically engage with the young people at the centre of its research:

> Resistance... was understood by the CCCS as the obvious reaction of young people to their social positioning. But were these rituals what the young people actually did, or were they representations of what the young people did as seen through the eyes of social scientists? Questions like these were rarely asked, let alone answered.

The collective solution to this omission of everyday youth cultural practice from academic discourse has been a turn to empirical work, in an attempt to understand how young people themselves '[construct] their identities as members of subcultures; and how they [construct] accounts of their relationship as members of subcultural groups to wider society' (Widdicombe and Wooffitt, 1995, p. 2).

The return of the native?

In turning to empirical work as a means of researching youth culture, many contemporary researchers have used their direct experience of and familiarity with particular youth cultural groups as 'a way in', that is to say, as a means of negotiating access to research settings, establishing field relations and collecting data. Indeed, several researchers have cited such pre-existing ties with their chosen research topic as a clear methodological advantage over researchers with no such connection. Thus, as Malbon (1999, p. 32) observes:

> ...my own background as a clubber was, I believe, crucial in establishing my credentials as someone who was both genuinely interested in and could readily empathise with [clubbers'] experiences rather than merely as someone who happened to be "doing a project" on nightclubs as his "job".

While there may indeed by certain advantages associated with the youth researcher's 'knowingness' of, interest in and genuine enthusiasm for the subject of his/her research, accounts concerning the effectiveness of such 'insider knowledge' remain largely circumspect and anecdotal. Moreover, there is little acknowledgement of the possible disadvantages of engaging in academic research on music and style-based youth cultures with an existing insider knowledge of the research topic. Indeed, ethnographers working in other areas of sociology have actively warned against, or at the very least, strongly questioned, the use of insider knowledge in the research process. Thus, as Whyte (1993, p. 371) observes in his landmark ethnographic study *Street Corner Society*: 'We may agree that no outsider can really know a given culture fully, but then we must ask can any insider know his or her culture.' Similarly, the degree to which insider knowledge facilitates acceptance in the field has also been questioned. For example, Armstrong (1993, p. 30), who used his links with the city of Sheffield and background as a Sheffield United football supporter as a means of gaining access to fans of the team, makes the following observation:

> There was certainly some ambiguity in my role. Because I was often out and about with the 'core' Blades[2] confusion over my true role could arise; one would joke when I was talking to him: 'Are we talking Blade to Blade? Which head have you got on, your journalist's or your hooligan's?'.

It seems reasonable to suggest that a similar ambiguity will pertain in the case of a former 'subculturalist' (Muggleton, 2000) who has 'stepped over the line' to become an academic researcher of youth, style and music and subsequently returns to the field to collect data. Thus, there is no guarantee that visual image and apparent 'knowingness' of particular musical genres and attendant 'subcultural' sensibilities will be sufficient to secure the researcher's acceptance into a particular youth cultural group. Questions may still be asked about the researcher's presence in the group and may also extend to the integrity of his/her claims to having a background in that youth cultural group.

Such problems of 'identity' may well be accentuated by the experience of the researcher him/herself. At the most fundamental level, anyone making the transition from youth cultural practitioner to academic researcher will go through a process of personal transformation, an inevitable part of the research training process (see Hobbs, 1993). This will involve an 'unlearning', or at least the objectification, of those 'taken for granted' attitudes and values which underpin the life of a committed youth stylist and music fan. Issues of musical and stylistic 'authenticity', which once seemed perfectly *natural*, will have been reappraised as 'constructs' based upon subjective reworkings of musical and stylistic resources in particular ways that suit the aesthetic values of particular youth cultural groups. Other factors may also play a part here, such as the researcher's modified attitudes towards the use of sexist and/or racist language or a desire to refrain from excessive consumption of alcohol or the use of drugs. Clearly, such factors will vary considerably depending on the personal outlook and professional ethic of the researcher. Nevertheless, they will, in some way, play a role in effecting a distance between the researcher and the researched, which even displays of 'subcultural capital' (Thornton, 1995) on the part of the researcher may well be unable to bridge.

Ethnography in 'cool places'

Quite apart from the issue of acceptance in the field, research on music and style-based youth cultures throws up a number of situational and contextual problems for the researcher which even those who intend using insider knowledge as 'a way in' may find problematic to deal with. A common point of departure for those involved in ethnographic work on music and style-based youth cultures are those places commonly frequented by young people, typically, dance clubs, concerts, bars or urban spaces appropriated by youth at certain times of the day or night.

A key advantage of conducting fieldwork in such 'youth spaces' is that it provides an opportunity to observe the research subjects in 'context'. At the same time, however, such spaces impose their own limits on the kinds of research which can be carried out there. Most importantly, the unwritten codes of the club or venue act to circumscribe the researcher's engagement with research subjects, the more unrestrained behaviour permitted in the club or venue and the emphasis upon enjoyment making one-to-one data gathering exercises inherently difficult to pursue.

This is particularly pronounced in dance club settings where the expectation that dancers have of 'losing themselves in the crowd' (Malbon, 1999) imposes a particular dynamic on the kinds of interaction which take place in the club. As a consequence, clubbers will feel far less inclined to try and communicate to a researcher what they will often perceive of as spontaneous displays of pleasure and emotion. The problems which this poses for the researcher are tellingly illustrated in the following account from Thornton (1995, p. 2):

> I was *working* in a cultural space in which everyone else (except the DJs, door and bar staff, and perhaps the odd journalist) were at their *leisure*. Not only did I have intents and purposes that were different to the crowd, but also for the most part I tried to maintain an analytical frame of mind that is truly anathema to the 'lose yourself' and 'let the rhythm take control' ethos of clubs and raves.

Although personal accounts of clubbing can be often acquired from informants in extra-club settings, such as cafes, bars or informants' homes, such accounts lack the direct phenomenological experience of the club, notably the heavily amplified pulse of the music resonating through the body, the collective motion of the crowd and the often exhilarating/disorientating effect of lighting and other special effects used to enhance the dance club atmosphere.

Similarly, the physical volume of the music performed by the DJ or band imposes its own restrictions, both on the ability of the researcher to converse with others in the club or venue and to overhear the conversations of others, a necessary, if not always acknowledged, aspect of the ethnographic process. This is undoubtedly why empirical studies which involve research in clubs and venues themselves tend to concentrate on the overall spectacle of the event (see, for example, Melechi, 1993; Fonarow, 1995). Herein, however, lies a central drawback with such studies as much of the rich subtext which accompanies the club cultural experience is lost. As Shumway (1992, p. 128) observes:

...in a club, the musicians may or may not be at the center of the audience's attention. Not only do patrons typically dance, but they usually eat, drink, and talk during the performance.

To Shumway's observations can be added a number of other 'extra-musical' (Bennett, 2000) activities engaged in by those who frequent music venues and dance clubs, including making new friends, finding a partner, getting to know important promoters, musicians and DJs, and 'swapping notes' about particular tracks and artists. In their own ways, each of these forms of participation in the music event add to the experience of those involved in such events and the significance they attach to the latter. Moreover, in ethnographic terms, such minutiae add significantly to the overall aim of achieving what Geertz (1973) refers to as rich description. As noted above, however, due to the practical methodological problems that apply to on-site club and venue research, this kind of rich detail is difficult to record in anything more than a relatively superficial and anecdotal fashion.

In a very real sense then, even those researchers with pre-formed insider knowledges of particular youth cultures and music scenes will be at a loss to penetrate certain layers of experience that characterise those settings in which youth cultural practice is performed. Clearly, researchers with insider knowledge of youth cultures and scenes may find ways of filling such gaps in their ethnographic narratives by applying their own experiences as a guide to the types of subtext which accompany the club experience. However, the question which then needs to be asked is to what extent the application of insider knowledge constitutes ethnography, or rather becomes 'a quasi-ethnographic research style' overlain with the researcher's own experiential narrative? (Chaney, 1994, p. 39).

Academic or populist?

In the case of those using their 'insider knowledge' of particular youth cultural groups, the problem of researching youth in context may well be exacerbated by the sense of unease experienced by researchers themselves when returning to settings they initially experienced as sites of leisure. Given this situation, researchers may well see it as an advantage to draw on their native knowledge and experience of those settings.

Having previously learned and adhered to the norms of club-cultural behaviour, these will readily suggest themselves to the researcher as a means of blending into the club setting. Indeed, the ability to engage in the clubbing experience in this way could be seen as a highly 'natural' form of participant observation. Clearly, however, if such 'native' conventions are to be used in this way in the pursuit of research, then it is important that they are effectively managed, that the researcher does not simply become so caught up in his/her experience that he/she assumes the role of 'subcultural' spokesperson. In recent years, the tendency of youth researchers to adopt this type of approach has resulted in a series of published studies which assume an overtly populist stance, for example, Richard and Krüger's (1998) account of the annual 'Love Parade' through the streets and Champion's (1997) study of the conflict between ravers and the local communities in Wisconsin.

Clearly, it is inevitable that where a level of individual investment in the subject of the research exists on the part of the researcher, he/she will often experience a confluence between 'personal and academic endeavours' (Green, 1993, p. 108). The issue of prior involvement with the research subject does not, however, in itself pose a problem. Indeed, it is now relatively taken for granted among researchers that the notion of 'objectivity' is itself an ideological construct and 'that data cannot be collected untainted by the hands of the researcher' (May, 1993, p. 75). More crucial here is the way in which the researcher manages his/her personal attachment to or ideological interest in the research matter. In the case of youth and music research, this problem is exacerbated due to the fact that those who retain a foot in each camp, being both youth cultural practitioners and researchers, often assume an authority to speak on behalf of those at the centre of the research. As I have noted elsewhere, missing from such accounts is any 'attempt...to assume a critical distance from the research setting and respondents, the descriptive authority of the researchers concerned becoming a one-dimensional voice which echoes the self-assumed "rightness" of the movement which each study seeks to describe' (Bennett, 2002, p. 457).

Rappert (1999, p. 715) has suggested that a key challenge for sociological research is the need to 'find a way of being reflexive without falling into conservativism'. In youth and music research, an equal danger is the risk of falling into what McGuigan (1992) describes as cultural populism, with academic writing on youth and music becoming little more than 'an uncritical celebration of mass culture which, like popular journalism, claims knowledge through an ability to identify with the "street level" sensibilities of particular scenes and audiences' (Bennett, 2002, p. 457).

Levels of performance

On-site research is not the only way in which ethnographers of music and style-based youth cultures collect data. In recent years, a wealth of data on contemporary youth cultural groups has been collected using a combination of various qualitative approaches, notably semi-structured interviews, focus groups and questionnaires (Malbon, 1999; Muggleton, 2000; Hodkinson, 2002). The issue of whether such methods of data gathering can be more effectively conducted by researchers who are similar in age and appearance to their informants remains unclear. What does seem clear, however, is that in using his/her personal knowledge of and/or competence in a particular form of youth cultural practice as a means of gaining the confidence of the informant, the researcher is forced into a new role characterised by a tension between personal attachment to the subject of the research and the need to generate data. Ultimately, the question which then arises is the extent to which the researcher remains an 'insider' or if, through the demands of the research process, the notion of being an insider is gradually eroded, the image and attendant sensibilities of the researcher becoming essentially a veneer, or what Goffman (1959) would term a 'presenting self'?

As ethnographic researchers openly concede, some level of deception is present in many types of ethnographic research (see, for example, Fountain, 1993), the most extreme cases being those where the researcher has undergone some form of visual transformation, including on occasion cosmetic surgery, in order to achieve an appearance commensurate with that of the research setting he or she hopes to enter. In many ways, however, the issue of deception in youth and music research carried out by the subculturalist-turned-researcher is different in kind to that experienced in social research on other areas of social life. To begin with, the researcher's outward appearance is ready-made rather than carefully nurtured to achieve the desired aim of blending in. Moreover, researchers who nurture an appearance generally do this with the aim of carrying out covert research. The youth and music researcher, on the other hand, will generally carry out overt research, the need for a covert approach being deemed unnecessary when a pre-existing continuity exists between the researcher's outward appearance and those who are to be studied. Indeed, such is the seamless transition that may be possible for the fan-researcher from the academic setting to the field, that he/she may feel no need to explain and account for themselves to the informants. This situation may be further reinforced by the raw enthusiasm often exhibited by those invited to take part in research on youth and music. Whereas researchers investigating more sensitive, personal or 'taboo' topics may need to invest considerable time in encouraging respondents to talk about their experiences, youth and music researchers generally find that respondents need little encouragement, especially when placed in the role of 'expert' or 'narrator'. This urge to surrender personal views and information to the researcher may be even more readily forthcoming when the researcher is perceived to be 'one of us'. Clearly, however, this aspect of youth and music research demands that even more attention is paid on the part of the researcher to ethical codes pertaining in the research process. Despite the personal ease that the researcher may feel in gaining acceptance in the field setting, he/she must ensure that the purpose of the research is fully explained to the research respondents, in order that they are able to make informed decisions on the nature and extent of the information they share with the researcher. Such a protocol should be observed even when it threatens to dampen the initial enthusiasm of research participants for the research project.

Insider knowledge as a method of research

Thus far, this chapter has examined a number of methodological issues associated with the use of insider knowledge as a means of gaining access to and conducting research on music and style-centred youth cultural groups. Issues so far discussed include the issue of insider knowledge and acceptance in the field, and the need for the researcher needs to manage his/her insider knowledge so that the ethics of conducting ethnographic research are not compromised. There is, however, another dimension to the use of insider knowledge in this type of work which warrants attention here. As noted earlier in this chapter, for a number of years research on music and style-based youth cultures assumed a 'top-down' perspective, the accounts of those involved in youth cultural groups at an everyday level being considered unnecessary to the task of unravelling the significance of youth culture as a late modern cultural form. More recent research, pursued by those with a more personal, 'hands on' investment in particular youth cultural groups, has taken issue with earlier researchers' apparent lack of concern with the social actors at the centre of their research. To this end, 'insider' knowledge has been promoted as a means of getting close to the research subjects and, thus, filling the empirical gaps apparent in previous research on youth culture. Contemporary research on youth culture is thus distinctively characterised by a level of commonality between the researcher and the researched. That is to say, ethnographic research in this field is 'co-produced' (Fountain, 1993) by researchers and informants whose leisure and lifestyle preferences are underpinned by a common stock of musicalised sensibilities. Given that this is the case, 'insider knowledge' may be the key to answering a series of questions which remain unanswered in the sociology of youth culture, relating to the role and significance of music in the mundane contexts of everyday life. In their attempts to provide overarching structuralist explanations of music and style, earlier studies of youth culture overlooked the micro-social, locally nuanced significance of musicalised life for young people. In an earlier study, I have noted the importance of going beyond structuralist accounts of music and focusing instead on music's significance for youth as a means of symbolically negotiating the everyday:

> The same music and style will often produce not one but a variety of responses on the part of young people to the particular local circumstances in which they find themselves, each response being underpinned by a common set of base knowledges relating to the local (Bennett, 2000, p. 67)

Youth researchers entering fieldwork settings with fully formed knowledges of particular musics and attendant discourses of fandom could effectively use this knowledge as a means of conducting a reflexive ethnography in which both the researcher and his/her respondents work through the processes via which music is transformed into a means of symbolically negotiating the everyday. At a theoretical level, justification for this type of approach in ethnographic work on youth and music is clearly established. The criticism of the CCCS and related approaches to the study of youth culture has led to a rejection of subcultural theory and its replacement by a series of theoretical frameworks which lay more emphasis on the significance of music as a reflexively used cultural resource. This, in turn has given rise to new terms of reference for music and style-based youth cultural groups, such as 'scene' (Straw, 1991), 'tribe' (Bennett, 1999) and 'taste culture' (Lewis, 1992). Although such new approaches have been criticised for their lack of consensus regarding the precise ways through which music functions as a means of collective expression for young people (see, for example, Hodkinson, 2004; Sweetman, 2004), at the very least they:

> ...allow for the greater heterogeneity now routinely identified with stylistically and/or musically demarcated groups. [Moreover these] new approaches [also] stress the significance of musical taste as one of a series of inter-related aesthetic values through which individuals both construct their own identities and identify with others who are seen to possess the same or similar values (Bennett, 2002, p. 462).

Problematically, while sociological research on youth and music has sought to understand and explain the significance of music in everyday life, the traditional tools of analysis it has conventionally relied on have produced explanations far removed from those young people for whom music 'matters' on a day-to-day basis. This problem of explanation is highlighted by Frith (1987, pp. 133–4, p. 144), who makes the following observation:

> There is no doubt that sociologists have tended to explain away pop music. In my own academic work I have examined how rock is produced and consumed, and have tried to place it ideologically, but there is no way that a reading of my books (or those of other sociologists) could be used to explain why some pop songs are good and others bad... how is it that people (myself included) can say, quite confidently, that some popular music is better than others?

Given Frith's comments, it is possible to see how an intimate knowledge, on the part of the researcher, of the aesthetic discourses used by members of particular youth cultures and scenes may be utilised both as a means of understanding the collective values attached by members of youth cultures to particular styles of music and encouraging them to talk about these on a biographical and introspective level. Cultural theorist Alasuutari (1995, p. 146) has suggested that a key concern for contemporary cultural studies 'is with things that people know about but of which they are not very conscious'. Another way of expressing this might be to say that individuals simply take those 'things', that they perceive as *natural*, for granted. The task for the youth and music researcher, then, becomes one of untapping this taken-for-grantedness as it applies to musical taste and attendant sensibilities of style at all levels. In her ethnographic research on uses of the Internet, Hine (2000, p. 10) suggests that: 'Conducting an ethnographic enquiry through the use of CMC [computer-mediated communication] opens up the possibility of gaining a reflexive understanding of what it is to be a part of the Internet.' In a similar way, through utilising their insider knowledges and attendant 'learned' discourses as an interpretive tool in the research process, youth researchers could begin to develop a more reflexive ethnographic understanding of what it means to be part of a particular scene. Using their experience and personal investment in particular musical and stylistic resources as a bridging device, researchers could encourage a more equal co-production of the fieldwork, with both the researcher and his subjects 'discover[ing] what is going on and the meaning of events and activities' that they collectively engage in as followers of particular musics and members of associated scenes (Fountain, 1993, p. 149).

Conclusion

This chapter has critically examined the use of 'insider' knowledge in research on contemporary music and style-based youth cultures. The first part of the chapter considered how theoretical accounts of youth culture, such as those published by the CCCS, have been succeeded by a more empirical approach where the emphasis has been upon the use of ethnography to engage with the accounts of youth cultural actors themselves. It was then noted how, in conducting ethnographic work, many youth researchers have relied upon their own knowledge and experience of particular youth cultural groups as a means of gaining access to these groups as objects of research. Consideration then turned to the issue of insider knowledge itself. With reference to accounts by ethnographers researching other areas of social life, it was argued that, even in the case of those with fully formed knowledges and experience of particular youth cultural groups, there is no guarantee that this alone will facilitate a ready acceptance on the part of research respondents. This was followed by an examination of some of the practical difficulties associated with researching 'youth spaces', which even those using 'insider' knowledge may find difficult to overcome. The next section of the chapter focused on the researcher him/herself. It was noted here that the researcher needs to manage his/her identity in the field, being open about his/her intentions in order that respondents are not deceived into providing information about themselves. Similarly, it was argued, caution needs to be taken on the part of the researcher to ensure that 'knowledge' does not equate with authority, that is, the authority to assume the role of 'subcultural spokesperson', thus falling into the trap of cultural populism. Finally, it was considered how insider knowledge might be productively used by the youth researcher as a means of engaging in a reflexive ethnographic approach in which respondents are encouraged to take a more interpretive role in explaining their values and actions, thus co-producing the fieldwork with the researcher.

Notes

1. Parts of this chapter are based on an article previously published in the *British Journal of Sociology* (see Bennett, 2002).
2. 'Blades' is the nickname given to fans of Sheffield United. The name originates from Sheffield's industrial history as a steel making town.

Bibliography

Acker, J., Berry, K. and Esseveld (1991) 'Objectivity and Truth: Problems in Doing Feminist Research', in M.M. Fonow and J.A. Cook (eds) *Beyond Methodology: Feminist Scholarship as Lived Research*. Bloomington and Indianapolis: Indiana University Press.

Ackeroyd, A. (1984) 'Ethics in Relation to Informants, the Profession and Governments', in R.F. Ellen (ed.) *Ethnographic Research: A Guide to General Conduct*. London: Academic Press.

Acland, C. (1995) *Youth, Murder, Spectacle – The Cultural Politics of Youth in Crisis*. Oxford: Westview.

Ainley, P. (1991) *Young People Leaving Home*. London: Cassell.

Ainley, P. and Rainbird, H. (eds) (1999) *Apprenticeship: Towards a New Paradigm of Learning*. London: Sage.

Alasuutari, P. (1995) *Researching Culture: Qualitative Method and Cultural Studies*. London: Sage.

Alford, F. (1989) *Melanie Klein and Critical Social Theory*. New Haven: Yale Press.

Allen, C. (2001) 'On the Social Consequences (and Social Conscience) of the 'Foyer Industry': A Critical Ethnography', *Journal of Youth Studies*, 4(4): 471–94.

Amit-Talal, V. and Wolf, H. (1995) *Youth Culture: A Cross National Perspective*. London: Routledge.

Anderson, M. (1983) *The Family*, Occasional Paper 31. London: OPCS.

Anderson, P. (1979) *Considerations on Western Marxism*. London: Verso.

Appadurai, A. (1998) *Modernities at Large*. Chicago: University of Chicago Press.

Archer, M. (1982) 'Morphogenesis Versus Structuration', *British Journal of Sociology*, 33(4): 455–83.

Archibald, W.P. (1976) 'Psychology, Sociology and Social Psychology: Bad Fences Make Bad Neighbours', *British Journal of Sociology*, 27(2): 115–29.

Armstrong, G. (1993) 'Like That Desmond Morris', in D. Hobbs and T. May (eds) *Interpreting the Field: Accounts of Ethnography*. Oxford: Clarendon Press.

Ashmore, M. (1989) *The Reflexive Thesis: Writing Sociology of Scientific Knowledge*. Chicago: University of Chicago Press.

Ashton, D. (1973) 'The Transition From School to Work: Notes on the Different Frames of Reference among Male Workers', *Sociological Review*, 21: 101–25.

Ashton, D. (1993) *The Vanishing Youth Labour Market*. London: Youth Aid.

Ashton, D.N., Maguire, M.G. and Spillsbury, M. (1989) *Re-Structuring the Labour Market: The Implications for Youth*. London: Macmillan.

Atkinson, P. (1990) *The Ethnographic Imagination*. London: Routledge.

Back, L. (1996) *New Ethnicities and Urban Youth Culture*. London: UCL Press.

Bakhtin, M. (1994) *The Bakhtin Reader*. London: Arnold.

Ball, S. (1998) 'Participant Observation with Pupils', in R. Burgess (ed.) *Strategies of Educational Research: Qualitative Methods*. Lewes: Falmer Press.

Ball, S. and Maguire, M. (2000) *Choice, Pathways and Transitions Post-16: New Youth, New Economies in the Global City*. London: Routledge.

Bibliography

Banks, M., Bates, I., Breakwell, G., Bynner, J., Emler, N., Jamieson, L. and Roberts, K. (1992) *Careers and Identities*. Milton Keynes: Open University Press.
Barber, T. (2001) 'Participation: Sowing the Seeds of Social Inclusion', *Scottish Youth Issues Journal*, 2: 89–104.
Barker, M. (1981) *The New Racism*. London: Junction Books.
Bartky, S.L. (1990) *Femininity and Domination: Studies in The Phenomenology Of Oppression*. London: Routledge.
Bates, I. (ed.) (1984) *Schooling for the Dole*. Basingstoke: Macmillan.
Bates, I. *et al.* (1984) *Schooling for the Dole? The New Vocationalism*. London: Macmillan.
Bates, I. and Riseborough, G. (1993) *Youth and Inequality*. Milton Keynes: Open University Press.
Bean, P. (1996) *Release Drugs and Dance Survey: An Insight into the Culture*. London: Release.
Beck, U., Giddens, A. and Lash, S. (1994) *Reflexive Modernisation*. Cambridge: Polity.
Beck, U. (1992) *Risk Society: Towards a New Modernity*. London: Sage.
Becker, H. (1971) *Sociological Work*. London: Allen Lane.
Becker, H.S., Greer, B., Hughes, E.C. and Strauss, A. (1961) *Boys in White*. Chicago: University of Chicago Press.
Bennett, T. (1994) 'Out in the Open: Reflections on the History and Practice of Cultural Studies', *Cultural Studies*, 10(1): 35–54.
Bennett, A. (1999) 'Subcultures or Neo-Tribes? Rethinking the Relationship Between Youth, Style and Musical Taste', *Sociology*, 33(3): 599–617.
Bennett, A. (2000) *Popular Music and Youth Culture: Music, Identity and Place*. Basingstoke: Macmillan.
Bennett, A. (2002) 'Researching Youth Culture and Popular Music: A Methodological Critique', *British Journal of Sociology*, 53(3): 451–66.
Bernstein, B. (1974) *Towards a Theory of Educational Transmissions, Vol. 3*. London: Routledge.
Bernstein, R. (1976) *The Restructuring of Social and Political Theory*. Penn: Pennsylvania Press.
Bernstein, B. (1996) *Pedagogy, Symbolic Control and Identity*. London: Taylor and Francis.
Bilson, A. and Barker, R. (1995) 'Parental Contact with Children Fostered and in Residential Care After the Children Act 1989', *British Journal of Social Work*, 25: 367–81.
Black, L. (2003) *The Political Culture of the Left in Britain*. Basingstoke: Palgrave.
Blackman, S. (1995) *Youth: Positions and Oppositions: Style, Sexuality and Schooling*. Aldershot: Avebury.
Blackman, S. (1998) 'The School: Poxy Cupid! An Ethnographic and Feminist Account of a Resistant Female Youth Culture: The New Wave Girls', in T. Skelton and G. Valentine (eds) *Cool Places*. London: Routledge.
Blackstone, T., Gales, K., Hadley, R. and Lewis, W. (1970) *Students in Conflict: LSE in 1967*. London: Weidenfeld and Nicolson.
Blair, T. (1993) Extract of speech given by Tony Blair MP to Wellingborough Constituency Party, 3 March, New Release, The Labour Party, 150 Walworth Road, London, in Heron and Dwyer op. cit.

Bibliography 203

Blair, T. (1998) *The Third Way*. London: Fabian Society.
Blundell, V., Shepherd, J. and Taylor, I. (eds) (1993) *Relocating Cultural Studies: Developments in Theory and Research*. London: Routledge.
Bordo, S. (1993) *Unbearable Weight: Feminism, Western Culture and the Body*. Berkeley: University of California Press.
Bourdieu, P. and Passeron, J.C. (1977) *Reproduction in Education Society and Culture*. London: Sage.
Bourdieu, P. (1984) *Distinction: A Social Critique of the Judgement of Taste*. Cambridge, Mass: Harvard University Press.
Bowles, S. and Gintis, H. (1976) *Schooling in Capitalist America*. London: Routledge.
Brah, A. (1996) *Cartographies of Diaspora: Contesting Identities*. London: Routledge.
Brake, M. (1980) *Sociology of Youth*. London: Routledge.
Brake, M. (1985) *Comparative Youth Culture: The Sociology of Youth Cultures and Youth Subcultures in America, Britain and Canada*. London: Routledge and Kegan Paul.
Brannen, K. and Smyth, E. (2000) 'Issues in Constructing a Comparative Database from National Transition Surveys', paper presented to the International Workshop on Comparative Data on Education-to-Work Transitions, Paris, June 2000.
Brauns, H., Gangl, M. and Scherer, S. (2001) 'Education and Employment: Patterns of Labour Market Entry in France, the United Kingdom and West Germany', Working Paper. Mannheim: University of Mannheim.
Bray, R. (1980) *Boy Labour and Apprenticeship*. London: Garland.
Breen, R. (1991) *Education, Employment and Training in the Youth Labour Market*. ESRI.
Brice Heath, S. (1983) *Ways with Words*. Cambridge: Cambridge University Press.
British Crime Survey (1984) London: HMSO.
British Crime Survey (1994) Home Office: Crime and Criminal Justice unit.
Brown, P. (1987) *Schooling Ordinary Kids: Inequality, Unemployment and the New Vocationalism*. London: Tavistock.
Brown, D. and Peddar, J. (1991) *An Introduction to Psychotherapy: An Outline of Psychodynamic Principles and Practice*. London: Routledge.
Buckingham, D. (1994) *Reading Audiences: Young People and the Media*. Manchester: Manchester University Press.
Burchell, B.L., Day, D., Hudson, M., Lapido, D., Mankelow, R., Nolan, J.P., Reed, I., Wichert, C. and Wilkinson, F. (1999) *Job Insecurity and Work Intensification*. York: Joseph Rowntree Foundation.
Burgess, R.G. (1985) 'Issues and Problems in Educational Research: An Introduction', in R.G. Burgess (ed.) *Issues in Educational Research: Qualitative Methods*. London: The Falmer Press.
Burr, V. (1995) *An Introduction to Social Constructionism*. London: Routledge.
Butcher, M. and Thomas, M. (2001) 'Generate: The Popular Culture of Middle Eastern and Asian Youth in Western Sydney', paper presented at the BSA Youth Study Group Conference, *Global Youth? Young People in the 21st Century Conference*, University of Plymouth, 3–5 September.
Bynner, J. (1997) 'A New Agenda for Youth Research', in J. Bynner, L. Chisholm, and A. Furlong (eds) *Youth, Citizenship and Social Change in a European Context*. Aldershot: Ashgate.
Bynner, J. (1998) 'Youth in the Information Society: Problems, Prospects and Research Directions', *Journal of Education Policy*, 13(3): 433–42.
Bynner, J. (2001) 'British Youth Transitions in Comparative Perspective', *Journal of Youth Studies*, 4(1): 5–24.

Bynner, J. and Ashford, S. (1992) 'Teenage Careers and Leisure Lives: An Analysis of Lifestyles', *Society and Leisure*, 15: 499–519.
Bynner, J. and Roberts, K. (eds) (1991) *Youth and Work: Transition to Employment in England and Germany*. London: Anglo-German Foundation.
Bynner, J., Chisholm, L. and Furlong, A. (eds) (1997a) *Youth, Citizenship and Social Change in a European Context*. Aldershot: Ashgate.
Bynner, J., Ferri, E. and Shepherd, P. (eds) (1997b) *Twenty-Something in the 1990s*. Aldershot: Ashgate.
Cabinet Office (1998) *Tackling Drugs to Build a Better Britain: The Government's 10-Year Strategy for Tackling Drug Misuse*. London: Stationery Office.
Calcutt, A. (1998) *Arrested Development: Pop Culture and the Erosion of Adulthood*. Basingstoke: Macmillan.
Calvey, D. (2000) 'Getting on the Door and Staying there: A Covert Participant Observational Study of Bouncers', in G. Lee-Treweek and S. Linkogle (eds) *Danger in the Field*. London: Routledge.
Cameron, C., Lush, A. and Meara, G. (1943) *Disinherited Youth*. Edinburgh: Carnegie Trust.
Campbell, N. (2000) *The Radiant Hour: Versions of Youth in American Culture*. Exter: Exeter University Press.
Cantelon, H. and Hollands, R. (eds) (1988) *Leisure, Sport and Working Class Cultures: Theory and History*. Toronto: Garamond Press.
Carrington, B. and Wilson (2002) 'Global Club Cultures: Cultural Flows and Late Modern Dance Music Culture', in M. Cieslik and G. Pollock (eds) *Young People in Risk Society: The Restructuring of Youth Identities and Transitions in Late Modernity*. Aldershot: Ashgate.
Catan, L. (2002) 'Making Research Useful: Experiments from the Economic and Social Research Council's Youth Research Programme', *Youth and Policy*, 76: 1–14.
CCCS Race and Politics Group (1982) *The Empire Strikes Back*. London: Hutchinson.
Centre for Social Markets (2002) *British Asians Today*. London.
Chamberlayne, P. and Wengraf, T. (2000) *The Turn to Biographical Methods in the Social Sciences*. London: Routledge.
Chamberlayne, P., Bornart, J. and Wengraf, T. (eds) (2000) *The Turn to Biographical Methods*. London: Routledge.
Champion, S. (1997) 'Fear and Loathing in Wisconsin', in S. Redhead, D. Wynne, and J. O'Connor (eds) *The Clubcultures Reader: Readings in Popular Cultural Studies*. Oxford: Blackwell.
Chaney, D. (1994) *The Cultural Turn: Scene Setting Essays on Contemporary Cultural History*. London: Routledge.
Chaney, D. (1996) *Lifestyles*. London: Routledge.
Chatterton, P. and Hollands, R. (2001) *Changing Our Toon: Youth, Nightlife and Urban Change in Newcastle*. Newcastle: Newcastle University Press.
Chernin, K. (1983) *Woman size: The Tyranny of Stenderness*. London: Women's Press.
Chernin, K. (1985). *The Hungry Self: Women, Eating and Identity*. New york: Times Books.
Christensen, P. and James, A. (eds) (2000) *Research with Children: Perspectives and Practices*. London: Falmer Press.
Cieslik, M. (2001) 'Researching Youth Cultures: Some Problems with the Cultural Turn in British Youth Studies', *Scottish Youth Issues Journal*, 2 (Spring): 27–47.

Cieslik, M. and Pollock, G. (2002) 'Introduction: Studying Young People in Late Modernity', in M. Cieslik and G. Pollock (eds) *Young People in Risk Society*. Aldershot: Ashgate.
Cieslik, M. and Pollock, G. (eds) (2002) *Young People in Risk Society: The Restructuring of Youth Identities and Transitions in Late Modernity*. Aldershot: Ashgate.
Clarke, J., Hall, S., Jefferson, T. and Roberts, B. (1976) 'Subcultures, Cultures and Class: A Theoretical Overview', in S. Hall and T. Jefferson (eds) *Resistance Through Rituals: Youth Subcultures in Post-War Britain*. London: Hutchinson.
Clifford, J. (1986) 'Partial Truths', in J. Clifford and G.E. Marcus (eds) *Writing Culture; the Poetics and Politics of Ethnography*. Berkeley: University of California Press.
Clifford, J. and Marcus, G. (eds) (1986) *Writing Culture*. Berkeley: University of California Press.
Cockburn, C. (1987) *Two Track Training*. Basingstoke: Macmillan.
Cockrill, A., Scott, P. and Fitz, J. (1999) 'Planning, Implementation and Practical Issues in Cross-National Comparative Research', in F. Coffield (ed.) *Why's the Beer Always Stronger Up North*. Bristol: Policy Press.
Coffield, F. (1986) *Growing Up at the Margins Milton Keynes*. Milton Keynes: Open University Press.
Coffield, F. (1999) *Why's the Beer Always Stronger Up North?* Bristol: Policy Press.
Cohen, P. (1984) 'Against the New Vocationalism', in I. Bates *et al.* (eds) *Schooling for the Dole*. London: Macmillan.
Cohen, S. (1987) *Folk Devils and Moral Panics: The Creation of the Mods and Rockers*, 3rd edn. Oxford: Basil Blackwell.
Cohen, P. (1997a) *Rethinking the Youth Question*. Basingstoke: Macmillan.
Cohen, P. (1997b) 'Labouring Under Whiteness', in R. Frankenberg (ed.) *Dislocating Whiteness*. Durham, NC: Duke University Press.
Cohen, P. (1999a) 'In Visible Cities', *Community Plural*, 3(1): 20–52.
Cohen, P. (1999b) 'Apprenticeship a-la-mode', in P. Ainley and H. Rainbird (eds) *Apprenticeship: Towards a New Paradigm of Learning*. London: Sage.
Cohen, P. and Ainley, P. (2000) 'In the Country of the Blind? Youth Studies and Cultural Studies in Britain', *Journal of Youth Studies*, 3(1): 79–95.
Coles, B. (2000) *Joined-Up Youth Research, Policy and Practice: A New Agenda for Change?* Leicester: Youth Work Press.
Coles, B. (1995) *Youth and Social Policy: Youth Citizenship and Young Careers*. London: UCL Press.
Collins, M. (1997) *Altered State: The Story of Ecstasy Culture and Acid House*. London: Serpent's Tail.
Consumers in NHS Research Support Unit (2000) *Involving Consumers in Research and Development in the NHS. Briefing Notes For Researchers*. Hampshire: Consumers in NHS Research Support Unit.
Corsaro, W. and Molinari, L. (1990) 'From Seggiolini to Discussione: The Generation and Extension of Peer Culture Among Italian Preschool Children', *International Journal of Qualitative Studies in Education*, 3: 213–30.
Cottle, T. (1973) 'The Life Study: On Mutual Recognition and the Subjective Inquiry', *Urban Life and Culture*, 2: 344–60.
Couppié, T. and Mansuy, M. (2001) 'The Position of Young People and New Entrants in the European Labour Markets', Working Paper January 2001. Comparative Analysis of Transitions from Education to Work in Europe.

Coxall, B. and Robins, L. (1998) *Contemporary British Politics*. Basingstoke: Macmillan.
Craine, S. (1997) 'The "Black Magic Roundabout": Cyclical Transitions, Social Exclusion and Alternative Careers', in R. McDonald (ed.) *Youth, the Underclass and Social Exclusion*. London: Routledge.
Csikszentmihalyi, M. and Rochberg-Halton, E. (1981) *The Meaning of Things*. Cambridge: Cambridge University Press.
Dalrymple, J. and Burke, B. (1995) *Anti-Oppressive Practice: Social Care and the Law*. Buckingham: Open University Press.
Davies, B. (1993) *Shards of Glass: Children Reading and Writing Beyond Gendered Identites*. New Jersey: Hampton.
Davies, B. (1999) *From Thatcherism to New Labour*. Leicester: Youth Work Press.
Daws, P. (1977) *Social Determinism or Personal Choice*. University of Keele: Studies in the Sociology of Vocational Guidance.
de Broucker, P., Gensbittel, M.H. and Mainguet, C. (2000) 'Educational Determinants and Other Aspects of the Transition Process', paper presented at the International Workshop on Comparative Data on Education-to-Work Transitions, Paris, June 2000.
Deakin, B. (1996) *The Youth Labour Market in Britain*. Cambridge: Cambridge University Press.
Denzin, N.K. and Lincoln, P. (1994) *Qualitative Research*. London: Sage.
Department of Health (1998) *Modernising Health and Social Services: National Priorities Guidance 1999/00–2001/02*. London: DoH.
Department of Health (2001) *Co-ordinated Service Planning for Vulnerable Children and Young People in England*. London: Stationary Office.
DfEE (1999) *All Our Futures: Creativity, Culture and Education*. London: HMSO.
Douglas, J. (ed.) (1976) *Investigative Social Research*. California: Sage.
DrugScope and DPAS (2001) *Assessing Local Need: Planning Services for Young People*. London: DPAS.
Du Bois-Reymond, M. (1998) '"I Don't Want To Commit Myself Yet": Young People's Life Concepts', *Journal of Youth Studies*, 1(1): 63–79.
Durkheim, E. (1897/1970) *Suicide*, G. Simpson (ed.). London: Routeledge and Kegan Paul.
Dwyer, P. (1998) 'Conditional Citizens? Welfare Rights and Responsibilities in the late 1990s', *Critical Social Policy*, 18(4): 493–517.
Education Group (1981) *Unpopular Education*. London: Hutchinson.
Education Group II (1991) *Education Limited*. London: Unwin Hyman.
Edwards, R. (1998) 'Mapping, Locating and Translating: A Discursive Approach to Professional Development', *Studies in Continuing Education*, 20(1): 23–38.
EGRIS (2001) 'Misleading Trajectories: Transition Dilemmas of Young Adults in Europe', *Journal of Youth Studies*, 4(1): 101–18.
Eichler, M. (1988) *Nonsexist Research Methods*. London: Allen and Unwin.
Eisentadt, S.N. and Curelaru, M. (1977) 'Macro Sociology: Theory, Analysis and Comparative Studies', *Current Sociology*, 25: 1–12.
Emond, R. (2000) 'Survival of the Skilful: An Ethnographic Study of two Groups of Young People in Residential Care', Unpublished PhD Thesis, University of Stirling.
Epstein, J.S. (ed.) (1998) *Youth Culture: Identity in a Post Modern World*. Oxford: Blackwell.
Erikson, E. (1971) *Identity, Youth and Crisis*. London: Faber.

Esping-Andersen, G. (1990) *The Three Worlds of Welfare Capitalism*. Cambridge: Polity Press.

European Commission (2002) Decision No. 1513/2002/EC of the European Parliament and of the Council. *Official Journal of the European Communities*, 232.

Evans, K. (2002) 'Taking Control Over Their Lives? Agency in Youth Adult Transitions in England and the New Germany', *Journal of Youth Studies*, 5(3): 245–71.

Evans, K. and Furlong, A. (1997) 'Metaphors and Youth Transitions: Niches, Pathways, Trajectories and Navigations', in J. Bynner, L. Chisholm and A. Furlong (eds) *Youth, Citizenship and Social Change in a European Context*. Aldershot: Ashgate.

Evans, K. and Heinz, W.R. (1993) *Becoming Adults in England and Germany*. London: Anglo-German Foundation.

Evans, K., Behrens, M. and Kaluza, J. (2000) *Learning and Work in the Risk Society*. Basingstoke: Macmillan.

Eygendaal, W. (1992) 'The Black Heart – A Qualitative Study of the Death Metal Culture in The Netherlands', paper presented to conference on *Internationalisation and Leisure Research*, Tilburg.

Farmer, J. and Chesson, R. (2001) 'Health Care Management: Models for Evidence Based Practice', *Journal of Management in Medicine*, 15(4): 266–82.

Featherstone, M. (1991) 'The Body in Consumer Culture', in M. Featherstone, M. Hepworth and B. Turner (eds) *The Body, Social Process and Cultural Theory*. London: Sage.

Featherstone, M., Hepworth, M. and Turner, B. (eds) (1991) *The Body, Social Process and Cultural Theory*. London: Sage.

Ferguson, R. (2001) 'On Goldfish Bowls and Oceans: A Comparison of the Attitudes of Young People With Those of Adults in Positions of Authority', *Scottish Youth Issues Journal*, 2: 105–26.

Fielding, N. (1993) 'Ethnography', in N. Gilbert (ed.) *Researching Social Life*. London: Sage.

Finch, J. (1984) 'Its Great To Have Someone to Talk To: The Ethics and Politics of Interviewing Women', in C. Bell and H. Roberts (eds) *Social Researching*. London: Routledge.

Fine, G.A. and Sandstrom, K.L. (1988) *Knowing Children: Participant Observation with Minors*. Sage University Paper Series on Qualitative Research Methods, Vol.15, Beverly Hills: Sage.

Finn, D. (1987) *Training Without Jobs*. Basingstoke: Macmillan.

Fonarow, W. (1995) 'The Spatial Organization of the Indie-guitar Music Gig', in K. Gelder and S. Thornton (eds) (1997) *The Subcultures Reader*. London: Routledge.

Fonow, M.M. and Cook, J.A. (eds) (1991) *Beyond Methodology: Feminist Scholarship as Lived Research*. Bloomington and Indianapolis: Indiana University Press.

Fornäs, J. and Bolin, G. (eds) (1995) *Youth Culture in Late Modernity*. London: Sage.

Foskett, D.J. (1979) *Introduction in Comparative Librarianship*. Bangalore: Sarada Rangathan Endowment for Library Science.

Foucault, M. (1977) *Discipline and Punish*. Harmondsworth: Penguin.

Fountain, J. (1993) 'Dealing with Data', in D. Hobbs and T. May (eds) *Interpreting the Field: Accounts of Ethnography*. Oxford: Clarendon Press.

France, A. (1998) 'Why Should We Care: Young People, Citizenship and Questions of Social Responsibility', *Journal of Youth Studies*, 1(1): 97–112.
France, A. (2000a) 'Towards a Sociological Understanding of Youth and their Risk-Taking', *Journal of Youth Studies*, 3(3): 317–32.
France, A. (2000b) *Youth Researching Youth. The Triumph and Success Peer Research Project*. Leicester: Youth Work Press.
Frank, T. (1997) *The Conquest of the Cool*. Chicago: University of Chicago Press.
Frankenberg, R. (ed.) (1997) *Dislocating Whiteness*. Durham, NC: Duke University Press.
Freire, P. (1970) *The Pedagogy of the Oppressed*. Harmondsworth: Penguin.
Frith, S. (1983) *Sound Effects: Youth, Leisure and the Politics of Rock 'n' Roll*. London: Constable.
Frith, S. (1987) 'Towards an Aesthetic of Popular Music', in R. Leppert and S. McClary (eds) *Music and Society: The Politics of Composition, Performance and Reception*. Cambridge: Cambridge University Press.
Frith, S. (1996) *Performing Rites*. Oxford: Oxford University Press.
Frosh, S., Pheonix, A. and Pattman, R. (2002) *Young Masculinities*. Basingstoke: Palgrave.
Frost, L. (2001) *Young Women and the Body: A Feminist Sociology*. Basingstoke: Palgrave.
Furedi, F. (1997) *Culture of Fear: Risk-Taking and the Morality of Low Expectation*. London: Cassell.
Furlong, A. (1993) *Growing Up in a Classless Society?* Edinburgh: Edinburgh University Press.
Furlong, A. and Cartmel, F. (1997) *Young People and Social Change: Individualization and Risk in Late Modernity*. Buckingham: Open University Press.
Furlong, A. and Cartmel, F. (2001) 'The Relationship Between Youth Unemployment and Social and Economic Marginalisation', in B. Furåker, (ed.) *Employment and Unemployment and Marginalisation: Studies in Contemporary Labour Markets*. Gothenburg: Gothenburg University Press.
Furlong, A. and McNeish, W. (2002) *Integration through Training*. Report to the European Commission.
Fuss, D. (1989) *Essentially Speaking: Feminism, Nature and Difference*. London: Routledge.
Gallie, D. and Paugam, S. (eds) (2000) *Welfare Regimes and the Experience of Unemployment in Europe*. Oxford: Oxford University Press.
Gangl, M. (2000) 'Education and Labour Market Entry Across Europe: The Impact of Institutional Arrangements in Training Systems and Labour Markets', Working Paper 25. Mannheim. University of Mannheim.
Garfinkel, P.E. and Garner, D.M. (1982) *Anorexia Nervosa: A Multi-dimensional Perspective*. New York: Brunner/Mazel.
Geertz, C. (1973) *The Interpretation of Cultures*. London: Hutchinson.
Gelder, K. and Thornton, S. (eds) (1997) *The Subcultures Reader*. London: Routledge.
Gibbons, M. (1994) *The New Production of Knowledge: The Dynamics of Science and Research in Contemporary Societies*. London: Sage.
Giddens, A. (1977) *Studies in Social and Political Theory*. New York: Basic Books.
Giddens, A. (1990) *The Consequences of Modernity*. Cambridge: Polity Press.
Giddens, A. (1991) *Modernity and Self-Identity: Self and Society in the Late Modern Age*. Cambridge: Polity Press.

Giddens, A. (1998) *The Third Way: The Renewal of Social Democracy*. Cambridge: Polity Press.
Giddens, A. (2000) *The Third Way and its Critics*. Cambridge: Polity Press.
Gilroy, P. (1987) *There Ain't No Black in the Union Jack*. London: Hutchinson.
Gilroy, P. (1993) *Small Acts*. London: Comedia.
Gipps, C. (1996) 'The Paradox of Pacific Rim Learners', *Times Educational Supplement*, 20 December.
Giroux, H. (1996) *Fugitive Cultures*. London: Routledge.
Goddard, E. (1997) *Young Teenagers and Alcohol in 1996. England*. London: Stationery Office.
Goffman, E. (1959) *The Presentation of the Self in Everyday Life*. London: Penguin Books.
Goldthorpe, J.H. (1998) 'Rational Action Theory for Sociology', *British Journal of Sociology*, 49(2): 167–92.
Gollan, J. (1937) *Youth in British Industry*. London: Lawrence and Wishart.
Gouldner, A. (1971) *The Coming Crisis of Western Sociology*. London: Heinmann.
Green, P. (1993) 'Taking Sides: Partisan Research on the 1984–1985 Miners Strike', in D. Hobbs and T. May (eds) *Interpreting the Field: Accounts of Ethnography*. Oxford: Clarendon Press.
Green, N. (2002) 'Outwardly Mobile: Young People and Mobile Technologies', paper presented at the BSA Youth Study Group seminar, Young People and New Technology, University of Surrey, Roehampton, November.
Griffin, C. (1985) *Typical Girls?* London: Routledge.
Griffin, C. (1986) 'Qualitative Methods and Cultural Analysis', in R. Burgess (ed.) *Field Methods in the Study of Education*. London: Falmer.
Griffin, C. (1993) *Representing Youth: The Study of Youth and Adolescence in Britain and America*. Cambridge: Polity Press.
Griffiths, V. (1984) 'Feminist Research and the Use of Drama', *Women's Studies International Forum*, 7: 511–19.
Grogan, S. (1979) *Understanding Body Dissatisfaction in Men, Women and Children*. London: Routledge.
Grogan, S. (1999) *Body Image*. London: Routledge.
Grossberg, L. (1997) *Bringing It All Back Home*. Durham, NC: Duke University Press.
Guerrero, T. (2001) *Youth in Transition*. Aldershot: Ashgate.
Hagood, M.J. (1939) *Mothers of the South: Portraiture of the White Tenant Farm Woman*. Charlottesville, VA, USA.
Hall, S. (1980) 'Cultural Studies: Two Paradigms', in T. Bennett, G. Martin, C. Mercer and J. Woollacott (eds) (1981) *Culture, Ideology and Social Process*. London: Open University Press/Batsford.
Hall, S. (1992) 'Cultural Studies and its Theoretical Legacies', in L. Grossberg (ed.) *The Cultural Studies Reader*. London: Sage.
Hall, S. and Jefferson, T. (eds) (1978) *Resistance Through Rituals: Youth Subcultures in Post-War Britain*. London: Hutchinson.
Hall, T., Williamson, H. and Coffey, A. (2000) 'Young People, Citizenship and the Third Way: A Role for the Youth Service?', *Journal of Youth Studies*, 3(4): 461–75.
Hammersley, M. (1992) *What's Wrong With Ethnography?* London: Routledge.
Hammersley, M. and Atkinson, P. (1983) *Ethnography. Principles and Practice*. London: Routledge.

Haraway, D. (1988) 'Situated Knowledges: The Science Question in Feminism and the Privilege of Partial Perspective', *Feminist Studies*, 14(3): 575–99.
Harden, J. and Scott, S. (1998) 'Risk Anxiety and the Social Construction of Childhood', paper presented at the International Sociological Association World Congress, Montreal, July 1998.
Harding, S. (ed.) (1987) *Feminism and Methodology*. Milton Keynes: Open University Press.
Hardt, M. and Negri, T. (2001) *Empire*. London: Random House.
Hargreaves, D. (1967) *Social Relations in a Secondary School*. London: Routledge.
Hargreaves, D. (1975) *Deviance in the Classroom*. London: Routledge.
Hart, R. (1995) 'Children as the Makers of a New Geography', in L. Karsten, T. Bongertman, G. de Haan, G. van der Straaten and I. Tom (eds) *Building Identities: Gender Perspectives on Children and Urban Space*. University of Amsterdam.
Hawes, D. (1998) 'A Short Archeology of the Chemical Age', in S. Champion (ed.) *Disco 2000*. London: Hodder and Stoughton.
Hazenkamp, J., Meers, W. and Poel, Y.T. (eds) (1998) *European Contributions to Youth Research*. Amsterdam: Free University Press.
Health Advisory Service (1996) *Children and Young People's Substance Misuse Services: The Substance of Young Needs*. London: HAS.
Health Advisory Service (2001) *The Substance of Young Needs Review 2001*. London: HAS.
Heath, S. and Kenyon, L. (1999) 'Upwardly and Geographically Mobile Young Professionals, the Labour Market and Shared Household Living', paper presented at European Sociological Association Conference, Amsterdam.
Hebdige, D. (1979) *Subculture: The Meaning of Style*. London: Routledge.
Hebdige, D. (1988) *Hiding in the Light: On Images and* Things. London: Comedia.
Heinz, W.R. (ed.) (1999) *From Education to Work: Cross-National Perspectives*. Cambridge: Cambridge University Press.
Helve, H. and Wallace, C. (eds) (2001) *Youth, Citizenship and Empowerment*. Aldershot: Ashgate.
Henderson, S. (1993) *Women, Sexuality and Ecstasy Use: The Final Report*. Manchester: Lifeline.
Henderson, S. (1997) *Ecstasy: Case Unsolved*. Cambridge: Cambridge University Press.
Hendry, L., Shucksmith, J., Love, J.G. and Glendinning, A. (1993) *Young People's Leisure and Life-styles*. London: Routledge.
Hendry, L.B., Shucksmith, J. and Philip, K. (1995) *Educating for Health: School and Community Approaches with Adolescents*. London: Cassell.
Henriques, J., Hollway, W., Urwin, K., Venn, C. and Walkerdine, V. (eds) (1984) *Changing the Subject: Psychology, Social Regulation and Subjectivity*. London: Methuen.
Henry, H. (1971) 'We Cannot Ask "why"', in H. Henry (ed.) *Perspectives in Management and Marketing Research*. London: Crosby Lockwood, 293–311.
Heron, E. and Dwyer, P. (1999) 'Doing the Right Thing: Labour's Attempt to Forge a New Welfare Deal Between the Individual and the State', *Social Policy and Administration*, 33(1): 91–104.
Hessler, M.H. (1992) *Social Research Methods*. St. Paul: West Publishing.
Hetherington, K. (1996) 'Identity Formation, Space and Social Centrality', *Theory, Culture and Society*, 13(4): 33–52.

Hetherington, K. (1997) *The Badlands of Modernity: Heterotopia and Social Ordering.* London: Routledge.
Hewitt, R. (1986) *White Talk, Black Talk.* Cambridge: Cambridge University Press.
Hey, V. (1997) *The Company She Keeps Ethnography of Girls' Friendships.* Buckingham: Open University Press.
Higgins, J. (1986) 'Comparative Social Policy', *Quarterly Journal of Social Affairs*, 2: 221–42.
Hine, C. (2000) *Virtual Ethnography.* London: Sage.
Hobbs, D. (1993) 'Peers, Careers, and Academic Fears: Writing as Field-Work', in D. Hobbs and T. May (eds) *Interpreting the Field: Accounts of Ethnography.* Oxford: Clarendon Press.
Hobcraft, J. and Kiernan, K. (1996) *Becoming a Parent in Europe.* Welfare State Programme 116, London School of Economics.
Hodkinson, P. (2002) *Goth. Identity, Style and Subculture.* Oxford: Berg.
Hodkinson, P. (2004) 'The Goth Scene and (Sub)Cultural Substance', in A. Bennett and K. Kahn-Harris (eds) *After Subculture: Critical Studies in Contemporary Youth Culture.* Basingstoke: Palgrave.
Hoggett, P. (2001) 'Agency, Rationality and Social Policy', *Journal of Social Policy*, 30(1): 37–56.
Holdsworth, C. and Elliott, J. (2001) 'The Timing of Family Formation in Britain and Spain', *Sociological Research Online*, 6: 2.
Holland, J. and Ramazanoglu, C. (1994) 'Coming to Conclusions: Power and Interpretation in Researching Young Women's Sexuality', in M. Maynard and J. Purvis (eds) *Researching Women's Lives from a Feminist Perspective.* London: Taylor and Francis.
Holland, R. (1977) *Self and Social Context.* London: Macmillan.
Hollands, R. (1985a) 'Working for the Best Ethnography', *CCCS Stencilled Paper*, No. 79.
Hollands, R. (1985b) 'Its Your Life!: Male Working Class Youths' Orientation Towards Educational Comics', in C. Points (ed.) *Working Papers for 16 + Media Studies*, Clywd Media Studies Unit.
Hollands, R. (1990) *The Long Transition: Class, Culture and Youth Training.* London: Macmillan.
Hollands, R. (1991) 'Losing: The Generation Game Revisited', *Youth and Policy*, 33: 38–42.
Hollands, R. (1995) *Friday Night, Saturday Night.* Department of Social Policy, University of Newcastle.
Hollway, W. (1984) 'Gender Difference and the Production of Subjectivity', in J. Henriques, W. Hollway, K. Urwin, C. Venn and V. Walkerdine (eds) *Changing the Subject: Psychology, Social Regulation and Subjectivity.* London: Methuen.
Hollway, W. (2001) 'The Psycho-social Subject in "Evidence-based Practice"', *Journal of Social Work Practice*, 15(1): 9–22.
Hollway, W. and Jefferson, T. (2000) *Doing Qualitative Research Differently: Free Association, Narrative and the Interview Method.* London: Sage.
Home Office (1995) *Tackling Drugs Together: A Strategy for England 1995–1998.* London: HMSO.
Hood-Williams, J. (2002) *Beyond Sex and Gender.* London: Sage.
Hooks, B. (1992) *Black Looks: Race and Representation.* Boston, MA: South End Press.

Hughes, J.A. (1976) *Sociological Analysis: Methods of Discovery*. London: Nelson.
Hutson, S. and Liddiard, M. (1994) *Youth Homelessness*. Basingstoke: Macmillan.
Irwin, I. (1995) *Rights of Passage*. London: UCL Press.
Irwin, S. (1995) 'Social Reproduction and Change in the Transition from Youth to Adulthood', *Sociology*, 29(2): 293–315.
Jackson, B. and Marsden, D. (1986) *Education and the Working Class*. London: Ark.
Jackson, S. and Scott, S. (2000) 'Childhood', in G. Payne, (ed.) *Social Divisions*. London: Macmillan.
Jans, M. and Percy-Smith, B. (1999) 'Towards interpretative professional practice', TSER Balancing competencies, *Working Paper*, available from the authors.
Janssens, C., Percy-Smith, B., Jans, M. and Wildemeersch, D. (2000) 'Towards an Interpretive Education, Training and Guidance Practice', Final Report, *Balancing Competencies*, Leuven: TSER EU Fourth Framework Programme.
Jacques, M. and Mulhern, F. (1982) *The Forward March of Labour Halted*. London: NLB.
Jeffs, T. and Smith, M.K. (1998) 'The Problem of Youth for Youth Work', *Youth and Policy*, 62: 45–66.
Jenkins, R. (1983) *Lads, Citizens and Ordinary Kids: Working-Class Youth Lifestyles in Belfast*. London: Routledge and Kegan Paul.
Jewkes, J. and Jewkes, S. (1938) *The Juvenile Labour Market*. London: Gollancz.
Johnson, R. (1983) 'What Is Cultural Studies Anyway?', *CCCS Stencilled Paper*, No. 74.
Johnson, V., Ivan-Smith, E., Gordon, G., Pridmore, P. and Scott, P. (1998) *Stepping Forward: Children and Young People's Participation in the Development Process*. London: IT Publications.
Jones, G. (1994) *Young People in and out of the Housing Market*. York: Joseph Rowntree Foundation.
Jones, G. (1995) *Leaving Home*. Buckingham: Open University Press.
Jones, S. (1998) *Black Culture, White Youth: The Reggae Tradition from JA to UK*. Basingstoke: Macmillan.
Jones, G. and Martin, C. (1999) 'The "Young Consumer" at Home: Dependence, Resistance and Autonomy', in J. Hearn and S. Roseneil (eds) *Consuming Cultures: Power and Resistance*. Basingstoke: Macmillan.
Jones, G. and Wallace, C. (1992) *Youth, Family and Citizenship*. Milton Keynes: Open University Press.
Julkunen, I. and Malmberg-Heimonen, I. (1998) *The Encounter of High Unemployment Among Youth*. Helsinki: Työministeriö.
Jupp, V., Davies, P. and Francis, P. (eds) (2000) *Doing Criminological Research*. London: Sage Press.
Karovnen, S., West, P., Sweeting, H., Rahkonen, O. and Young, R. (2001) 'Lifestyle, Social Class and Heath-Related Behaviour: A Cross-Cultural Comparison of 15 Year olds in Glasgow and Helsinki', *Journal of Youth Studies*, 4(2): 101–19.
Keat, R. and Urry, J. (1975) *Social Theory as Science*. London: Routledge.
Kelly, L., Burton, S. and Regan, L. (1994) 'Researching Women's Lives or Studying Women's Oppression', in M. Maynard and J. Purvis (eds) *Researching Women's Lives from a Feminist Perspective*. London: Taylor and Francis.
Kelly, P. (2000) 'Youth as an Artefact of Expertise: Problematising the Practice of Youth Studies in an Age of Uncertainty', *Journal of Youth Studies*, 3(3): 301–16.

Kemmis, S. (n.d.) *Interrupt and Say: Is it Worth Doing? Communicative Action – Developments Inspired By Habermas.* Interview with Steven Kemmis.
Kerr, M. (1970) *The People of Ship Street.* London: Routledge.
Kiernan, K.E. (1995) *Transition to Parenthood: Young Mothers, Young Fathers – Associated Factors and Later Life Experiences.* Welfare State Programme 113, London School of Economics.
Kinder, K., Wakefield, A. and Wilkin, A. (1996) *Talking Back: Pupil Views on Disaffection.* Slough: NFER.
King, R. and Wincup, E. (eds) (2000) *Doing Research on Crime and Justice.* Oxford: Oxford University Press.
Kirby, P. (1999) *Involving Young Researchers: How to Enable Young People to Design and Conduct Research.* York: Joseph Rowntree Foundation/York Publishing Services.
Kirby, P. and Bryson, S. (2002) *Measuring the Magic? Evaluating and Researching Young People's Participation in Public Decision Making.* London: Carnegie Young People Initiative.
Kohn, M.L. (1989) 'Cross National Research as an Analytical Strategy', in M.L. Kohn (ed.) *Cross-National Research in Sociology.* Newbury Park: Sage.
Kriesi, H. (1992) 'The Rebellion of Research Objects', in M. Diani and R. Eyerman (eds) *Studying Collective Action.* London: Sage.
Lagree, J.C. (1996) 'Youth in Europe: Cultural Patterns of Transition', *Berkeley Journal of Sociology*, 41(2): 67–101.
Landry, C. and Bianchini, F. (1996) *The Creative City.* London: Demos.
Landry, C. and Ransom, S. (1999) *The Learning City in the Learning Age.* London: Demos.
Langman, L. (1992) 'Neon Cages: Shopping for Subjectivity', in R. Sheilds (ed.) *Lifestyle Shopping.* London: Routledge.
Lash, S. (1990) *Sociology of Postmodernism.* London: Routledge.
Laufer, M. and Egle, M. (1984) *Adolescence and Developmental Breakdown.* New Haven: Yale University Press.
Lave, J. and Wenger, E. (1991) *Informal Situated Learning.* Cambridge: Cambridge University Press.
Lawford, G. and Lawford, J. (eds) (1992) *Ravescene Yearbook.* London: Yage Corporation.
Lawrence, E. (1982) 'Just Plain Common-Sense: The "Roots" of Racism', centre of contemporary cultural Studies, 47–94, *The Empire Strikes Back: Race and Racism in 70s Britain*, 47–92. London: Hutchinson.
Leadbetter, C. (1997) *The Rise of the Social Entrepreneur.* London: Demos.
Lee, D. and Turner, B. (1996) *Conflicts about Class.* London: Longman.
Lee, R.M. (1993) *Doing Research on Sensitive Topics.* London: Sage.
Lees, S. (1986) *Losing Out: Sexuality and Adolescent Girls.* London: Hutchinson.
Lee-Treweek, G. (1996) *Discourse, Care and Control: An Ethnography of Residential and Nursing Home Elder Care Work*, unpublished PhD, University of Plymouth.
Lee-Treweek, G. (2000) 'The Insight of Emotional Danger: Research Experiences in a Home for Older People', in G. Lee-Treweek and S. Linkogle (eds) *Danger in the Field.* London: Routledge.
Lensin, D. (1995) *On Drugs.* Minneapolis: University of Minneapolis Press.
Leonard, D. (1980) *Sex and Generation.* London: Tavistock.
Levine, P. (1979) *Family Formations in Nascent Capitalism.* New Haven: Yale University Press.

Levitas, R. (1996) 'The Concept of Social Exclusion and the New Durkheimian Hegemony', *Critical Social Policy*, 46: 5–20.
Lewis, G.H. (1992) 'Who Do You Love?: The Dimensions of Musical Taste', in J. Lull (ed.) *Popular Music and Communication*, 2nd edn. London: Sage.
Lewis, J. (1992) *The Road to Romance and Ruin*. London: Routledge.
Lingis, A. (1994) *Foreign Bodies*. London: Routledge.
Littlewood, P. and Herkommer, S. (1999) 'Identifying Social Exclusion', in P. Littlewood, with I. Glorieux, S. Herkommer and I. Jönsson (eds) *Social Exclusion in Europe: Problems and Paradigms*. Aldershot: Ashgate.
Local Government Management Board (1996) *Local Agenda 21 Roundtable guidance: Local Agenda 21 and Young People*. Luton: LGMB.
Lofland, J. and Lofland, L.H. (1984) *Analysing Social Settings*, 2nd edn. Belmont, CA: Wadsworth.
Lupton, D. (1999) *Risk*. London: Routledge.
Mac an Ghail, M. (1988) *Young Gifted and Black*. Milton Keynes: Open University Press.
Macdonald, N. (2001) *The Graffiti Subculture: Youth, Masculinity and Identity in New York*. Basingstoke: Palgrave.
MacDonald, R. (1998) 'Youth Transitions and Social Exclusion: Some Issues for Youth Research in the UK', *Journal of Youth Studies*, 1(2): 163–76.
MacDonald, R. (ed.) (1997) *Youth, Social Exclusion and the Underclass*. London: Routledge.
MacDonald, R. and Coffield, F. (1991) *Risky Business: Youth and the Enterprise Culture*. London: Falmer.
MacDonald, R. and Marsh, J. (2001) 'Disconnected Youth?', *Journal of Youth Studies*, 4(4): 373–91.
MacDonald, R. and Mason, P. (2001) 'Snakes and Ladders: In Defence of Studies of Youth Transition', *Sociological Research Online*, February.
MacDonald, R., Mason, P., Shildrick, T., Webster, C., Johnston, L. and Ridley, L. (2001) 'Snakes and Ladders: In Defence of Studies of Youth Transitions', *Sociological Research Online*, 5(4).
MacKenzie, J. (2001) 'Teacher Have to Win all the Time: New Directions in the Pursuit of Social Justice in the Classroom', *Scottish Youth Issues Journal*, 2: 67–88.
MacSweeney, M. (1993) *Anorexic Bodies: A Feminist and Sociological Perspective on Anorexia Nervosa*. London: Routledge.
Malbon, B. (1999) *Clubbing: Dancing, Ecstasy and Vitality*. London: Routledge.
Malson, H. (1998) *The Thin Woman: Feminism, Post-Structuralism and the Social Psychology of Anorexia Nervosa*. London: Routledge.
Marcus, G. and Fischer, M. (1986) *Anthropology as Cultural Critique*. Chicago: University of Chicago Press.
Marriott, J. (1991) *The Culture of Labourism*. Edinburgh: Edinburgh University Press.
Marsh, C. (1982) *The Survey Method: The Contribution of Surveys to Sociological Method*. London: George, Allen and Unwin.
Marx, K. (1985) *Grundrisse*. London: Penguin.
May, T. (1993) 'Feelings Matter: Inverting the Hidden Equation', in D. Hobbs and T. May (eds) *Interpreting the Field: Accounts of Ethnography*. Oxford: Clarendon Press.

May, T. (1997) *Social Research: Issues, Methods and Process*. Buckingham: Open University Press.
Maynard, M. and Purvis, J. (eds) (1994) *Researching Women's Lives from a Feminist Perspective*. London: Taylor and Francis.
Mays, J.B. (1954) *Growing up in the City*. Liverpool: Liverpool University Press.
McDonald, M. (1994) *Gender, Drink and Drugs*. Oxford: Providence.
McGuigan, J. (1992) *Cultural Populism*. London: Routledge.
McKenna, P. (1996) *Nightshift*. Dunoon: ST Publishing.
McLeod, J. and Malone, K. (2000) *Researching Youth*. Tasmania: Australian Clearing House for Youth Research.
McNamee, S. (1998) 'Youth, Gender and Video Games: Power and Control in the Home', in T. Skelton and G. Valentine (eds) *Cool Places: Geographies of Youth Culture*. London: Routledge.
McRobbie, A. (1982) 'The Politics of Feminist Research: Between Talk, Text and Action', *Feminist Review*, 12: 46–57.
McRobbie, A. (1991) *Feminism and Youth Culture: From Jackie to Just Seventeen*. Basingstoke: Macmillan.
McRobbie, A. (1994) *Post Modernism and Popular Culture*. London: Routledge.
McRobbie, A. (ed.) (1997) *Back to Reality: Social Experience and Cultural Studies*. Manchester: Manchester University Press.
Melechi, A. (1993) 'The Ecstasy of Disappearance', in S. Redhead (ed.) *Rave Off: Politics and Deviance in Contemporary Youth Culture*. Aldershot: Avebury.
Melly, G. (1989) *Revolt into Style*, 3rd edn. Milton Keynes: Open University Press.
Melucci, A. (1989) *Nomads of the Present*. London: Hutchinson.
Miles, S. (1995) 'Towards an Understanding of the Relationship Between Youth Identities and Consumer Culture', *Youth and Policy*, 51: 35–45.
Miles, S. (1998) *Consumerism as a Way of Life*. London: Sage.
Miles, S. (2000) *Youth Lifestyles in A Changing World*. Buckingham: Open University Press.
Mintel (1996) *Nightclubs and Discotheques*. London: Market Intelligence International Group Ltd.
Mirza, H. (1992) *Young, Female and Black*. London: Routledge.
Mitscherlich, A. and Mitscherlich, M. (1973) *Society Without the Father*. London: Tavistock.
Mitterauer, M. (1992) *A History of Youth: Family, Sexuality and Social Relations in Past Times*. Cambridge: Blackwell.
Mizen, P. (1995) *The State, Young People and Youth Training*. Basingstoke: Macmillan.
Mizen, P. (2002) 'Putting the Politics Back into Youth Studies: Keynesianism, Monetarism and the Changing State of Youth', *Journal of Youth Studies*, 5(1): 5–20.
Moore-Gilbert, B. (1997) *Post Colonial Theory*. London: Verso.
Moretti, F. (1987) *The Way of the World*. London: Verso.
Muggleton, D. (1997) 'The Post-Subculturalist', in S. Redhead, J. O'Connor and Wynne, D. (eds) *The Clubcultures Reader*. Cambridge: Blackwell Press.
Muggleton, D. (2000) *Inside Subculture: The Postmodern Meaning of Style*. Oxford: Berg.
Mullan, R., Sherval, J. and Skelton, L. (1997) 'Young People's Drug Use at Rave/Dance Events. Evaluation of Crew 2000's Safer Dancing Outreach Service': (Rezerection, Ingliston Edinburgh April 1996, September 1996), Edinburgh: Crew 2000.

216 Bibliography

Müller, W. and Shavit, Y. (1998) 'The Institutional Embeddedness of the Stratification Process: A Comparative Study of Qualifications and Occupations in Thirteen Countries', in Y. Shavit and W. Müller (eds) *From School to Work. A Comparative Study of Educational Qualifications and Occupational Destinations*. Oxford: Claredon Press.

Mungham, G. and Pearson, G. (eds) (1976) *Working Class Youth Cultures*. London: Routledge and Kegan Paul.

Munt, S. (ed.) (2000) *Cultural Studies and the Working Class*. London: Cassell.

Murray, C. (1990) *The Emerging British Underclass*. Institute of Economic Affairs, London.

Murray, C. (1994) *Underclass: The Crisis Deepens*. Institute of Economic Affairs, London.

Nolan, J. (1996) *The American Culture Wars*. Arlington: University of Virginia Press.

O'Shea, A. (1998) 'A Special Relationship? Cultural Studies, Academia and Pedagogy', *Cultural Studies*, 16(1): 22–40.

Oakley, A. (1981) 'Interviewing Women: A Contradiction in Terms', in H. Roberts (ed.) *Doing Feminist Research*. London: Routledge and Kegan Paul.

Oakley, A. (1998) 'Gender, Methodology and People's Way of Knowing: Some Problems with Feminism and the Paradigm Debate in Social Science', *Sociology*, 32(4): 707–31.

Oliver, B. (2002) 'Links in the Chain: An Analysis of the Participatory Methodology being used to Develop the Role of Connexions Personal Advisor', *Youth and Policy*, 76: 29–38.

Oliver, J.P.J., Huxley, P.J. and Butler, A. (1989) *Mental Health Casework: Illuminations and Reflections*. Manchester: Manchester University Press.

Orbach, S. (1978) *Fat is a Feminist Issue*. New York: Berkeley Books.

Osborne, T. (1997) 'Body Amnesia-Comments of Corporeality', in D. Owen (ed.) *Sociology after Postmodernism*. London: Sage.

Owen, D. (ed.) (1997) *Sociology After Postmodernism*. London: Sage.

Oyen, E. (1990) 'The Imperfection of Comparisons', in E. Oyen (ed.) *Comparative Methodology: Theory and Practice in International Social Research*. London: Sage.

Palkulski, J. and Waters, M. (1996) *The Death of Class*. London: Sage.

Parker, H. (1974) *The View from the Boys*. London: David & Charles.

Parker, H., Measham, F. and Aldridge, J. (1995) *Drugs Futures: Changing Patterns of Drug Use Amongst English Youth*. ISDD Research Monograph 7, London: Institute for the Study of Drug Dependence.

Pawson, R. and Tilley, N. (1997) *Realistic Evaluation*. London: Sage.

Pearce, M. and Hillman, M. (1998) *Wasted Youth: Raising Achievement and Tackling Social Exclusion*. London: IPPR.

Pearson, G. (1983) *Hooliganism: A History of Respectable Fears*. Basingstoke: Macmillan.

Percy-Smith, B. (1999) 'Multiple Childhood Geographies: Giving Voice to Young People's Experience of Place', Unpublished doctoral thesis, University College Northampton.

Percy-Smith, B. (2002) 'Responding to Underachievement and Disaffection: Lessons from New Start for Educational Reform', paper presented at the YOUTH 2002: Research, Practice and Policy conference, Keele University, July.

Percy-Smith, B. and Weil, S. (2002) 'New Deal or Raw Deal? Dilemmas and Paradoxes of State Interventions into the Youth Labour Market', in M. Cieslik

and G. Pollock (eds) (2002) *Young People in Risk Society: The Restructuring of Youth Identities and Transitions in Late Modernity*. Aldershot: Ashgate.
Perri, 6, Jupp, B., Perry, H. and Laskey, K. (1997) *The Substance of Youth: The Role of Drugs in Young People's Lives Today*. York: Joseph Rowntree Foundation/York Publishing Services.
Phoenix, A. and Rattansi, A. (1998) 'Youth Research in Britain', in J. Bynner, L. Chisholm and A. Furlong (eds) *Youth, Citizenship and Social Change*. London: Ashgate.
Pickvance, C. and Pickvance, K. (1994) 'Towards a Strategic Approach to Housing Behaviour: A Study of Young People's Housing Strategies in South-East England', *Sociology*, 28(3): 657–77.
Pile, S. and Thrift, N. (1995) *Mapping the Subject*. London: Routledge.
Pinchbeck, I. and Hewitt, M. (1969) *Children in English Society*, 2 Vols. London: Routledge.
Polhemus, T. (1994) *Street Style from Sidewalk to Catwalk*. London: Thames and Hudson.
Polsky, H. (1962) *Cottage Six: The Social System of Delinquent Boys in Residential Treatment*. New York: John Wiley.
Portelli, A. (1997) *The Battle of Valle Giulia: Oral History and the Art of Dialogue*. Madison: University of Wisconsin Press.
Porter, R. (1997) *Drugs and Narcotics in History*. Cambridge: Cambridge University Press.
Punch, M. (1986) *The Politics and Ethics of Fieldwork*. London: Sage.
Puuronen, V. (2001) 'Youth Research at the Beginning of the New Millennium', in V. Puuronen (ed.) *Youth on the Threshold of the 3rd Millennium*. Karelian Institute, University of Joensuu, Joensuu.
Raabe, B. (1993) 'Constructing Identities: Young People's Understanding of Power and Social Relations', *Feminism and Psychology*, 3(3): 369–73.
Raffe, D. (1988) *Education and the Youth Labour Market*. London: Falmer.
Raffe, D. (2000) 'Strategies for Collecting Cross-National Data on Education-To-Work Transitions: Recommendations of the Catewe Project', paper presented at the International Workshop on Comparative Data on Education-to-Work Transitions, Paris, 21–23 June, 2000.
Rampton, B. (1995) *Crossing-Language and Ethnicity Among Adolescents*. London: Longman.
Rappert, B. (1999) 'The Uses of Relevance: Thoughts on a Reflexive Sociology', *Sociology*, 33(4): 705–23.
Rattansi, A. and Phoenix, A. (1997) 'Rethinking Youth Identities: Modernist and Postmodernist Frameworks', in J. Bynner, L. Chisholm and A. Furlong (eds) *Youth, Citizenship and Social Change in a European Context*. Aldershot: Ashgate.
Redhead, S. *et al.* (eds) (1993) *Rave Off! Politics and Deviance in Contemporary Youth Culture*. Aldershot: Ashgate.
Redhead, S. (1998) *Subculture to Clubculture*. Aldershot: Avebury.
Rees, G., Gorard, S. *et al.* (2000) 'Participating in the Learning Society: History, Place and Biography', in F. Coffield (ed.) *Differing Visions of a Learning Society: Research Findings, Vol. 2*. Bristol: Policy Press.
Rees, T.L. and Atkinson, P. (eds) (1982) *Youth Unemployment and State Intervention*. London: Routledge.

Reimer, B. (1995) 'Youth and Modern Lifestyles', in J. Fornäs and G. Bolin (eds) *Youth Culture in Late Modernity*. London: Sage.
Reinhartz, S. (1992) *Feminist Methods in Social Research*. Oxford: Oxford University Press.
Release (1997) *Release Drugs and Dance Survey: An Insight into the Culture*. Release: London.
Richard, B. and Krüger, H.H. (1998) 'Ravers' Paradise?: German Youth Cultures in the 1990s', in T. Skelton and G. Valentine (eds) *Cool Places: Geographies of Youth Culture*. London: Routledge.
Richter, H. (1964) *T.H. Green and the Politics of Conscience*. London: Weidenfeld.
Ridge, T. (2002) *Childhood, Poverty and Social Exclusion: From a Child's Perspective*. Bristol: Policy Press.
Roberts, K. (1975) 'The Developmental Theory of Occupational Choice: A Critique and an Alternative', in G. Esland, G. Salaman and A.M. Speakman (eds) *People and Work*. Edinburgh: Holmes McDougall.
Roberts, H. (ed.) (1980) *Doing Feminist Research*. London: Routledge and Kegan Paul.
Roberts, K. (1986) *The Changing Structure of the Youth Labour Market*. London: Routledge.
Roberts, B. (1995) *Biographical Research*. Milton Keynes: Open University Press.
Roberts, K. (1995) *Youth and Employment in Modern Britain*. Oxford: Oxford University Press.
Roberts, K. (1996) 'Individualisation and Risk in East and West Europe', in H. Helve and J. Bynner (eds) *Youth and Life Management: Research Perspectives*. Helsinki: Helsinki University Press.
Roberts, K. (1997) 'Structure and Agency: The New Youth Research Agenda', in J. Bynner, L. Chisholm and A. Furlong (eds) *Youth, Citizenship and Social Change*. Aldershot: Ashgate, 56–67.
Roberts, K. (1998) 'School to Work Transitions in Former Communist Countries', *British Journal of Education and Work*, 11(2): 221–38.
Roberts, T. (1998) 'Built for Speed', at http://hyperreal.org/rdugs/stimulants.
Roberts, K. (1999) *Leisure in Contemporary Society*. Wallingford: CAB International.
Roberts, B. (2001) *Biographical Research*. Buckingham: Open University Press.
Roberts, K. and Jung, B. (1995) *Poland's First Post-Communist Generation*. Aldershot: Avebury.
Roberts, K. and Parsell, G. (1991) 'Young people's Sources and Levels of Income, and Patterns of Consumption in Britain in the Late-1980s', *Youth and Policy*, 35: 20–5.
Roberts, K. and Parsell, G. (1992) 'Entering the Labour Market in Britain: The Survival of Traditional Opportunity Structures', *Sociological Review*, 30: 727–53.
Roberts, K., Clark, S.C. and Wallace, C. (1994) 'Flexibility and Individualisation: A Comparison of Youth Transitions into Employment in England and Germany', *Sociology*, 28(1): 31–54.
Robins, D. and Cohen, P. (1978) *Knuckle Sandwich: Growing Up in the Working Class City*. Harmondsworth: Penguin.
Robins, K. (1994) 'Forces of Consumption: From the Symbolic to the Psychotic', *Media, Culture and Society*, 16: 449–68.
Robinson, P. (1984) 'Languages in Data Collection: Difficulties with Diversity', *Journal of the Market Research Society*, 26(2): 159–69.
Roche, J. and Tucker, S. (eds) (1997) 'Introduction', *Youth in Society: Contemporary Theory, Policy and Practice*. London: Sage.

Roche, J. and Tucker, S. (eds) (1997) *Youth in Society: Contemporary Theory, Policy and Practice*. London: Sage.

Roker, D. and Coleman, J. (1997) 'Education and Advice About Illegal Drugs: What Do Young People Want?', *Drugs: Education, Prevention and Policy*, 4(1): 53–64.

Roker, D., Player, K. and Coleman, J. (1999) *Challenging the Image: Young People as Volunteers and Campaigners*. Leicester: Youth Work Press.

Roszak, T. (1969) *The Making of a Counter Culture: Reflections on the Technocratic Society and its Youthful Opposition*. London: Faber and Faber.

Rudd, P. and Evans, K. (1998) 'Structure and Agency in Youth Transitions: Student Experiences of Vocational Further Education', *Journal of Youth Studies*, 1(1): 39–62.

Rutherford, J. (ed.) (1997) *Young Britain*, Soundings 6. London: Lawrence and Wishart.

Rutter, M. and Smith, D.J. (1995) *Psychosocial Disorders in Young People: Time Trends and Their Causes*. Chichester: John Wiley.

Sanders, D. (1997) 'Voting and the Electorate', in P. Dunleavy, A. Gamble, I. Holliday and G. Peele (eds) *Developments in British Politics*. Basingstoke: Macmillan.

Sassen, S. (1991) *The Global City*. Princeton: Princeton University Press.

Saunders, N. (1995) *Ecstasy and the Dance Culture*. Exeter: BPC Wheatons.

Sayer, A. (2000) 'For Postdisciplinary Studies: Sociology and the Curse of Disciplinary Parochialism and Imperialism', in J. Eldgridge (ed.) *For Sociology: Legacies and Prospects*. Durham: Sociology Press.

Scheler, M. (1954) *The Nature of Sympathy*. London: Routledge and Kegan Paul.

Scheper-Hughes, N. (2000) 'Ire in Ireland', *Ethnography*, 1(1): 117–40.

Seabrook, J. (1978) *What Went Wrong?* London: Gollancz.

Seale, C. (1998) *Researching Society and Culture*. London: Sage.

Sefton-Green, J. (ed.) (1998) *Digital Diversions*. London: Routledge.

Sennett, R. (1998) *The Corrosion of Character*. New York: Norton.

Serres, M. (1997) *The Troubadour of Knowledge*. Ann Arbor: University of Michigan.

Sewell, T. (1997) *Black Masculinities and Schooling*. Stoke on Trent: Trentham.

Shavit, Y. and Muller, W. (eds) (1998) *From School to Work: Comparative Study of Educational Qualifications and Occupational Destinations*. London: Clarendon Press.

Shields, R. (1992) 'The Individual, Consumption Cultures and the Fate of Community', in R. Shields (ed.) *Lifestyle Shopping: The Subject of Consumption*. London: Routledge.

Shumway, D. (1992) 'Rock and Roll as a Cultural Practice', in A. DeCurtis (ed.) *Present Tense: Rock and Roll and Culture*. Durham, North Carolina: Duke University Press.

Skeggs, B. (1994) 'Situating the Production of Feminist Ethnography', in M. Maynard and J. Purvis (eds) *Researching Women's Lives from a Feminist Perspective*. London: Taylor and Francis.

Skeggs, B. (1997) *Formations of Class and Gender*. London: Sage.

Skeggs, B. (2001) 'Feminist Ethnography', in P. Atkinson, A. Coffey, S. Delamont, J. Lofland and L. Lofland (eds) *Handbook of Ethnography*. London: Sage.

Skelton, T. (2002) 'Research on Youth Transitions: Some Critical Interventions', in M. Cieslik and G. Pollock (eds) *Young People in Risk Society: The Restructuring of Youth Identities and Transitions in Late Modernity*. Aldershot: Ashgate.

Skelton, T. and Valentine, G. (eds) (1998) *Cool Places: Geographies of Youth Culture*. London: Routledge.
Soderquist, T. (1991) 'Biography or Ethnobiography?' in F. Steier (ed.) *Research and Reflexivity*. London: Routledge.
Springhall, J. (1971) *Youth, Empire and Society*. London: Croom Helm.
Springhall, J. (1998) *Youth, Popular Culture and Moral Panics 1830–1996*. Basingstoke: Macmillan.
Stacey, K. (2001) 'Achieving Praxis in Youth Partnership Accountability', *Journal of Youth Studies*, 4(2): 209–32.
Stacey, L. and Mignot, P. (2001) 'The Discourse of the Careers Guidance Interview: From Public Policy to Private Practice', *Youth and Policy*, 70: 25–39.
Stanley, L. and Wise, S. (1983) *Breaking Out: Feminist Consciousness and Feminist Research*. London: Routlege and Kegan Paul.
Steier, F. (ed.) (1991) *Research and Reflexivity*. London: Routledge.
Strauss, A. and Corbin, J. (1998) 'Grounded Theory Methodology', in N. Denzin and Y. Licoln (eds) *Strategies of Qualitative Inquiry*. Thousand Oaks, CA: Sage.
Straw, W. (1991) 'Systems of Articulation, Logics of Change: Communities and Scenes in Popular Music', *Cultural Studies* 5(3): 368–88.
Sweetman, P. (2004) 'Tourists and Travellers? "Subcultures", Reflexive Identities and Neo-Tribal Sociality', in A. Bennett and K. Kahn-Harris (eds) *After Subculture: Critical Studies in Contemporary Youth Culture*. Basingstoke: Palgrave.
Sztompka, P. (1988) 'Conceptual Frameworks in Comparative Inquiry: Diversity or convergent?', *International Sociology*, 3(3): 207–18.
Tait, G. (1993) 'Re-assessing Street Kids: A Critique of Subcultural Theory', in R. White (ed.) *Youth Sub-cultures: Theory, History and the Australian Experience*. Hobart: National Clearinghouse for Youth Studies.
Tennant, M. (1997) *Psychology and Adult Learning*. London: Routledge.
Tesch, R. (1990) *Qualitiative Research*. London: Falmer.
The Routes Project Team (2001) *Young People as Researchers: Possibilities, Problems and Politics*. Leicester: Youth Work Press.
Thompson, R., Bell, R. Holland, J., Henderson, S., McGrellis, S. and Sharpe, S. (2002) 'Critical Moments: Choice, Chance and Opportunity in Young People's Narratives of Transition', *Sociology*, 36(2): 335–54.
Thornton, S. (1995) *Club Cultures: Music, Media and Subcultural Capital*. Oxford: Polity Press.
Touraine, A. (1979) 'Political Ecology: A Demand to Live Differently Now', *New Society*, November, 26–8.
Travis, A. (1999) 'Sex in the 90s: The Young Take a Moral Stand', *Guardian*, 29 December, 3.
Urry, J. (1990) *The Tourist Gaze*. London: Sage.
Valentine, G., Skelton, T. and Chambers, D. (1998) 'Cool Places: An Introduction to Youth and Youth Cultures', in T. Skelton and G. Valentine (eds) (1998) *Cool Places: Geographies of Youth Culture*. London: Routledge.
Vogler, C. (2000) 'Social Identity and Emotion: the Meeting of Psychoanalysis and Sociology', *Sociological Review*. Oxford: Blackwell.
Wade, H., Lawton, A. and Stevenson, M. (2001) *Hear by Right: Setting Standards for the Active Involvement of Young People in Democracy*. London/Leicester: Local Government Association/National Youth Agency.

Walkerdine, V. (1997) *Daddy's Girls: Young Girls and Popular Culture*. Basingstoke: Macmillan.
Walkerdine, V. (2001) *Growing Up Girl*. Basingstoke: Palgrave.
Wallace, C. and Kovatcheva, S. (1998) *Youth in Society: The Construction and Deconstruction of Youth in Eastern and Western Europe*. London: Macmillan.
Ward, L. (1997) *Seen and Heard: Involving Disabled Children and Young People in Research and Development Projects*. York: Joseph Rowntree Foundation/York Publishing Services.
Waters, M. (1997) 'Class', in D. Owen (ed.) *Sociology After Postmodernism*. London: Sage.
Weil, S. (1989) 'Influences of Lifelong Learning on Adult's Expectations and Experiences of Returning to Formal Learning Contexts', Unpublished doctoral thesis, University of London.
Weil, S. (1997) 'Rhetorics and Realities in Public Service Organisations: Systemic Practice and Organisational Learning as Critically Reflexive Action Research (CRAR)', *Systemic Practice and Action Research*, 11(1): 37–61.
Weil, S. (1999) 'Strangers on the Shore? Living and Learning New Cultures of Inquiry', *Professorial Inaugural Lecture*, University College, Northampton, May.
Weinstein, D. (2000) *Heavy Metal: The Music and its Culture*, 2nd edn. London: Da Capo Press.
Wenger, E. (1998) *Communities of Practice: Learning, Meaning and Identity*. Cambridge: Cambridge University Press.
Westmarland, L. (2000) 'Taking the Flak: Operational Policing, Fear and Violence', in G. Lee-Treweek and S. Linkogle (eds) *Danger in the Field*. London: Routledge.
White, M. (1994) *The Material Child: Coming of Age in Japan and America*. Oxford: Free Press.
White, R. (1999) *Australian Youth Subcultures: On the Margins and in the Mainstream*. Hobart: Australian Clearinghouse for Youth Studies.
Whyte, W.F. (1955/1981/1993) *Street Corner Society: The Social Structure of an Italian Slum*. Chicago: University of Chicago Press.
Widdicombe, S. and Wooffitt, R. (1995) *The Language of Youth Subcultures: Social Identity in Action*. Hemel Hempstead: Harvester Wheatsheaf.
Wiener, M. (1985) *English Culture and the Decline of the Industrial Spirit*. Harmondsowth: Penguin.
Wildemeersch, D. (1996) 'Social Learning for Reconstruction and Development: Perspectives on Experimental Learning for Social Transformation', paper presented at the *5th ICEL Conference*, Cape Town.
Wilkinson, S. (1998) 'Focus Groups in Feminist Research: Power, Interaction, and the Co-construction of Meaning', *Women's Studies International Forum*, 21(1): 111–15.
Williams, R. (1976) *Keywords*. London: Fontana.
Williamson, H. and Butler, I. (1995) 'No one Ever Listens to Us: Interviewing Children and Young People', in C. Cloke and M. Davies (eds) *Participation and Empowerment in Child Protection*. Chichester: Wiley.
Williamson, H. and Middlemiss, R. (1999) 'The Emperor Has No Clothes: Cycles of Delusion in Community Interventions with Disaffected Young Men', *Youth and Policy*, 63: 13–25.
Willis, P. (1977) *Learning to Labour*. Farnbourgh: Saxon House.
Willis, P. (1980) 'Notes on Method', in S. Hall *et al.* (eds) *Culture, Media, Language*.

Willis, P. (1985) *The Social Condition of Young People in Wolverhampton in 1984*. Wolverhampton Council.
Willis, P. (1990) *Common Culture*. Milton Keynes: Open University Press.
Willow, C. (1997) *Hear! Hear! Promoting Children and Young People's Democratic Participation in Local Government*. Local Government Information Unit.
Wilmott, P. (1966) *Adolescent Boys in East London*. London: Routledge and Kegan Paul.
Winlow, S. (2002) *Badfellas*. London: Berg Press.
Winnicott, D.W. (1984) *Deprivation and Delinquency*. London: Tavistock.
Wood, S. and Forrest, D. (2000) 'Participatory Action Research: An Empowering Methodology for Work with Marginalised Young People', *Scottish Youth Issues Journal*, 1: 63–86.
Wyn, J. and Dwyer, P. (1999) 'New Directions in Research on Youth in Transition', *Journal of Youth Studies*, 2(1): 5–22.
Wyn, J. and White, R. (1997) *Rethinking Youth*. London: Sage.
Young, M. (1994) *The Rise of the Meritocracy*. London: Transaction.
Zizek, S. (1998) *Pleasure and Popular Culture*. London: Verso.

Index

abstracted empiricism 42

Beck, Ulrich 175
Bernstein, Basil 31
bio-politics 46
black cultural studies 37
black youth culture 34
Blairism 33
body hatred 120, 134
Bourdieu, Pierre 31, 142
Bowles, Stanley and Gintis,
  Herbert 31
British Crime Survey 139
British Household Panel Survey 26
British National Child Development
  Study 93
British Sociological Association 4

Centre for Contemporary Cultural
  Studies (CCCS) 22–5, 159, 187,
  196–9
Chicago School 115
citizenship 7, 19–21, 41, 47, 66–9
club cultures 71, 104, 138–53
Cohen, Stanley 186
communicative action spaces 5,
  73, 80
confidentiality 105, 109
Connexions 66–7, 70
consumer culture 176
  citizenship 178
consumption 6, 9, 14, 21, 32,
  170–85
critically reflexive action research 78
cultural studies 19–42, 158
  capital 46, 172
  identities 176
  turn 32–42

data analysis 103, 107
  collection 91–2, 109, 118, 189
de-industrialisation 6
dialogics 46–51

diaspora 44
dissemination 88
drug
  education 56
  prevention 50, 63
  use 5, 56, 138–53, 172
Durkheim, Emile 70

ecstasy 138–53
education 31, 71, 88, 95, 120
embodiment 121, 142, 149
empowerment 8, 47, 70, 80, 87,
  106, 128, 134, 173
epistemological dilemmas 9
ethnographic turn 186
ethnography 26, 34–7, 41,
  103–19
  critical 39, 158
  structural 158
evaluation 59, 63
evidence-based policy 46
evidence-based practice 63, 67

feminisation 44
fieldwork 91, 107–8, 117, 128,
  136, 196
  relations 5, 117, 189
  social relations of 9, 157–69
Foucault, Michel 36

gay rights 46
Geertz, Clifford 192
Giddens, Anthony 50, 89,
  157, 188
girls cultures 34
globalisation 2, 41, 88–9, 175
Goffman, Erving 107, 194
Goldthorpe, John 24

Hammersley, Martin 109, 158
HIV 18
home boys 44
homelessness 19

identity politics 39
individualisation 8, 23, 45, 68, 174
informants 48–9
insider knowledge 150–2, 186–99
interview process 126–9, 146
 schedules 104–5

justice system 19–21

Labour Force Survey 95
Lacan, Jacques 36
lifecourse 8, 42
lifestyles 8, 68–70, 74, 90, 187

Mods 32–4
multi-agency collaboration 83
Murray, Charles 15

neo-tribes 8
New Deal 69–74, 83
New Labour 3, 50–1
New Right 38, 160
new social movements 20, 39, 160
normalisation 18, 150

objectivity 121, 143, 193

participant observation 103, 160
participative methodologies 5
peer education 56–7
 groups 39–40
pilot studies 104–5
policy interventions 6, 56–61, 66, 77
politics 20, 86
post-Fordism 19, 23, 33
 adolescents 180
 modernism 32–9, 135–7, 173
 structuralism 8, 36, 48, 135
 subcultures 8
power relations 5, 60, 128–35, 157–69
psychoanalysis 36–7, 129–33
psychotherapy 127
punks 35

questionnaires 58–9, 90–2, 123, 194

reflexivity 2–5, 32, 45, 49, 78, 118, 150, 158, 174
research
 access 107, 128
 action 164
 applied 56
 biographical 8
 collaborative 68
 commissioning of 56, 61–2
 comparative 7, 18, 27, 85–101
 covert 194
 design 3
 ethics 3, 139
 feminist 136, 165–7
 interdisciplinary 48
 overt 194
 participative 56, 63–5, 67, 109
 practice based 68
 process 3, 55, 61, 129, 136
 qualitative 5–7, 24–7, 194
 quantitative 24–7, 89–90
 relations 110, 114, 123
risk 17, 45, 68, 70, 140, 174–85
Rockers 32–4

sampling 92
scenes 196–9
secondary analysis 93–7
sexual identities 15, 45
Skinheads 34
social exclusion 5–7, 14, 50, 93
 capital 39
 inclusion 67–9, 93
structure and agency 24, 45, 88, 158
subcultural capital 190
subjectivity 121
survey research 60, 139

Teds 34
thick description 115
Third Way 50, 74
tribes 196

underclass 14, 29, 33
unemployment 18, 87, 93–5

welfare systems 10, 88
Whyte, William Foote 5, 189

youth
  citizenship   19–20
  cohort studies   26, 94
  crime   5
  cultures   2, 9, 21–2, 31, 40,
    88, 138, 152, 186–99
  education   14
  employment   170–1
  fashions   31
  identities   2, 120, 125,
    161–3
  interventions   68, 82
  policy   59–63, 66, 69
  problems   7, 75
  service   63
  studies   6, 29
  style   35–40, 195
  subculture   171, 178, 190
  training   2, 29, 160, 170
  transitions   7, 16–19, 69, 88, 94,
    104, 160–3, 176
  underclass   5, 15, 45, 172
  unemployment   15–18, 171
  work   64
  youth problem, the   15
  youth question, the   30–4, 160